Gilad Ben-Nun is Marie Curie Individual Fellow at Verona University's Department of Public International Law and holds a PhD from the University of Leipzig. He is also the author of *The Fourth Geneva Convention: The History of International Humanitarian Law* (I.B.Tauris, forthcoming).

"Fascinating, even gripping ... [the book] sheds rare light onto the drafting process of the most important treaty on refugees."

Pierre Hazan, Special Advisor on Transitional Justice, Centre for Humanitarian Dialogue (Geneva) and Associate Professor, Neuchâtel University

"No moment could be more appropriate for tackling this topic than today, when all of Europe, inside and outside of the EU, and the Mediterranean region, are helpless and in disarray facing the refugee crisis. Gilad Ben-Nun dares a twin-track strategy of making us aware about the section of international law that has become so critical after World War II and the period of decolonization, and the role the young state of Israel played in writing and commenting this law: that is one track. The other is the application of international and national law on refugees to Israel. The second track can be observed as a paradigmatic oscillation between universalism – i.e. also a global commitment to conventions and rules of supranational law – and a fall-back into old and new nationalisms ... This book is pioneering in several ways."

Michael Daxner, Professor, Freie Universität Berlin and former Principal International Officer, United Nations Interim Administration Mission in Kosovo (UNMIK)

"This book demonstrates convincingly that knowing about global history is essential for understanding current international events. By analyzing the conflict between judges and government in Israel concerning the treatment of refugees, the author has made visible the deep roots of today's migration policies."

Matthias Middell, Professor of Global History, University of Leipzig

SEEKING ASYLUM IN ISRAEL

Refugees and the History of Migration Law

GILAD BEN-NUN

I.B.TAURIS
LONDON · NEW YORK

Published in 2017 by
I.B.Tauris & Co. Ltd
London • New York
www.ibtauris.com

Library of Modern Middle East Studies 193

ISBN: 978 1 78453 760 9
eISBN: 978 1 78672 133 4
ePDF: 978 1 78673 133 3

A full CIP record for this book is available from the British Library
A full CIP record is available from the Library of Congress

Library of Congress Catalog Card Number: available

Typeset in Garamond Three by OKS Prepress Services, Chennai, India
Printed and bound by CPI Group (UK) Ltd, Croydon, CR0 4YY

FSC www.fsc.org MIX Paper from responsible sources FSC® C013604

To Keren:

האוהב אחת היא ואתה

Maimonides, Commentary on the Mishna, Avot A. 6.

CONTENTS

LIST OF ILLUSTRATIONS

Map

Graph

ACKNOWLEDGEMENTS

The origins of my interest in forced migration stem from personal circumstances. My father was born in Morocco to a religious Jewish family whose origins trace back to the exiled Jews of Spain. The Banon family, originally from a village carrying that name some 60 km south of Zaragoza, received asylum in Morocco – a Muslim welcome which lasted four-and-a-half centuries, as they first settled in Marrakesh, and later moved south to the region of Agadir and Tiznit. My mother's family were Lithuanian Jews, who fled to South Africa in early twentieth century after experiencing anti-Jewish riots during the rise of East-European nationalism. I was born in Jerusalem, to where my parents – Jews born on the opposite ends of the African continent – emigrated to. My father-in-law was born in Israel to a German-speaking Jewish family who fled Nazi Berlin in the late 1930s. My mother-in-law was born in Alexandria to Jews originally also from Spain. She was exiled from Egypt after the ousting of Egypt's Jews by Gamal Abdel Nasser.

My first direct contact with non-Jewish exile was that of Palestinian refugees, during my years of service in military intelligence and work in East Jerusalem's security sector during the Oslo years. My empathy towards Palestinian refugees grew during my years in Peace Now and later in the UN. From 2008 onwards one gradually began to see more and more black African migrants arrive in Israel. By 2011, this initial trickling of Africans had become a mass influx. I could now see a refugee crisis happening "in real time", and not just hear about it and meet its descendants *post eventum.* Most importantly, I witnessed first-hand the visceral societal reactions which this influx of foreign refugees generated in a host society. I thus went searching for a doctoral program which would provide a sound academic housing and a nourishing intellectual environment to ponder this societal reaction. I found this stimulating environment and more – in Leipzig.

Ever since I unassumingly knocked on his door, Matthias Middell – the Director of Leipzig University's Global and European Studies Institute (GESI) and its Centre for Area Studies (CAS) has been a mentor and friend. His counsel on the need to break the boundaries of traditional academic disciplines in the study of a multi-faceted field such as forced migration, has rendered a new meaning to my understanding of what Global Studies is all about. At GESI, Martina Keilbach's wisdom and advice were of special importance, and Stefan Troebst provided much needed guidance. Over the past four years, I have had the privilege of teaching at the joint MA and PHD program in Global Studies of Leipzig University and Addis Ababa University's Institute for Peace and Security Studies (IPSS). Significant segments of this book were written during my extensive stays in Addis at IPSS. I owe a special debt to Ulf Engel for his friendship and unparalleled knowledge of Africa, for privileging me with this experience of being close to my students from the African continent, and for reading and commenting on the entire manuscript.

I was blessed to have received the generous support of the Ernst Ludwig Ehrlich Foundation (ELES) who shouldered, both financially and thematically, this entire project from its outset. Special thanks to Eva Lezzi and Dimitry Belkin. Michael Daxner has had a special impact on this book, thanks to the hours he accorded me - picking his brain and vast experience, both as an academic and as a former senior UN diplomat.

Looking back, I understand the impact which my years at the UN and living in Geneva have had on my life. Pierre Hazan has had a profound influence on this book, on its engagement with issues of Universalism and Exceptionalism, and more generally on my intellectual development over the past fifteen years. I owe him a lot, and this is a good venue to mention it. In Geneva, I owe a special debt of gratitude to Jasna, Roland and Emmanuelle. In addition to the portions of this book written in Leipzig, and Addis, many ideas were shaped during discussions on the kitchen table in Jussy, and over coffee tables in Meinier and Cologny.

Over the years quite a number of people have contributed to my thoughts, and I apologize to the ones not mentioned due to space limitations. Many thanks to: Amr Abdalla, Aline Angoustures, Claudia Baumann, Haim Ben-Noun, Alain Bittar, Vincent Chetail, Antje Dietze, Selamawit Girmay, Nahla Haidar, Maurice Krigel, Patricia Lewis (former UNIDIR now Chatham House for getting me started on all this), Jean-Marc Liling, Steffi Marung, Dietmar Müller, Etu Mulugeta, Katja Naumann, Sunday Okello, Gad Ortar, Liad Ortar, Gali and Friederike Schir, Kathleen Schlütter, Adam Skordos, Rana Taha, Caroline Vuillemin (and that wonderfully important institution-Fondation Hirondelle), David Whittlesey, and Antje Zettler.

In Verona, a special thanks to Annalisa Ciampi for her guidance and her insistence upon the relevance of historical research to the interpretation and application of modern international law.

I owe a special thanks to civic artist Ilana Salama Ortar for sharing her work and ideas on migration, forced migration, and on how feelings and notions of uprootedness can and ought to be conveyed, in both artistic and literary forms.

Looking back, I understand the important role my education at the Hebrew University has played in shaping my thoughts and being. It has been over two decades since I began studying on Mount Scopus, and only now do I truly appreciate the quality of intellectual rigour which I was fortunate enough to have received there. My teachers – the late Michael Heyd, Steve Aschheim, Esther Cohen, Rina Peled, Moshe Zimmermann, and especially Avihu Zakai, as well as classmates like Eran Shalev are still an unflinching source of academic inspiration. Another source of inspiration are my children, Tamar and Raz. As this book has a lot to do with law and judges, it is only now that I understand Maimonides' comment, that a prerequisite requirement to qualify for judiciary in ancient Jewish law was to have children "due to the virtue of compassion". Thank you for compelling me to think in these terms.

Some of the materials included in Part 1 of this book have been published in *the Journal of Refugee Studies* 27 (1) & 28 (1), and in *Refugee Survey Quarterly* 34 (2). Many thanks to Oxford University Press for permissions to draw upon these materials. At I.B.Tauris I have enjoyed working with a remarkable team of editors who took on this project from its early stages all through to publication. Thanks to Maria Marsh (now with Cambridge University Press), Azmina Siddique, and foremost to Tom Stottor for all his support. Ian McDonald has pulled off his usual magic in turning my half-baked first draft into polished language.

My last and most sincere debt is to Keren, to whom this book is dedicated. Thank you for teaching me about empathy, for supporting this project all along, and for your insights into the nexus between the Jewish and the universal – so much of which have gone into it.

INTRODUCTION

The image on the cover of this book was captured during a demonstration of non-Jewish African asylum seekers in February 2014. The demonstrators partially painted their faces white, so as to protest the Israeli Government's discriminatory approach towards them as "black skinned" African asylum seekers, in comparison to the more favorable treatment accorded to other "white skinned" non-Jewish occidental migrants at the very same time. To most Jews, this image is deeply disturbing. It epitomizes the Israeli state's deeply embedded racial discrimination against African non-Jewish "others" who fled persecution and death on account of their race, only to be incarcerated en masse, in a country which was supposed to provide them asylum. The sight of their half-painted faces against the backdrop of the Israeli flag, which carries the Star of David – that perpetual sign of suffering through the ages, on account of Jewish "otherness" – is almost irreconcilable.

Between 2005 and 2014, well over 60,000 African asylum seekers, mainly from genocide-stricken Darfur (Sudan) and authoritarian Eritrea, fled to Israel and received temporary asylum there. This human influx tugged at the heart and guts of the Israeli social psyche. Israeli reactions towards the coming of these migrants exhibited stringently polarized characteristics, from wholehearted acceptance on the one hand to outright rejection on the other. This study examines these reactions. It sets them against the historical backdrop of the development of International Refugee law in the early 1950s, which was significantly influenced by Jewish and Israeli delegates. Understanding Israel's societal reactions to their full extent, and the challenges the nation faced due to this incoming African migration, requires a conceptual framework. In an effort to explain these twofold reactions, this book focuses on the tension between two ideological sets of values: universalism and exceptionalism. These two concepts form a fundamental part of our global attitudes towards Third World migrants who clandestinely attempt to enter Western countries – be they in Israel, nations in the North Atlantic and European hemisphere, or Australia.

In the case of Israel, universalism and exceptionalism have cohabited in various forms since the creation of the State in 1948. Designated a "Jewish State" by the United Nations in the 1947 UN Partition plan, Israel has stood at the extreme end of the ethnocultural versus civic-pluralist citizenship debate.[1] Over the years, Israeli naturalization policies have invariably meant the granting of citizenship to Jews or people with Jewish origins only. The obtaining of Israeli citizenship has always been inordinately difficult for non-Jews, let alone for Palestinians or Arabs who, once perceived as the enemies of the Jewish state, have suffered all the more so. In a world split between civic national citizenships based upon *jus soli* (paradigmatically, the US and France) and ethno-cultural belongings based upon *jus sanguinis* (Germany prior to the 1999 reforms, Armenia, and Bulgaria), Israel empathically belongs to the latter group.

From the mid-1990s onward, as Israel ascended economically to the status of a developed country, it began receiving large populations of non-Jewish and non-Arab transnational migrants from the developing and underdeveloped world. With severe refugee crises taking place in East Africa in its geographical proximity, and with it being the only Western-style developed and politically stable country in its region, Israel began, from the early 2000s, receiving growing numbers of asylum-seeking African migrants, mainly from Eritrea and Sudan. To its surprise, Israel found itself, somewhat unknowingly, bound by international treaties it had signed and ratified some six decades earlier concerning forced persecuted migration – foremost among them, the 1951 Refugee Convention. Habitually, this ought not to have had any particular significance, given Israel's traditionally antagonistic approach to international relations and UN treaties, as the country has consistently maintained that these do not apply in its case – especially with regard to the effects of the Palestinian–Israeli conflict.

Yet this time round, it was not so much the world that demanded the implementation of the universalist values enshrined in UN instruments, but rather Israeli civil society itself, along with its significant NGO (nongovernmental organization) sector, which actively and forcefully mobilized public support in favor of the African asylum seekers. These NGOs defied governmental pressures, and coerced the government to cave in and ultimately submit to international norms imposed upon it by the Israeli Supreme Court. In January 2014, fourteen months after the 2012 Anti-Infiltration Act came into force, media outlets around the world reported the mass demonstrations by African asylum seekers along with ordinary Israeli citizens. The pro-migrant NGO lobby demanded the implementation of international human rights norms, denied to the African migrants by the Israeli Government.[2]

Between Universalism and Exceptionalism: The Research Problem

At the heart of this study stands the age-old conundrum, also existent in Judaism, of two conflicting ideological traits: universalism and exceptionalism. This dilemma dates back to biblical times, and is best captured by the theological dichotomy between Israel as "a light unto the nations" and the vision of the Jewish people as those who "shall dwell alone and shall not be reckoned among the nations."[3] These bipolar tendencies of Israel, drifting between being an integral participant in the international world order and its exceptionalist tendencies of Jewish ethnocentric supremacy, defying international norms and UN resolutions, have been at the heart of Israel's foreign policy since its inception.[4] To be sure, the Israeli exceptionalist ethos has also been exacerbated by the reciprocal tendency of the UN and international bodies to deal unevenly with Israel, especially with regard to the Arab–Israeli conflict. The designation of Zionism as a form of racism by the UN General Assembly in 1975 served as the epitome of this trend, granted that the revocation of that notorious resolution was usually much less acknowledged in Israeli circles.[5] To a large extent, the abstruse relations between Israel and the international community can be traced back to the very origins of both the United Nations and the Jewish state between 1945 and 1949.[6] The creation of Israel, following the 1947 UN Partition plan and the end of the British Mandate in

Palestine, was also followed by the assassination of the very first UN Special Representative of the Secretary General (SRSG), Folke Bernadotte, by Jewish militants possibly led by the later Israeli prime minister, Yitzhak Shamir, in Jerusalem.[7]

With its war of independence extracting an immense human toll, immediately after the Holocaust trauma, Israeli foreign policy had become hostage to the Arab–Israeli conflict, precluding any possibility of the normalization of its conduct in world affairs. From the 1967 dictum of "throwing the Jews into the Sea," through then-Defense Minister Moshe Dayan's metaphor of "the destruction of the Third Temple" during the dark early hours of the Yom Kippur War, and with Iranian President Mahmoud Ahmadinejad's calling for its erasure off the face of the earth in 2006, Israel's existential fears were well grounded to say the least.[8] These threats, posed by the Arab environment towards Israel's very existence, alongside the consistent hostile automatic majorities it faced at the UN, precluded any possibility of the country's adherence to normal universal benchmarks. To say that UN–Israeli relations were tainted as a result would be an understatement.

Late 2005 and early 2006 saw the beginning of what was to become a considerable population flow of African asylum-seeking migrants into Israel, mainly from Sudan's genocide-stricken Darfur, South Sudan, and Eritrea. As these migrants began crossing the southern Israeli border with Egypt on foot, following atrocious experiences they had endured in the Sinai Desert, the Israeli authorities and Israeli society at large found themselves confronted with a situation hitherto unknown to them. Never before had Israel been forced to deal with a humanitarian catastrophe that was not in any way connected to the Arab–Israeli conflict. For the first time, Israeli authorities began cooperating with International agencies, in this case with UNHCR (the Office of the United Nations High Commissioner for Refugees), the largest UN agency, without any political agenda serving as a hindrance to these working relations.

In this new and unknown condition, liberated from the "context heaviness" of the Arab–Israeli conflict and free of the security threats constantly infringing upon its well-being, which set of values would Israeli society ultimately embrace? Confronted with these refugee pleas, which ethos would ultimately prevail: universalism or exceptionalism?

It is here, confronted with the plight of scores of helpless and harmless African asylum-seeking migrants, that the conflicting dichotomy between the universalist tendencies of "a light unto the nations" and the exceptionalist tendencies of "a nation who shall dwell alone" would ultimately be tested.

One of the clearest and most venerable Israeli voices to capture this unfolding conundrum was the Jerusalem-based sociologist Eva Illouz.[9] As the African migrants tugged at the heartstrings of Israeli society in mid-2012, with violent anti-migrant demonstrators confronting pro-migrant activists on the streets of south Tel Aviv, Illouz emerged as the prime protagonist advocating for universal values against ethnicity-driven concepts. In a series of articles published in *Haaretz* newspaper, illustrating her academic and intellectual clout, Illouz encapsulated the universalist/exceptionalist conundrum. Arguing against the racial slanders voiced by the Israeli interior minister, Eli Yishai, against the African migrants, Illouz commented:

> The issue of refugees and illegal migrants is a very good way to understand the state of the norms that regulate the speech of our public representatives. Since antiquity, the way in which it treated foreigners was viewed as a sign of a country's morality. Ancient cultures and the medieval Church recognized the right of persecuted foreigners to find shelter in their midst. Modern and peaceful nation-states mark their membership in the community of civilized states by showing moral concern for refugees and by treating even illegal workers with humanity. Its attitude to foreigners – legal and illegal – is a crucial litmus test of a country's morality. Sure, the regulation of citizenship has been, historically, the prerogative of nation-states. Immigration is and perhaps must be monitored. This is Israel's right, as is the case in other countries. But the legitimate regulation of immigration cannot be carried out in a way that betrays the norms that the world community has come to view as universal [...] the interior minister's recent comments and behavior regarding the issue of illegal migrants cannot be tolerated in a democratic country because a great deal of democracy rests on universal principles, on the recognition [that] there is a fundamental equality of all human beings. Eli Yishai is someone even Marine Le Pen, the leader of the

> French extreme right, would be reluctant to stand near [...] What he means by "Zionist dream" is the ethnic and religious purity of the country, a concern shared by very large segments of Israel's citizenry [...] Racism is not behind the view that ethnic–religious purity must be preserved, but the other way around: It is the view of citizenship based on religion and ethnicity that produces racist worldviews. Israel is the country of the Jews, but this does not mean we cannot and should not adopt and institutionalize the idea of a universal citizenship that is already in effect in many European countries.[10]

Illouz wrote the article from which the above extract is taken in the midst of the hottest anti-migrant onslaught following violent demonstrations against them in south Tel-Aviv, marking the highest point of ethno-national exceptionalist tendencies. This contextualization is important if only to stress the fact that at no time did these exceptionailst tendencies ever prevail over Israel's universalist ones. What seemed a long, hot, triumphant summer for the ethnocentric forces in Israeli politics tuned out to be a colossal failure, as the Israeli Supreme Court unanimously revoked the governmental anti-migrant legislation in its entirety merely a year later.[11] Israeli attitudes towards the African migrants were by no means consistent and one-sided, as both universalist and exceptionalist attitudes coexisted simultaneously.

The Structure of this Book

The general pattern of relations between universalism and exceptionalism is one of a parabolic nature, along which the parts of this book are construed. Part I illustrates how Israeli policies vis-à-vis alien non-Jewish migrants began in the early 1950s with a stern universalism at heart. This universalism was largely theoretical and was devoid of any practical implications, given that no neutral non-Jewish alien refugees, who were not enemy nationals, actively made their way to Israel.

Part II explores the seemingly conclusive triumph of exceptionalism over universalism from 2006 until 2014. As the African migrant influx into Israel increased, Israeli policies and attitudes became more ethnically grounded, along with the rise of an Israeli extreme-right political faction. This resulted in an open onslaught against the African migrant community. Israel's usage against these migrants of emergency legislation from a time of bygone military threats, in a similar fashion to France's actions during its 2005 riots, and its application of "venue shopping" policies (explained in Part III), parallel similar policies exercised by other Western developed countries in their tackling of migrant issues.

Part III analyzes the return of universalism to the foreground, in direct opposition to the exceptionalist tendencies previously observed in Part II. The Israeli Parliament's (Knesset's) recurring attempts to re-enact the amendment to the Anti-Infiltration Act failed as the Israeli Supreme Court consistently revoked these laws on the grounds of their unconstitutionality. The situation where parliament became directly pitted against the supreme court signaled an ensuing constitutional crisis, and was symptomatic of the contrast between the court's universalism and the Knesset's exceptionalism.

Beyond the chronological periodization, the division of this study into its three parts is also due to the employment of different methodological approaches which were needed to do justice to each part's very different thematic specificities. As Part I is mainly engaged with events which took place some 60-odd years ago, the primary focus here was upon the uncovering of archival sources, hitherto not examined by researchers, concerning the origins of the 1951 Refugee Convention – and, more specifically, the vital part played by Israeli and Jewish diplomats in the drafting thereof.

The intermediary triumph of exceptionalism over universalism explored in Part II proved to be a considerable methodological challenge, given the radical shift of Israeli policies not only vis-à-vis the original humanitarian ethos of the early diplomats (described in Part I), but more so in light of the humanitarian tendencies existent *within* the immediate timeframe of the decade between the beginning of the African migrant influx (2005) and the present. The solution to this conundrum lay in exploring the broader Israeli social tendencies of growing extremism and radicalization per se. Once this general process of "extremization" was set forth, the focus on the specificities of the onslaught against the African refugees began to make sense. As such, Part II emphasizes the sociological characteristics which played their part in the extrimization of Israeli society. This radicalization found its voice and form in the harsh remaking and application of severe anti-infiltration legislation, which came to be directed against the mostly harmless and vulnerable African migrants.

The return to the fore of universalism, through the Israeli Supreme Court's revocation of the governmentally instigated anti-infiltration legislation, demanded yet another methodological approach – namely, annotated legal commentary. Nevertheless, given that the Israeli legal system is a hybrid of both British and ancient Jewish legal codes, one could not explain the rationale of the high court without delving deeply into historical sources, some of them dating back to Talmudic and medieval Jewish religious fundamentals. While Part III somewhat resembles Part I in its historicist explorations of judicial and legal positions, it is in fact the backdrop provided by Part II, upon which Part III rests, which makes the recurring revocation of governmental anti-migrant legislation by the Israeli Supreme Court all the more dramatic.

Initial Israeli Legislation Concerning Migrants and Aliens from the 1950s to the 1990s

The prima facie conjuncture of Israel as the state of the Jewish people, in direct relation to the European Holocaust, and the Jewish refugees expelled from the Arab countries after 1948, found its legislative expression in the Jewish Law of Return (August 1950). According to it all Jews, people of Jewish decent, or people connected through direct family ties to Jews are entitled to immigrate to Israel and later apply for Israeli citizenship. Jewish immigrants were demarked as "Olim," which is literally derived from the Hebrew biblical term for pilgrimage, a connotation which has remained intact ever since.[12] Though over the years this law has been adapted, and judicial rulings have elaborated upon its stipulations and criteria, the Law of Return has remained an indispensable pillar of the Israeli and Jewish psyche.[13] This is all the more potent given the plight of Palestinian refugees who have been demanding the exact same right of return in the exact same linguistic formulation for three generations now, most of whom live in sight of the land of their forefathers to which they wish to return.[14]

As per the general legislative drive of the Knesset to formulate the legal foundations of the newly created Israeli state, the Law of Entry into Israel was enacted in 1952. Setting forth the legal stipulations of border crossing, visa requirements and policies, and the legal categories of sojourn, the aim of this law was to regulate the procedural regime of entry and residence within the country.[15] With the newly created state just after its war of independence, and with Holocaust-surviving refugees and penniless Jewish refugees from Arab states being housed in makeshift refugee shanty towns (*maabarot*), no voluntary immigration of non-Jews to Israel was either envisaged or legislated for at the time. The poverty-stricken Israel of 1952 simply did not draw any non-Jewish immigration. Beyond the ideological importance of the Law of Return and its extension in the Law of Entry into Israel, other important aspects were the termination of refugee status for European Jews under the auspices of UNHCR and the cases of Jews from Arab states who transited through camps such as the Camps Arenas in Marseille.[16] Referencing Article 34 of the 1951 Refugee Convention, concerning the naturalization of refugees and their resettlement, the Government of Israel officially informed UNHCR of the naturalization papers it had issued to Jewish refugees, and their loss of refugee status through naturalization in early 1953.[17]

Nevertheless, for over 600,000 Palestinian refugees – the "nemesis" of Jewish immigration – that very same poverty-stricken Israel, with its food rationing and Jewish refugee towns, was the ultimate wishful destination. Aspiring to return to their mostly destroyed homes, the Palestinian diaspora, with the support of the defeated Arab armies of Egypt and Jordan, embarked on a large-scale border war from 1949 until 1956.

In his authoritative study of Israel's border wars, Benny Morris convincingly demonstrates that at the time these border conflicts were perceived to be the highest existential threat to the nascent Israeli state, established only eight years earlier with the Holocaust at its background. The border conflict with the Palestinian Fada'ayun militias eventually prompted Israel to embark on a full-scale war, in which it ultimately occupied the entire Sinai Peninsula.[18] Significantly, the pattern of this border conflict was one of continuous infiltrations and incursions into Israeli territory, first by unarmed civilians (1949–50), followed by an armed guerilla campaign (1950–5), which ceased only after the end of the Suez Canal crisis. Though the skirmishes took place on both the Jordanian (eastern) and Egyptian (southern) fronts, the latter theatre was significantly more challenging to the Israeli military establishment, causing over three quarters of Israeli deaths and injuries, and inflicting financially crippling costs.

By 1956, as Israel embarked on the full scale Sinai Campaign, 538 Israelis had been killed and approximately the same amount injured during the seven-year period between the signing of the armistice agreements of March 1949 and October 1956.[19] With no adequate legislation at hand, the Israeli Government quickly found itself in an untenable legal situation concerning captured infiltrators. The penalties and stipulations of the Law of Entry into Israel (1952) provided lenient and insufficiently punitive measures when concerned with armed attacks on whole villages and kibbutzim. By late 1953, many of these settlements began to be deserted by their civilian inhabitants, with the armed forces occupying them in their stead – resulting in an extreme burden over an already overstretched Israeli Army, stationed along four major fronts.[20] Under the State of Emergency declared in 1948, the Knesset passed the 1954 Anti-Infiltration Act.[21]

This new law stipulated harsh penalties of 5 to 15-year jail terms and heavy financial fines for trespassers who transgressed the Israeli state borders, now internationally recognized under the 1949 UN-brokered Rhodes armistice agreements ("The Green Line"). Border transgressors were not entitled to petition Israeli state courts, but rather were to be court-martailed by military courts and judged by military ranking officers. As per the grave security threat posed at the time by the Fada'ayun guerilla infiltrators, this legislation was to be administered by the minister of defense, and executed by the Israeli Army, rather than by the civilian authorities of the interior or justice ministries. This was in deliberate contrast to the treatment of other border transgressors who would be tried in accordance with the terms stipulated in the Law of Entry into Israel of 1952. Under this more lenient law, justice was administered by the civilian state courts, with the detention and coercion responsibilities administered by the Israeli Police (rather than the Army), all under the ministerial oversight of the Interior Ministry.

The definition of an infiltrator, as opposed to any other border transgressor, relied heavily on an examination of the trespasser's country of origin. The military Anti-Infiltration Act of 1954 was applied only to nationals or residents of enemy countries openly and officially at war with Israel. As per his responsibilities and potencies, it was the then-minister of defense, Pinchas Lavon, who presented the 1954 Anti-Infiltration Act before the Knesset:

> The clandestine war waged against us by the Arab countries, which is coined as "infiltration", has accompanied the life of our country for years. From the side of the Arab countries and as auxiliaries to this war, both political and criminal elements are administered. By negating any constructive solution to the Palestinian refugee problem, some sons of the Arabs turn towards terrorist actions and transgression into Israeli territory. The aim of this infiltration is to deliberately destabilize our existence. This goal is not and shall not be achieved, since we are improving our defense manners.[22]

Thus, the clandestine illegal border trespassers of the mid-1950s were not treated or perceived as civilian refugees towards whom the 1951 Refugee Convention was applied. Both sides, Israel and the Palestinians alike, saw this border transgression as a "continuum of diplomacy by military means" à la Clausewitz. Consequently, the framing of the Israeli counter-legislation aimed against these border crossers bore a strict security-based agenda. So long as the trespassers were enemy nationals, and the frontier they were transgressing was under military authority, the harsh hand of the 1954 Anti-Infiltration Act was to be applied. In 2012, it was precisely the blurring of this fundamental distinction between military and civilian characters that invited the heavy criticism of the Israeli Supreme Court.

The Fada'ayun infiltrators ceased their attacks following the Suez Canal crisis of October 1956, and the resulting checking and balancing of Egyptian power along with the reopening of the canal to international shipping routes. While low-intensity conflicts between Israel and the neighboring Arab countries continued, border transgressions and human infiltration stopped almost entirely.[23]

The Arrival of Foreign Labor in Israel during the mid-1990s

Prior to the African wave of non-Jewish migrants, Israeli society had already accumulated ample experience with non-Jewish labor migration. During the early 1990s, Israel significantly altered its unskilled labor market and for the first time began to import unskilled foreign labor from Africa, Latin America, and East Asia.[24] Reversing its two-decade dependency on Palestinian guest laborers since the early 1970s, the State opted for imported foreign laborers from underdeveloped countries the world over. This change in policy stemmed first and foremost from the disruptions to the Israeli labor market caused by the first Palestinian uprising against Israeli occupation – "the first Intifada, 1987–91."[25] An Israeli border regime and permit-control system was enacted in the Occupied Palestinian Territories (OPT) in direct response to the extensive terror attacks and the bombing campaign unleashed on buses and public places during the mid-1990s. These terror attacks and their corresponding closures led to significant shortages of unskilled Palestinian workers in the construction and agricultural sectors, hitherto totally dependent on Palestinian guest workers.[26] By late 2001, approximately 160,000 migrants (roughly 3.5 percent of Israel's population, and almost 10 percent of the country's workforce) had become foreign and non-Jewish in origin.[27] As the new Sharon Administration came into power in 2001, it embarked on a significant campaign to reduce the numbers of, and forcefully deport, these labor migrants – ultimately causing over 140,000 of them to leave the country.[28] By 2005, as the influx of the East African asylum seekers into Israel began, existing African foreign migrants in Israel numbered 14,000.[29] These mostly West African migrants were primarily cared for by Israeli NGOs charged with serving the general foreign-worker communities, whose largest ethnic groups were drawn from Eastern European, Filipino, Latin American, and African societies.[30]

The Rise of Clandestine African Refugee Migration under Sharon and Olmert, 2005–9

Between 2005 and the end of 2013, over 60,000 East Africans – primarily from Sudan (Darfur), South Sudan, and Eritrea – entered Israel clandestinely after crossing the Sinai Desert on foot. The overwhelming majority of the new migrants, who quadrupled Israel's non-Jewish African population, were conflict-fleeing asylum seekers in contrast to the distinctly labor-migrating character of the African communities existent in Israel prior to 2005.[31] The key triggers for this significant rise in numbers of African asylum seekers from 2005 onwards were the harsh events in Egypt and the massacring of mainly Sudanese and Eritrean migrants near the UNHCR headquarters in Cairo in December 2005.[32]

Even allowing for the importance and impact of the Cairo events, longer-term immigration trends from the African continent towards the developed countries of southern Europe had been at play long before the shootings in front of the UNHCR offices. The immigration of East African asylum seekers to Israel must be understood in a comparative perspective with the general trend of African clandestine migration towards countries where migrants would not suffer torment. While Israel retained a similar GDP per capita as that of Spain, for example, it was geographically far more attached to the African continent with its 240 km long and contiguous land border with Egypt, the longest landmass connection of any developed country with Africa.[33]

An examination of data from the European agency for statistics (EUROSTAT), cross-checked with newspaper and media sources, confirms the long-known trends of clandestine African migration towards mainland Europe. Southern European countries – most notably Spain, Malta, Italy, and Greece – have been the primary landing grounds for African sea-ferrying migrants attempting to set foot on the continent.

Three of the main maritime hubs of entry into Europe – Malta, Italy, and Spain – show the same correlative annual trends in African migration between 2004 and 2009. While the period between 2004 and 2008 saw a steep rise in migrant entries into Europe, late 2007 and 2008 were the turning years with a sharp decline in migrant entries into all three countries, mainly attributed to actions of the EU border control agency – FRONTEX.[34] This decline was attributed to a fundamental tightening of the European border regime administrated by FRONTEX, once the Schengen Agreement came into force in 2006.[35] Interestingly, the exact same African migratory trends toward mainland Europe between 2004 and 2008 could be observed into Israel, as African migrants crosed the Israeli–Egyptian border in evergrowing numbers during those years. The sharp decline in migratory patterns, observed in the European hemisphere, was also witnessed correlatively in Israel.

The reasoning linking the 2005 Cairo shootings to the subsequent steep rise in African migration to Israel has already been qualitatively

vote for his nomination at the UN. Lobbying on behalf of his old friend's bid with his superior, Foreign Minister Sharett, Robinson referred to Larsen's and his own positive contribution to the success of the 1951 Refugee Convention:

> Regarding your letter to the High Commissioner for Refugees dated 14th March 1952, M/32400, in light of the nomination of Mr Knud Larsen to the post of Deputy High Commissioner, I would like to inform you that this Mr Larsen held a very senior position in the Danish Ministry of the Interior. He was my closest associate in all my work concerning the creation of the Offices of the High Commissioner for Refugees and the making of the Convention concerning the legal status of refugees. By the way he headed the convention in Geneva last summer. He published a two-volume study concerning the Danish citizenship legal code. I was the one who reviewed his publication in the *American Journal of International Law.* I thought you might be interested in these details.[19]

The review referred to in the text is overwhelmingly positive, and appeared in print during the three-week period of the Conference of Plenipotentiaries in July 1951.[20] In the above letter to Foreign Minister Sharett, Robinson credits Larsen and himself with no less than the creation of UNHCR and the "making" of the 1951 Refugee Convention. These are far-reaching claims of credit voiced by an ambassador to his foreign minister. Both the Director of the Bureau for International Organizations at the Israeli Foreign Ministry, and the Israeli ambassador to the UN, Abba Eban, were copied in on this letter. Eban had been well acquainted with Robinson ever since he had established the Israeli mission to the UN in New York in late 1947, with Robinson as the mission's off-counsel legal advisor. Eban was also well versed in the UN and its institutions, serving as the vice president of the General Assembly in 1952 and overseeing the beginning of the ratification process of the 1951 Refugee Convention by UN member states.[21] Given Eban's extremely close working relationship with Sharett, and his deep acquaintance with the UN Secretariat and structures, any inconsistencies in Robinson's reporting would have immediately surfaced, and would probably have been communicated to the Foreign Minister. However, prima facie, all the archive materials examined thus far have not yielded any such inconsistencies concerning Robinson's reports.

Who, then, was Jacob Robinson? How did he come to play such a leading role in consolidating and driving forward the 1951 Refugee Convention?

Born in 1889 in Lithuania to a practicing religious Jewish family, Jacob Robinson graduated from the Law Faculty of the University of Warsaw in 1914, and was elected to the Lithuanian Parliament as the head of the Jewish faction in the newly created Seimas, the Lithuanian House of Representatives, in 1922. In 1931, Robinson acted as the senior legal advisor to the Lithuanian Foreign Ministry, winning the legal case on behalf of the German-speaking Memel province of Lithuania against Germany at the Permanent Court of International Justice in The Hague in 1934.[22] It was during this period that Robinson first became acquainted with Knud Larsen, who would later become the president of the Refugee Conference of Plenipotentiaries. In 1941, following his escape from Europe, Robinson founded the Institute for Jewish Affairs (IJA) as part of the World Jewish Congress (WJC) in New York. A few years later, in 1945, Robinson was appointed as a senior legal advisor to the prosecution team under US Chief Counsel Robert H. Jackson at the Nuremberg trials for Nazi war criminals. Robinson supplied the prosecution with considerable volumes of data collected by the IJA concerning the annihilation of the Jewish communities of Europe under the Nazis.[23] During 1946 and 1947, Robinson was commissioned by the newly created UN Secretariat to help draft the legal framework for the Human Rights Commission. In 1948, following the passing of UN Resolution 181, Prime Minister David Ben-Gurion and Foreign Minister Sharett enlisted Robinson as the legal advisor to the Israeli mission to the UN in New York. Although not an Israeli citizen at the time, Robinson was given the diplomatic rank of ambassador plenipotentiary, reporting directly to Sharett in coordination with Abba Eben.[24]

With Robinson assuming his Israeli ambassadorship, his younger brother, Dr Nehemiah Robinson, became the director of the IJA that same year. In this capacity, Nehemiah Robinson would cooperate with his older brother, representing the WJC at the 1951 Refugee Conference of Plenipotentiaries and later publishing the first extensive legal commentary on the Refugee Convention under the auspices of the IJA.[25]

It was during these years that Jacob Robinson became acquainted with the well-known Jewish international jurist Louis Henkin, who at the time was serving in the US State Department's UN division. Henkin was the US representative to the Ad Hoc Committee on Statelessness, and was instrumental in securing US support for the Refugee Convention at the Conference of Plenipotentiaries in July 1951.[26] Both Henkin and Robinson had previously cooperated with Raphael Lemkin in the promotion of the 1948 Genocide Convention, which came into force as the negotiations were materializing for the Refugee Convention in early 1951. Robinson met Lemkin initially during his role at the Nuremburg trials in 1946, where Lemkin was lobbying for genocide indictments.[27]

Jacob Robinson's decision to accept the request to act as the representative of the State of Israel was by no means an easy one, all the more so because he was neither an Israeli citizen nor part of the Israeli political establishment. Any ambassadorial role is complicated – especially one representing a country in a declared state of war, not to mention the ample archive evidence pointing to the difficulties that Robinson experienced due to the rivalry between his superiors, Sharett and Ben-Gurion.[28] Indeed, he almost resigned his ambassadorial post due to the delay in Israel's ratification of the 1951 Refugee Convention, a delay caused by the animosity between the two.[29] His selection for an Israeli ambassadorship should be seen in the context of his roles in the international arena. Only as a full ambassador of a member state could he influence the wording of international legal instruments – that is, from within the drafting bodies of these conventions. Only as an ambassador for a UN member state could he take part in all five drafting organs of the 1951 Refugee Convention. Robinson was at the height of his long international career, a world expert regarding political minorities and state arrangements to accommodate them.[30] In 1958, he was awarded the highest honor any international lawyer could achieve, as he delivered the summer semester course at the Academy of International Law in The Hague.[31]

As he commenced his work as a member-state representative in the drafting organ of the Ad Hoc Committee on Statelessness, his main counterpart from within the UN establishment was the IRO representative to that committee, who was also another member of the like-minded, humanitarian Robinsonian network: his former employee and protégé, Paul Weis.

Born in Vienna in 1907, Weis graduated with a PhD in International Law from Vienna University in 1930, having studied under the well-known legal theorist Hans Kelsen. Following the Austrian *Anschluss* in March 1938, Weis was incarcerated in Dachau concentration camp, but was fortunately released due to an entry-visa application which he obtained for the UK in April 1939.[32] In late 1942, Weis joined the WJC, working as the secretary of its legal division, becoming the institution's key technical expert on the reclamation of Jewish property in various European countries and their respective legal systems. At the WJC, Weis' direct superiors were Jacob and Nehemiah Robinson. As their working relationships intensified, Weis became something of a protégé of the Robinson brothers. In parallel to his duties at the WJC, Weis joined the Free Austria Movement and completed his second PhD, in Nationality and Statelessness Law at the London School of Economics, which was published a few years later.[33] Weis maintained his connection with the IJA for the rest of his life, acting as a board member in the late 1960s after his retirement from UNHCR and overseeing the institute's relocation from New York to London.[34] In 1949, Weis assumed his first UN role as director of protection for the IRO, reporting directly to the renowned Swiss jurist Gustav Kullman. Kullman was a veteran of the League of Nations, having served that organization during the interwar period. He also acted as the Deputy High Commissioner for Refugees before and during World War II. Kullmann was charged with the overall responsibility within the UN Secretariat for the preparation of the preliminary IRO draft of the Refugee Convention.[35] As Weis' archive material clearly demonstrates, Kullman turned over many of the drafting responsibilities to his subordinate, Paul Weis, and it was Weis who undertook most of the textual coordination of the English and French versions of the proposed text.[36]

The next member of the Robinsonian network's inner circle was the UK representative to the Conference of Plenipotentiaries, Sir Samuel Hoare. Hoare's experience with refugee issues and his humanitarian approach to them dated back to 1928, when he acted as the deputy high commissioner for refugees in the League of Nations under Fridtjof Nansen.[37] In 1938, as the *Anschluss* in Austria unfolded, Hoare was the British home secretary who granted thousands of immigration visas to Jewish refugees from Austria and Germany while fighting adamantly in the House of Commons for further concessions for Jewish immigrants.

Often bitterly criticized by the backbenchers of his own Conservative Party, Hoare consistently maintained that the arrival of highly educated Jewish refugees, who were renowned experts in their fields, was a blessing for Britain.[38] Consequently, he went on to grant special asylum visas to people such as the ageing Dr Sigmund Freud and the well-known neurologist Dr Ludwig Guttman, the initiator of the Paralympics. In 1939, among the hundreds of residence permits issued by the British Home Office to Jews from Austria, Hoare granted asylum to yet another Jewish PhD holder, upon his conditional release from Dachau. His name was Paul Weis.[39]

The Robinson network's last member, somewhat in its outer circle, was the Refugee Convention's vice president and Belgian delegate, Albert Herment.[40] An old wartime friend of the UK delegate, Sir Samuel Hoare, Hermant was in fact an administrative senior bureaucrat within the Belgian foreign service, serving in his last post as the inspector general of the ministry before his retirement. By 1950, Herment had already reached the highest echelons of the Belgian foreign service, earning the Medaille Civile 1st Class in 1938, and designated an Officier de l'ordre de Léopold in 1945. Herment spent most of World War II, from December 1939 to December 1944, in London. His entire correspondence at the Belgian archives is written on the letterhead of the Belgian Embassy in London at 105 Eaton Square, across the road from Buckingham Palace.[41] In 1940, Herment was joined by Hubert Pierlot's exiled Belgian Government, which operated out of the very same compound because it was immediately recognized by Churchill to be the legitimate representation of the Belgian people. After World War II, Herment directed most of the Belgian Foreign Ministry's policies vis-à-vis the newly created UN, especially concerning the issue of refugees and stateless persons.[42] In December 1949, upon reaching the mandatory retirement age of 55 as a Belgian civil servant, Herment was honorably discharged to retirement.[43]

The next entry in Herment's personal service file (PERS: 2159) is somewhat irregular. Upon the extraordinary request of Belgian foreign minister, Paul Van Zeeland, and following a decree issued by King Leopold III dated April 27, 1950, Herment was reinstated with the rank of director at the prime minister's office (SPF Chancellerie du Premier Ministre). His sole task was to be the Belgian delegate to ECOSOC's (The UN's Economic and Social Council's) Ad Hoc Committee on Statelessness.

The Robinsonian network also included NGO representatives, who received observer status and were entitled to submit draft memoranda for consideration by the plenary both at the Ad Hoc Committee and the Conference of Plenipotentiaries. These NGOs included trade unions, intergovernmental organizations (such as the Inter-Parliamentary Union), religious organizations, and a significant group of Jewish NGOs headed by Nehemiah Robinson of the WJC. Within these Jewish advocacy circles, Jacob Robinson's reputation was well known, with Ben-Gurion often referring to him as "the most important Jew from Lithuania."[44] From Jacob Robinson's perspective, the NGOs could float ideas and texts which he did not wish to put forward in his role as the Israeli representative. However, there was coordination between the Jewish NGOs and Jacob Robinson which enabled a multi-pronged approach to the tabling of different ideas for consideration by the plenary. Reporting to Sharett, Robinson shared the fact that he was synchronizing his actions with those of the Jewish NGOs:

> Participating in the conference are non-governmental organizations with an advisory status to ECOSOC and within them three important Jewish organizations [. . .] Self-evidently I am in connection and coordination with these Jewish NGOs and on Saturday morning we had a meeting at my house in order to exchange views and consolidate what was important to us from the Jewish point of view.[45]

Recent scholarship has highlighted the large number of international jurists and technical experts concerned with refugees who participated in the various drafting stages of the 1951 Refugee Convention.[46] As I have shown above, many of these participants and jurists were interconnected into a like-minded network, with the explicit and premeditated objective of making the convention text as conducive and supportive as possible to refugee needs. Einarsen correctly points to the presence of Henkin, Robinson, and Weis at the different drafting stages of the convention. What new archive material yields, and which goes beyond Einarsen's description, is the fact that they were all interpersonally connected, with the convention president, Knud Larsen, as the most senior member of this network, which was actively coordinated by Jacob Robinson and strongly supported by Samuel

Hoare. Importantly, Larsen, Jacob Robinson, Weis, Hoare, Nehemiah Robinson, Henkin, and probably others were all connected before the Refugee Convention proceedings started – and, moreover, they actively continued their cooperation for many years thereafter. The archive material clearly highlights that the premeditated efforts of, and prior coordination between, these actors who I have called the Robinsonian network were key to their success in the 1951 Refugee Confention's drafting and eventual ratification. However, this success was anything but assured at the time, and it was secured only after a bitter and hard campaign.

Europeanists, Universalists, and the Threats to the 1951 Convention

The question as to the true motives of the drafters of the 1951 Refugee Convention does not have a single, straightforward answer. As G. Goodwin-Gill and J. McAdam have pertinently observed:

> While clear statements of drafting intentions are rare, the debates may provide a fascinating insight into the politics of a highly sensitive and emotive issue: if some sentiments and statements seem frozen in time, others show the continuity of concern and, perhaps too rarely, confirmation of a pervasive humanitarianism.[47]

Nevertheless, the humanitarian motivations of the Israeli drafters were crystal clear, and provided for in one of those "rare statements frozen in time," referred to by Goodwin-Gill and McAdam. At the very outset of the Plenipotentiaries' Conference, which established the 1951 Refugee Convention, Robinson tacitly shared with Moshe Sharett his motivating thoughts:

> What is the mission of our delegation to this Conference? At the strategic level [...] not to bring any new changes into the Convention text but rather – only to keep and guard the existing draft! And, to vote always for the current draft and for sensible improvements of the current draft and against any attempts to assassinate the soul of the Convention.[48]

Robinson was an extremely accurate writer, all the more so when he communicated with his Foreign Minister. Yet he used strong language when explaining to Sharett the obstacles in the way of the convention's success. Robinson's strategy was very clear: its underlying principle was that of "preventive drafting," and he only shifted towards affirmative drafting when improvements to the text – for example, in relation to the amelioration of refugee conditions – were in sight. However, overall, this drafting strategy was primarily defensive and designed for a hostile diplomatic environment in which the chances of harm coming to the convention text were far greater than those for its improvement. Why was Robinson employing a defensive drafting strategy and why was the diplomatic environment hostile in the first place? Who was trying, in his strong words, to "assassinate the soul of the convention"?

Robinson's main worry was the prospect of the failure and total collapse of the Refugee Convention due to the schism between the European nations and those countries that operated selective immigration policies. These two camps held diametrically opposed viewpoints. While the former was represented by France, the latter was headed, at the Conference of Plenipotentiaries, by Australia, with Canada and New Zealand as additional members.[49] With large quantities of refugees in many European countries, European interests were directly opposed to those of the selective immigration-receiving nations. The latter seemed to draw up regulations at the expense of the Europeans, who were expected to bear the brunt of policies devised by countries not burdened with large numbers of postwar refugees in refugee camps within their territory. The selective-immigration countries were seen as "cherry picking" only those refugees potentially beneficial for their demographic objectives. It seemed unfair to the Europeans that the countries not burdened with the refugees should design the international legal tool devised to regulate international refugee policy. In European eyes, the selective-immigration countries ought to have shouldered more of the refugee burden before tailoring this international refugee-policy tool according to their own demographic wishes.

Mapping this political path at the Conference of Plenipotentiaries, Robinson created its linguistic jargon, naming the selective-immigration countries "Universalists," and demarking the group headed by France and Belgium as "Europeanists."[50] These terms were later officially adopted throughout the conference.[51] For the Robinson network, victory lay in bridging both sides of the "Europeanist–Universalist" divide between France and the immigration countries: Canada, Australia, and their supporters.

The main objective of the French vis-à-vis this scope of the proposed Refugee Convention was, in diplomatic terms, to "kill it softly".[52] Robinson explained to Sharett this threat to the Convention emanating from the European camp:

> The French (and especially their delegate at the Conference) are planning to drown the Convention so as to prove that this issue is not for the UN to solve, but rather that it really belongs to the "Council of Europe", {which} not for nothing was invited as an observer to the Conference by Belgium, and {which} has been engaged with this very problem over the past few weeks. Accordingly, the French deliberately overstate (and the Belgians follow suit) the differences between the asylum countries (Europe) and the selective immigration countries overseas.[53]

If the threat posed by the Europeanists was one of total rejection of the Refugee Convention, that posed by the universalists was that of a dilution of the convention's articles, rendering its protective qualities effectively meaningless. The Australian and Canadian delegations, as representatives of immigrant-receiving countries with a selective strategy, were openly seeking to achieve a lowering of the international standards of refugee protection so as to enable them to carry on picking and choosing only those migrants suited to their demographic needs. Explaining these policy agendas to Sharett, Robinson exposed his deep concerns about the dilution of the potencies of the convention articles by Australia and Canada, strongly echoing Paul Weis' skepticism and the IRO's corresponding concerns:

Therefore two major evils hang over the Convention:

(a) The threat of lowering the international humanitarian standards which were devised during the first session of the Ad Hoc Committee (this process has already begun in the second session and is proceeding in an exasperatingly alarming pace through this Conference).

(b) The threat of the objections and exemptions which have been filed in the dozens and who knows how the respective national parliaments will ever ratify the Convention if at all.[54]

Of primary importance was the establishment of an initial working-draft text for the Conference of Plenipotentiaries. Through his overlapping roles in the different drafting committees, Robinson managed to secure the acceptance of Paul Weis' IRO draft as the base working document for the conference, thus scoring his first diplomatic victory – albeit a technical one:

> During the 2nd session of the Conference I suggested an order of procedure for the plenary sessions, one of its pillars being the principle that the draft of the Ad Hoc Committee (including all the amendments and corrections of ECOSOC's 5th assembly) be designated as the base text for the Conference. This procedural proposal of mine, and others, were all accepted by the Conference plenary.[55]

As per the Europeanists' strategic goal to "drown the Convention" (to use Robinson's words), the French representative immediately attempted to slow down the discussions by initiating a debate regarding the definitions in Article 1 and Article 2. At the sixth session during the very first week, the Belgian delegation proposed a total redrafting of Article 2 concerning the obligations of refugees. At this point, Larsen and Robinson initiated a procedure, which went on to become routine, of referring textual problems to specialized drafting committees consisting of both Europeanist and universalist member-state representatives who were in disagreement with one another over the wording of the text. These smaller drafting committees were tasked with rewording the contentious articles and returning to the plenary with the revised texts agreed upon by all parties, for its ultimate endorsement. This incremental approach enabled the conference to continue its discussions regarding other articles, thus sidestepping this delaying tactic of the French and the Belgians. Larsen's and Robinson's hidden agenda lay in the composition of these smaller drafting committees. On these subcommittees, the members of the Robinsonian network always significantly outnumbered the opponents of the convention.

Robinson explains how this somewhat manipulative procedural mechanism was first applied to Article 2:

> in the Plenary, I successfully counter-argued against the Belgian proposal to redraft Article 2 and the Belgian ambassador withdrew his proposal. In the meanwhile, however, the French delegate inserted his own proposal which I counter-argued against twice during the 7th session. The Conference, upon the President's recommendation, decided to turn over the whole issue to a drafting committee consisting of Israel, France and the UK.[56]

Thus, the three members of the drafting committee for Article 2 were Robinson (Israel) and Hoare (UK), both from the inner circle of the Robinsonian network, against Robert Rochefort (France). With Article 2 referred to a subcommittee, Larsen and Robinson avoided the conference being hampered, and this gave them the opportunity to tackle those delegates who opposed their preferred content for Article 3.

Fragmentation or Unity? The UN Notion of "Universalism" versus the League of Nation's Heritage of Particularism

The rift between the "universalist" concept of a refugee and its "Europeanist" nemesis mirrored the deep dichotomy between the particularistic heritage of the League of Nations and the "universal" ideals of the nascent UN. Under the League of Nations, Europe took the lead in resolving international affairs the world over – be it through the mandate system, as in Palestine, Syria and Lebanon; via the Permanent Court of International Justice, as in the case of Lithuania's German-speaking Memel province; or through geographically localized solutions, such as those concerning the Sanjak of Alexandretta and the Vilayet of Mosul.[57] One of the league's fundamental working paradigms was the provision of solutions to international problems case by case. Arguably, the organization's working ethos was essentially based on a fragmentary vision of international affairs. Each problem addressed by the league was dealt with *ad rem*.

The paradigm of this fragmented approach to international relations was the league's stance on the problem of national minorities, which, as Michael Marrus observed, was closely related to refugee issues.[58] From the outset, the league's covenant was supposed to include an overarching and explicit general provision for the problem of national minorities as declared in US President Woodrow Wilson's "Fourteen Points" statement and South African statesman Jan Smuts' plan. Wilson's language, two days after he opened the Paris Peace Conference on 8 January 1919, was distinctly "universal." He demanded that all the league's member states without exception accord to national and religious minorities within their territories the same "treatment and security both in law and in fact" as that accorded to the majority.[59] Yet during the lengthy deliberations over the covenant, it evidently became impossible to incorporate a fundamental reference principle, let alone a universally designated article such as that desired by Wilson for the protection of minorities. Consequently, the entire issue of minority treaties was executed on an ad hoc basis, with different conditions in each case for minorities within different countries.[60]

While some attempts were made to review and revive "universal" paradigms within the league, especially concerning refugees (as with the 1933 Convention), these were by and large doomed to failure. The death of the charismatic first high commissioner for refugees, Fridtjof Nansen, in 1930, together with the already ingrained "particularistic" ethos of the league, confirmed the permanency of the organization's ad hoc culture.[61]

For many of the diplomats involved, the birth of the UN signified nothing more than a return to "business as usual," where "usual" meant a reversion to the League of Nation's cultural ethos. The list of delegates present at the 1951 Refugee Convention's Conference of Plenipotentiaries serves as a good example of this attitude.

The convention president, Knud Larsen, was legal advisor to the Danish Foreign Ministry throughout the 1930s, and worked with the League of Nations' secretariat almost daily.[62] Jacob Robinson was the Lithuanian Foreign Ministry's legal advisor throughout the 1930s, after being a parliamentary delegate for the Jewish minority bloc in the Lithuanian Seimas. Robinson was the representing attorney who pleaded and won Lithuania's case over Memel province against Germany, under the league's auspices at the Permanent Court of International Justice in The Hague in 1933–4. The UK delegate, Sir Samuel Hoare, was no less than Fridtjof Nansen's deputy high commissioner for refugees (Russian and Armenian) under the League of Nations in 1928. Lastly, the Belgian convention's vice president, Albert Herment, had studied law at the

Sorbonne in Paris, graduated in 1919, and joined the Belgian foreign service as a junior officer in 1920.

The French delegate, Robert Rochefort, was no different from the rest of his peers, being similarly a product of the era of the League of Nations (1919–39). As such, he was a stern advocate for a fragmented, particularistic vision of international affairs, and deeply suspicious of any attempt to universalize this field. As the 1951 Conference of Plenipotentiaries continued, Rochefort emphatically argued against the futility of trying to bind together artificially all the different refugee situations in the world under one "universal" legal-refugee regime:

> It might be thought, if the problem was viewed from a theoretical standpoint, that provisions covering all refugees in general could be embodied in a single text. Such a view would, however, be unrealistic, since conditions varied in different countries [...] What countries would in fact consider extending the benefits of the Convention to Arab refugees in Palestine? The immigration countries? Their laws did not provide for the immigration of refugees from countries outside Europe. The European countries? They already had to bear a very heavy load of refugees. Even the European countries which were interested in obtaining international assistance in that field, knew that even if the Convention granted it to them, their case would not be considered by the United Nations in the face of problems of current world importance such as, for example, the reconstruction of Korea or the relief of famine in India. The truth was that progress in the international field was necessarily slow. One region in the world was ripe for the treatment of the refugee problem on an international scale. That region was Europe. One problem was ready to form the subject of an international convention, namely, the problem of the European refugees.[63]

In Rochefort's view, all member states would be better off were they to aim for an achievable and realistic objective for the proposed Refugee Convention, rather than trying to chase a theoretically "universal" and unified solution to all the world's refugee problems, which in his view was simply unattainable:

> All refugee problems could not be dealt with in the same convention, for to do so would be to risk jeopardizing what could certainly be done for the sake of something which could not perhaps be achieved. France, for her part, was responsible for too great a number of refugees to seek to extend her generosity to parts of the world which took no interest in the solution of such problems.[64]

Rochefort reiterates his point here in simple terms. This refugee convention ought to remedy the condition of the remaining European refugees who did not have access to specialist UN agencies such as UNRWA for the Palestinians (created in 1949), or UNKRA (the United Nations Korean Reconstruction Agency) for the Koreans (created in 1950). In his eyes, the body best suited to care for European refugees was the newly created Council of Europe. Some five weeks prior to Rochefort's address at the Geneva Conference of Plenipotentiaries, the French former prime minister and foreign minister, Robert Schuman, had secured the first supranational European Treaty of the Coal and Steel Community – The Treaty of Paris (signed on April 18, 1951). Rochefort was Schuman's protégé at the Quai D'Orsay (location of the French Ministry of Foreign Affairs) and a stern supporter of his new European regionalism, as envisaged a year earlier in the Schuman Declaration of May 9, 1950. This vision of regionalism ran counter to the UN's desired "universal" reach. Writing to Sharett in Jerusalem, Robinson explained this clash between the European regionalist preferences and the UN's global approach, notwithstanding the personality issues involved:

> it is known that the High Commissioner refused to accept Mr Rochefort as his deputy and that Schuman gave him only the alternative of either Rochefort or nobody [. . .] The whole argument between France and the UK led bloc may be considered as the continuation of the fight between these two countries for or against a Council of Europe with wide jurisdiction. It was rumored that France wanted to demonstrate at this Conference that the UN is incapable of producing a satisfactory solution for the refugee problem and that this problem belongs properly to the Council of Europe.[65]

In a previous interim report on the first week of the Conference of Plenipotentiaries, Robinson had been pessimistic about the chances of the Refugee Convention coming to fruition, and so reported to Sharett,

One ought not to have high hopes for this conference for the following reasons:

(a) The Convention is deeply tied to the High Commissioner for Refugees. However, this High Commissioner has no support, neither in the US, nor in France.
(b) The French (and especially their delegate) wish to bring down this Convention, thus proving that the refugee problem cannot be solved by the UN, but rather fundamentally belongs with the Council of Europe.[66]

The Robinsonian Network and the Drafting of Article 3 of the Refugee Convention

Celebrating 60 years since the Refugee Convention's creation, UNHCR issued a special edition of its text along with a dedicated preface. Explaining the acute importance of this instrument for the protection of refugees, the High Commissioner reiterated the three principles that comprise the bedrock of refugee protections: Non-Discrimination (Article 3), Non-Penalization (Article 31), and Non-Refoulement (Article 33).[67]

While the main opponents of Article 2 were the Europeanists, the main challenges to Article 3 came from the universalists, led by Australia and Canada. By now the Larsen Robinson mechanism of delegating the drafting complexities to smaller subcommittees had become an almost standardized procedure, and Robinson explained to Sharett how this principle was applied to the drafting problems of Article 3:

> Concerning Article 3 (Non-Discrimination) I explained to the plenary that this Article's meaning is to deliberately avoid discrimination between one refugee and another on the basis of his race, religion or place of origin, and I pointed out the variations of the English and French texts which could lead to contradictions with Article 23 and others. The issue was referred to yet another subcommittee which I am part of.[68]

Sensing the urgency and importance given by all the delegates to the issue of non-discrimination, Knud Larsen, as the conference president, nominated himself to preside over the deliberations and the drafting committee for Article 3.[69] The original Ad Hoc Committee text of Article 3 was plain and straightforward:

> The Contracting States shall not discriminate against a refugee on account of his race, religion or country of origin, or because he is a refugee.[70]

After seven days of deliberations and nine extensive drafting sessions, the drafting committee returned to the plenary with a unanimously chosen, completely new, wording for Article 3, subsequent to five earlier failed alternative versions, as evidenced in the report document UN A/ CONF.2/72 to the plenary dated July 11, 1951. The text adopted by the plenary and endorsed in the final act reads:

> The Contracting States shall apply the provisions of this Convention to refugees without discrimination as to race, religion or country of origin.[71]

The new text was more accommodating and palatable to the universalists, since it followed the fundamental distinction between a forbidding – preventive legal clause and an application of a positivist – performing clause, especially concerning governmental public law. Forbidding clauses are far narrower and, by nature, less open to legal interpretation. A legal clause demanding application of a certain condition is open to legal interpretation, since application can be executed in different manners – especially when it is governmental policy which is to be applied. The new text achieved a balance between the humanistic desire for universal non-discrimination and an understanding that the application of this universal principle would ultimately be the responsibility of the UN member states. Writing to Sharett on July 22, 1951, two days before the signing of the final act by President Larsen, Robinson refers to the textual compromise opening the now infamous Article 3 for member-state interpretation:

> A compromise has been found between the Europeanists and the Universalists (the terminology is my own and was adopted by all

> the speakers at the Conference), to allow every signatory member state to determine the scope of implementation of this Convention within its territory.[72]

It is this tolerance and "legal elasticity" that provided the lowest common denominator and enabled a rapprochement between the Europeanists and the universalists, calming the objections of both sides.

After some further proposals by the French and replies from the UK, the new version of Article 3 was finally adopted by 21 votes to zero with three abstentions at the 24th meeting of the conference. This was an achievement that cannot be underestimated; as commentators on the convention have pointed out, no such clause regarding non-discrimination between different refugees, or between refugees and other aliens, had existed in previous international instruments.[73] Robinson's confidential report to Sharett, dated July 11, 1951, concerning the drafting process of Article 3 provides a dramatic account of this process, which, as we shall see, somewhat contradicts that found in existing commentaries and scholarly literature:

> The drafting committee has concluded its work. On Tuesday morning as we convened, the President suggested we accept our failure and announce to the plenary that we could not find a textual formula for Non-Discrimination which satisfied all the drafting committee members. At this moment I proposed my version (which appears in the report as option number 6) and it was accepted unanimously [. . .] I was charged with composing the report to the plenary and you shall find it annexed as UN document A/CONF.2/72. It is interesting to note that no changes to my wordings, both in the English and French versions were requested.[74]

Modern-day commentary has, to a large extent, described Article 3 as an accessory to the other articles in the convention.[75] R. Marx and W. Staff see Article 3 as being highly technical in nature and somewhat symbolic – albeit less contentious than the other articles, most notably Article 32 (expulsion) and Article 33 (non-refoulement).[76] They correctly conclude that in contrast to articles 32 and 33, Article 3 has attracted much less legal attention, with far fewer instances concerning its violation.[77]

It should be noted that A/CONF.2/72, as drafted by Robinson, is the base document of the legal commentaries to the 1951 Refugee Convention, from the early commentary by A. Grahl-Madsen through the well-known Weis commentary to the most recent by Marx and Staff, as is evident from the footnotes of all these commentators.[78]

Without access to the newly discovered archive material mentioned above, Marx and Staff adequately summarize Robinson's description of the drafting process of Article 3 as it appears from Robinson's own document A/CONF.2/72, as follows:

> [Article 3] was finally referred to a drafting group. This group offered six choices for Art. 3 to the Conference of Plenipotentiaries. At its 24th meeting, the Conference of Plenipotentiaries discussed the sixth alternative reading.[79]

A reading of Robinson's UN document A/CONF.2/72 confirms the descriptive accuracy of the account by Marx and Staff, as well as the obvious contradiction between Robinson's two accounts – namely, his confidential account to Sharett and his official UN version, which he tabled to the plenary.[80]

At the 18th session, and as a direct result of Robinson's linguistic compromise, the Canadian delegation broke ranks with Australia through its acceptance of Robinson's formula, and fractured the universalist camp:

> Ambassador Chance [Canada] expressed his appreciation for the work accomplished by the committee, which had devoted much time and thought to a most contentious problem. For his part he would be prepared to accept the sixth alternative text submitted to the conference.[81]

UN documents almost never relay a positivist reality along the lines of Leopold von Ranke's exhortation to describe an event as "wie es eigentlich gewesen war [how it really was]." Rather, they usually convey a selective account, an exercise in commonly negotiated truth management with particular statements included or excluded according to protocol, thus providing for an agreed text rather than a description of what actually took place. Yet even within these parameters, Robinson's report to Sharett and its discrepancies and inconsistencies with his own drafting of UN document A/CONF.2/72 are striking. Thus, his affirmative drafting of Article 3 did not end with the article itself but continued with his affirmative drafting of the official conference records for the plenary. The archive material examined thus far has not yielded any clues as to Robinson's reasons for providing two very different accounts of events – one, official, to the UN plenary; the other, confidential, to his foreign minister. What is clear is that Sharett was indeed cognizant of these discrepancies, since A/CONF.2/72 was annexed to Robinson's confidential report to him. Yet the UN plenary was obviously not aware of what Robinson disclosed to Sharett. Faced with no archive material concerning this contradiction, one can only posit a logical assumption as to why Robinson drafted two strikingly different accounts and the motivations behind his selective reporting to the plenary. Robinson knew full well that the Refugee Convention would become a cardinal document in international law, if and when it was adopted. In his first report to Sharett, he openly shared his concern regarding the eventual future interpretation of the Refugee Convention.[82] Robinson and Larsen knew they were drafting an international instrument which did not enjoy full international consensus, which is why, as was shown earlier, Robinson and the IRO officials were skeptical and somewhat pessimistic regarding their chances of success. My assumption is that with this skepticism in mind, Robinson wished to deliberately "iron out" all the heated thematic disagreements that took place behind closed doors in the internal discussions of the small drafting committee for Article 3, away from the watching eyes of the whole Plenipotentiary Conference plenary. Robinson deliberately omitted the drafting committee's imminent risk of failure, and presented the deep thematic internal disagreements as mere technical, linguistic issues.

I believe Robinson knowingly misrepresented what really transpired since he wanted the UN record, destined to be retained for posterity, to convey as far as possible an overall sense of agreement and unanimity between all the drafting parties. The more unanimous and consensus-based the official UN record, the less it would be prone to divisive future legal interpretations. Indeed, Robinson succeeded in the sense that Article 3 has not been opened up to too much legal questioning over the years. This is partly due to the fact that our only official UN record of the *travaux préparatoires* concerning the work of the drafting committee for Article 3 is Robinson's own A/CONF.2/72, which, as we have seen in the footnotes of the commentators, has been the bedrock of all subsequent legal scholarship over this issue for the past 60 years. We are only aware of what really took place in the drafting committee for Article 3 due to Robinson's obligation to report the proceedings to his minister truthfully, in correspondence that he knew would remain highly confidential for decades to come.

Furthermore, given the close relations between Larsen and Robinson, I believe that they jointly and premeditatedly coordinated the drafting of this agreed version of events with Larsen as head of the Article 3 drafting committee. Larsen's tasking of Robinson to write UN A/CONF.2/72 for the plenary was in breach of the UN rules of procedure, and directly opposed the mandate given to the Executive Secretary of the Conference to perform this role, as nominated by the UN Secretary-General. Article 7 of the rules of procedure leaves very little room for interpretation:

> The Executive Secretary of the Conference, appointed by the Secretary-General, shall be responsible for making all arrangements connected with the meetings of the Conference [. . .] The Secretariat shall draw up a summary record in the working languages of each meeting of the Conference.[83]

Why would Larsen task Robinson, a member-state representative and partisan by definition, with a non-partisan drafting responsibility reserved for the UN Secretariat? What reason could have driven Larsen to breach the UN rules of procedure on this issue?

My feeling is that Larsen and Robinson wished to bury the disagreements exposed in the deliberations over Article 3, and minimize external knowledge and exposure of these disagreements. The most secure way to achieve this was by tasking a member of the Robinsonian network with the production of the official record. The minute the disagreements were omitted from the official record, they were lost to posterity. And what better proof of this point than over 60 years of scholarly legal commentary, devoid of the existence of these disagreements, to prove their success. This point is all the more pertinent given that two of the four significant legal commentaries upon the 1951 Convention were written by members of the Robinsonian network, personally very close to Jacob Robinson and present during the drafting stages between 1949 and 1951. Whether Weis and Nehemiah Robinson were aware of the drama and prospects of failure existent in the drafting committee for Article 3, or whether Jacob Robinson managed to keep even his closest companions in the dark regarding these events, is of little relevance here. The final result is the glaring absence of any account concerning the possible drafting failure of Article 3 from the two contemporary commentaries. Robinson's success in concealing the drama of Article 3 had already been sealed as early as 1953, with the publication of the first commentary by his brother, Nehemiah Robinson.

The Robinsonian Network and the Drafting of Article 6 of the Refugee Convention

The main issue perturbing the universalists appears to have been relatively straightforward. The selective-immigration countries were opposed to any attempt by the convention drafters to enact changes that would significantly influence their selective immigration regimes. This view was highlighted by the action of Ambassador Shaw of Australia when he tabled his radical amendment (A/CONF.2/20), which would have virtually nullified the potency of Article 3. The Australian amendment, had it been endorsed, would have done significant harm to the convention text because it demanded that refugees comply *a priori* with immigration procedures and the requirements for sojourn in Australia. Acceptance of any part of the Australian revision would have, in effect, rendered meaningless the various protections granted to refugees when fleeing for their lives, a process which necessarily entails crossing borders and illegally trespassing on the territory of a member state. As Ambassador Shaw explained to the plenary during the conference's second day:

> in the absence of a general provision in article 2 safeguarding the position of the Australian authorities, it seemed from the Australian point of view that article 3 would be vague and dangerous without the provision contained in the amendment. A reservation on the part of the Australian Government would not be appropriate; it was amendment of the text that was required.[84]

At the fifth session, a mere two days after the opening of the conference, France and Australia exchanged strong words concerning the way in which refugees who illegally crossed the border into the territory of a signatory member state of the convention should be treated.[85] Robinson's sixth-option compromise for the wording of Article 3 provided a solution that both Europeanists and universalists could live with – although, in the event, Australia abstained from the vote on this article.

The Robinsonian compromise also led to the birth of the hitherto non-existent Article 6 of the Refugee Convention text. Initially referred to as Article 3(b), Article 6 began life as an extension designed to appease the universalists' concerns. The Australians came to perceive Article 3 as a potential infringement of their immigration policies, viewing it as granting equal status to refugees and lawfully admitted aliens. The article was thus designed to set out the legal requirements for refugees and aliens alike. In their recent commentary on Article 6, although they mistakenly refer to Article 3(b) as Article 6(b) in two references, Marx and F. Machts explain that Article 6 did not exist in any draft form prior to the Conference of Plenipotentiaries of July 1951.[86] They further correctly assert that Article 6 was jointly drafted by Robinson and Hoare.[87] Although the article was designed to appease the Australian delegation, Robinson and Hoare still managed to safeguard their underlying motive, which was consistent in all their reworking of the 1951 Refugee Convention text. In the case of Article 6, their drafting motive of ameliorating the status of refugees wherever possible was achieved by exempting refugees from requirements they could not fulfill, thus overriding the idea that refugees should be treated in the same way as other aliens.

Article 6 took shape at the fifth plenary session of the Conference of Plenipotentiaries, the very same session at which President Larsen established the drafting committee for Article 3 with himself as its head, in light of the strong universalist opposition to that Article.[88] At the plenary meeting, the Australian Ambassador initially tabled an amendment calling for the removal of "any possible ambiguity with regard to the interpretation of the term 'discriminate'."[89] However, Robinson forcefully intervened against the Australian amendment, because in his view refugees were more vulnerable than other aliens. Indeed, at times refugees could not fulfill certain requirements due to their being, *inter alia*, refugees. He gave one example of this dilemma, stressing that in many central European countries aliens were only entitled to social benefits if they fulfilled what was known as *Heimatrecht* (laws of sojourn and residence), which refugees by their mere definition could not fulfill.[90, 91] Robinson and Hoare thus suggested that the article be redrafted, to which President Larsen responded by tasking them with participating in yet another drafting committee to finalize the text for review by the plenary.[92] As Robinson reported to Sharett, as with the UN document (A/CONF2.72) concerning Article 3, this document (A/CONF.2/84) concerning Article 6 was also drafted by him, with Hoare later reviewing it before its submission to the plenary:

> In the meanwhile I have drafted the report on the Article of "In the same circumstances" and once finalized with the representative of the UK we will submit it to the plenary [. . .] the number of times I took the floor was significantly reduced this week, given that I was burdened with the writing of two reports [Article 3 and Article 6] as well as negotiations with the other delegates on different issues.[93]

Once again overstepping Article 7 of the rules of procedure, Larsen charged Robinson with the drafting of the report to the plenary rather than giving the secretariat the task. Robinson's later statement concerning Article 32 (Non-Penalization) makes it evident that he was consistently determined to relieve refugees of requirements that they might be hard-pressed to fulfill in comparison to other aliens. In this statement, Robinson provided another rare insight into his true motives as a senior drafter of the Refugee Convention, motives of a heartfelt humanitarian who empathized with refugees and their precarious condition:

> there should be a great distinction between the treatment of aliens in general and the treatment of refugees. In the case of aliens, their own country was responsible for social cases; in the case of refugees, the answer was, no country. It seemed to him that countries should accept refugees as human beings, with all the infirmities and weaknesses inherent in the human condition, and should treat them accordingly when they had offended against national laws.[94]

The Robinsonian Legacy Revisited: Israel 2006

Back at the Israeli southern border in early 2006, the Holocaust context of refugee protections was once again called upon. This time it was not to protect Jewish refugees, but rather to have Israel uphold the commitments Jacob Robinson signed and ratified 50 years earlier on its behalf. With the influx of thousands of Sudanese and Eritrean asylum seekers, the Israeli Government found itself navigating uncharted waters, lacking any policy tools, legislation, or institutional experience to draw upon.[95] Fleeing from the Darfur Genocide and Eritrean dictatorial oppression into Egypt as a first country of asylum, the migrants began their journey to Israel as their second asylum destination. Though they had suffered consistent maltreatment at the hands of the Egyptian authorities, beforehand most scholars see the December 2005 violence wrought upon them by Egyptian security forces as a turning point.[96] While demonstrating in front of the UNHCR regional bureau in Cairo, between 30 and 200 migrants were shot dead and scores arrested, with reports of torture and arbitrary detention inflicted upon them.[97]

With no policy at hand, the Israeli security establishment, which was in charge of patrolling the border, devised a hybrid strategy of forcefully returning the refugees immediately to Egyptian territory, and detaining without trial all other asylum seekers. With most migrants carrying Sudanese identity documentation and others carrying UN identification papers for stateless persons ("Nansen passports"), as recognized refugees in Egypt, the Israeli military concluded they were to be detained as a threat to national security. Sudan's perpetual state of war with Israel, and its confirmed terrorist infrastructure, were seemingly sufficient grounds for the immediate tagging of all Sudanese migrants as enemy nationals.[98]

The detention of the Sudanese asylum seekers and the governmental position that, as enemy nationals, they had no right of standing in Israeli courts triggered an immediate habeas corpus appeal by Israeli human rights NGOs. As is mandatory in habeas corpus cases, the appeal was pleaded directly at the highest Israeli judicial level – the bench of the High Court of Justice.[99] At the court session, Chief Justice President Dorit Beinish reprimanded the State for the unlimited incarceration of all migrants, in what she coined a "haphazard arrangement," unjustifiable irrelevant of the nationality of the detainee. She ordered the State to provide its legal grounding and substantiate its arguments for the court's next session.

Upon the plaintiff's request, and with the court's blessing, an expert opinion concerning the humanitarian background and status of the Darfur refugees was prepared by the Israel Prize laureate Professor Yehuda Bauer. A world authority on Holocaust and genocide studies, and chairman of Yad Vashem Holocaust memorial (a post that Jacob Robinson held during the late 1960s), Bauer's opinion to the court was instrumental in the ultimate success of the NGO habeas corpus plea. The State, in turn, submitted its legal grounding, based upon a security assessment provided by the internal secret service (the Shin Bet) claiming that all Sudanese nationals must be detained on grounds of national security. The secret service claimed that the migrants were well acquainted with the smuggler routes of the Sinai Peninsula, which supplied arms and terrorist infrastructure to the Gaza strip, and that these could be brought into Israeli territory by the Sudanese asylum seekers.[100]

With no migrant ever having approached the border with firearms or resisted army arrest, and with the Israeli state social services itself administering humanitarian assistance to the African migrants, the State's defense argument was somewhat weakened. Yet the ultimate blow leading to the plea's success was Professor Bauer's opinion to the court. Referring to the legal and human conditions of the Sudanese refugees, Professor Bauer insisted that

> Their condition is not qualitatively different from the fate of tens of thousands of German Jews who felt their very souls were threatened when they fled from the Nazi regime and arrived in England seeking refuge. These refugees were first treated as enemies and were put in custody, but British authorities soon realized this [. . .] moral injustice and changed their attitude in favor of the refugees of the Nazi regime.[101]

Professor Bauer's paralleling of the Darfur Genocide and the Holocaust echoed loudly some 50 years after the latter tragedy, calling upon the memorandum submitted by Nehemiah Robinson concerning Article 9 on behalf of the WJC to the 1951 Refugee Conference. Article 9 dealt precisely with national security and the provisional measures to be taken during times of war by contracting states against refugees. At the convention, the UK and Australia had been among the main advocates of strong prerogatives for member states vis-à-vis refugees, a position countered by the WJC and other NGOs. Knowing the personal history and views of his interlocutor, Nehemiah Robinson told Sir Samuel Hoare that his comments

> were not directed against the United Kingdom which had generously given shelter to large numbers of refugees. He submitted that the clause suggested by the UK went too far. Everyone could agree that a Government in a time of crisis might be forced to intern refugees in order to investigate whether they were genuine or not and therefore a possible danger to the security of the country.[102]

At the same time, and from within the exclusive member-states "club," Jacob Robinson's position dovetailed with his younger brother's line of argument. Thus, member states could only draw on Article 9 in case of war or due to an extreme national emergency (*crise grave nationale* in the French text). National security was not to be used as a pretext for infringing upon the liberties of refugees at the State's convenience.

Hegel explained that history does not repeat itself in the strict sense of the term but rather, advances in a spiral-like mode while retaining the similarities of current events to comparable instances in the past. Here too then, the historical cycle ironically overlaped in its usual Hegelian manner. Jacob Robinson, the farsighted Israeli ambassador who had helped draft the 1951 Refugee Convention, deliberately undermined "National Security," the very tool with which the Israeli state was attempting to justify its actions against genocide-fleeing refugees 55 years later. No less ironic was the overturning of governmental policy by the Israeli Supreme Court in 2006, releasing from automatic detention those African migrants caught on the Israeli side of the border. The legal opinion tabled to the high court by Yehuda Bauer – Jacob Robinson's protégé, successor, and collaborator on the Holocaust memorial – reiterated, four decades later, the dictum of his illustrious forbearer. Humanitarianism was universal. It was not to be sacrificed on the altar of the false argumentative tabernacle of "national security."[103]

CHAPTER 2

THE ORIGINS OF THE NON-REFOULEMENT PRINCIPLE

The principle of non-refoulement in international law is intended to prevent a recipient country or entity from returning refugees into the hands of their tormentors, or placing them where they shall be subjected to persecution and maltreatment.

In a recent decision regarding the debatable legality of forcibly returning asylum seekers on the high seas, the European Court of Human Rights ruled that Italy had breached its legal obligations for refugee protection.[1] The Italian Coast Guard's action of forcibly returning African asylum seekers to the shores of Libya in 2009 ran counter to the country's obligations under the European Convention for the Protection of Human Rights and Fundamental Freedoms. In his concurring legal opinion, Judge Pinto de Albuquerque analyzed the exterritorial applicability of Article 33, better known as the "Non-Refoulement principle" of the 1951 Refugee Convention, to asylum seekers on the high seas. Albuquerque's opinion was based on his extensive study of the principle of non-refoulement, amply drawing from the 1951 Refugee Convention's *travaux préparatoires*.[2] As I have demonstrated elsewhere, the drafters of the 1951 Refugee Convention definitely intended for non-refoulement to apply on the high seas and explicitly referred to maritime "push back" operations of the late 1930s as illegal under the upcoming new convention.[3] The judge criticized the contrasting rulings by the US Supreme Court, the Australian High Court, and the British House of Lords, which in his view unjustifiably rejected the exterritorial reach of non-refoulement at sea.[4] The contrast between the European Court's ruling and those of its peers across the Atlantic and the English Channel merely denoted that the debate concerning non-refoulement's extraterritorial applicability is alive and kicking. This fundamental rift begs for the uncovering of the original sources and motivations which underpinned the work of the drafters of Article 33 of the 1951 Refugee Convention as we know it today.[5]

The Europeanist–Universalist Divide and the Geography of Refoulement

To say that non-refoulement was seen as yet another important issue in the eyes of the drafters of the 1951 Refugee Convention would be an understatement. In the second session of the Ad Hoc Committee (August 1950), the deliberations over the text of Article 33 (then still known as Article 28) intensified and overheated. The Cold War-related fears of espionage and political sabotage began to instigate a diluting of the protective language of Article 28 as it has been formulated six months earlier, during the Ad Hoc Committee's first session (February 1950).[6] Faced with this alarming development, President Knud Larsen exposed his deepest convictions about the overriding importance of what he himself later dubbed "non-refoulement." Reminding the other members that he was speaking on behalf of Denmark, which received thousands of refugees as a country of first asylum, Larsen stated his views and those of the Danish Government in no uncertain terms, remarking that:

> Even if the work of this Committee, resulted in the ratification by a number of countries of Article 28 alone, it would have been worthwhile. He himself would regret any changes to the wording.[7]

A few moments earlier in the same session, replying to the Swiss delegate's query as to how states should react towards a refugee who caused problems in his country of asylum, the Israeli delegate, Jacob Robinson, explained the *raison d'être* underpinning non-refoulement:

> The basic idea behind Article 28 was that in some circumstances the greatest possible evil for a refugee was to be returned to

> his country of origin. Governments were to be entitled for some remedy in cases where an individual was a public nuisance, but they were not to send him back to the country where death awaited him.[8]

The initial text concerning non-refoulement, incorporated into the draft IRO Convention text, read as follows:

> Each of the High Contracting Parties undertakes not to expel or in any way turn back refugees to the frontiers of territories where their life or freedom would be threatened on account of their race, religion, nationality or opinions.[9]

Robinson's protégé and former employee, Paul Weis, who represented the IRO in the very same debate, clarified further. Article 28 meant exactly what it said. It "imposed a negative duty forbidding the expulsion of any refugee to certain territories."[10]

Reading the statements of President Larsen, Robinson, and Weis concerning non-refoulement, one is not struck by any severe complexity or ambiguity. If anything, Article 28 contained the basic tenet of all humanitarian decrees. States were simply not allowed to return exiled innocent human beings to places where they would be tormented.

So, why not state it just like that? If non-refoulement was so vital, why didn't Larsen, Robinson, and Weis simply use the words "anywhere" or "any place"? Such a textual usage would have inherently included refugees at sea – or on the moon, for that matter, since that too belongs under the designated term "place." Jacob Robinson possessed an outstanding talent for drafting International treaties.[11] The problem of exiled people at sea, let alone for Jews like himself, was anything but foreign to him. One need only to recall the 1938 voyage of the *St. Louis*, full of German Jews, looking for a port of embarkation to no avail, only to be returned to Germany. In order to answer this conundrum, as to why the words "anywhere" or "any place" were not used, one would have to reconstruct the *a priori* geographical premises of the drafters of the 1951 Refugee Convention.

Robinson's final confidential report from the Ad Hoc Committee's first session in February 1950 provides us with important information as to the interrelationships between the geographical positioning of states and the issue of refoulement. In its opening paragraphs, Robinson explains the growing schism between the two parties present at the Ad Hoc Committee, later referred to by himself as "Europeanists" and "Universalists." As I have shown above, and as is also confirmed from UK archive sources, this vitally important fracture perturbed and threatened the very existence of the Refugee Convention from its nascent stage until the endorsement of the final act 18 months later in 1954.[12] On one side of this divide stood countries already housing significant numbers of refugees, such as France and Belgium. On the other side stood those countries that selectively accepted refugees as immigrants, but did not suffer the incoming of mass population flows. This second group was headed by Australia and included Canada, New Zealand, and some Latin American states as well.[13]

Robinson begins by explaining the interrelationships and problems regarding the geographical positioning of European countries versus overseas nations which voluntarily receive refugees:

> If we consider the members who took part in the deliberations of the Ad Hoc Committee from the view point of the refugee problem, we will easily discover that they belong to distinct categories:
>
> - The category of so-called reception countries (Belgium, Denmark, France, UK).
> - The category of so called immigration countries (Brazil, Canada, USA).
>
> The countries of reception are the European countries which by their geographic position and/or by their tradition, have been bound during the last three decades, to receive refugees and keep them there, not having any chance of shipping them away. The immigration countries, while in a way also giving shelter to refugees, do so only to selected categories in accordance with their immigration laws. While Canada, for instance, might have given shelter to a greater number of refugees than the UK the difference between them is that the UK – as a rule – did not select them, while Canada did.[14]

The geographical implications are clear here. Countries which are connected by land to places where mass refugee flows originate from are forced to receive refugees whether they would like to or not. The issue here is a fundamental one of geographical location. Canada or Australia did not have to deal with the problem of fleeing refugee masses at their borders, since they geographically did not have borders with war-torn lands after World War II.

The actual act of refoulement – that is, the turning back of persecuted refugees to the place they fled from – often occurred at a geographically landlocked border post, crossing, or fence. In a subsequent passage, Robinson testifies to the vital importance attributed to the idea of non-refoulement, already salient at this early stage of drafting. He then provides a fascinating insight into the intricate relations between refoulement and the geographical separation afforded by the high seas:

> The conflict of the two categories of countries interested in refugees made itself felt in the work of the Ad Hoc Committee as well as in some other organs including the General Assembly [. . .] the most manifest of these contradictions between the two categories came out when the problem of *non refoulement* was discussed. The countries of immigration were very enthusiastic against refoulement, but they made it clear that the turning back of illegal immigrants would not be considered *a refoulement*. The ocean protects the countries of immigration also against the need of refoulement, which exists only in countries with contiguous frontiers with other countries from where the stream of refugees comes.[15]

So there we have it. Australia, Canada, and the US could afford to advocate non-refoulement since they did not have to bear its demographic and social consequences. These would be borne by the European countries alone. Admirably though, it is partly thanks to the persistence of the UK, Belgium, and the Netherlands – the very countries who were bearing the brunt of the postwar European refugee crisis – that the 1951 Refugee Convention was eventually endorsed. In his final report to Cabinet, Sir Samuel Hoare explained who sided with the UK for the benefit of refugee protections at the Plenipotentiaries' Conference:

> Mr Larsen proved on the whole a very successful chairman. He was inclined to be slow but his patience and good humour were of

> particular value in preventing serious disruption of the conference by the provocative outbursts of the French representative Rochefort [...] of the representatives present the Belgian, Mr Hermant, was our greatest ally [...] The Netherlands' delegate Baron van Boetzelaer was also helpful and generally shared our point of view. Mr Robinson, the representative of Israel, made many useful contributions to the debate.[16]

Concerning the Australian position, Hoare remarked,

> The Australian representative, Mr Shaw, made such heavy weather of difficulties which the Australian government felt about certain provisions of the Convention as to give the impression that Australia's adherence to the Convention was not very likely.[17]

Robinson confirms Hoare's prognosis when he reports,

> the Australians were very restrictive during the first week of the conference, introducing numerous amendments to the detriment of the refugees.[18]

Most of the Australian amendments were aimed at blocking the adoption of clauses that contradicted Australian (and Canadian) immigration laws. With the European states housing most of the refugees from World War II, this position seemed morally untenable. If all states had equal humanitarian obligations, the limiting of these via selective immigration policies, leaving Europe to deal with vast postwar refugee populations, seemed rather unfair. In order not to lose diplomatic face, many of the Australian amendments were advocated under the pretext of national security needs, limiting the access possibilities for refugees whom Australia in fact did not desire.[19] In the fifth and sixth sessions of the Plenipotentiaries' Conference, Herment of Belgium and Rochefort of France amassed considerable diplomatic pressure against the Australian delegate, ultimately questioning his intellectual integrity.[20]

In order to avoid a total collapse of the Plenipotentiaries' Conference, and careful not to humiliate the Australian delegate by unmasking the true immigration-policy motivations behind his national security-driven amendments, Robinson stepped up to the podium. As the plenary blocked the Australian reductions of refugee protections, Robinson carefully maintained the debate on an *ad rem* level, preventing Rochefort from descending into *ad hominem* arguments, which would have triggered an Australian resignation from the Refugee Convention as a whole, as feared by Hoare. As for the problematic usage of the term "national security" as an all-inclusive "basket" clause, Robinson reported to Sharett:

> During the 6th session I did my utmost best to weaken as much as possible the element of "National Security" as an element which would enable member states to treat refugees harshly, and I therefore successfully pleaded against the Australian revision which was struck down by the conference.[21]

To the detriment of Australia and the US, since the early 1970s these so-called immigration countries which Robinson thought were protected by the ocean, have found themselves faced with considerable refugee flows – arriving, this time, by boats over the high seas. Subsequently, as these refugees began clandestinely transgressing US and Australian territorial waters both countries began forcefully returning them back to the high seas. The debate as to whether *territorial waters* are *territories* in themselves, as referred to in Article 33, since they are at sea, is beyond the scope of this book.

This text does, however, examine the hypotheses that the recent decision against Italy by the European Court of Human Rights falls directly in line with the original humanitarian intentions of the drafters of Article 33. In his concurring opinion, Justice Pinto de Albuquerque explicitly made the point of returning to the historical settings of World War II and its aftermath, with a specific reference to the saving of Jews by Raoul Wallenberg and the Portuguese consul, Aristides de Sousa Mendes, as the adequate standard of humanitarian behavior.[22] Judge Albuquerque's deliberations in the same verdict over the applicability of non-refoulement to maritime asylum seekers, as grounded in the *travaux préparatoires*, alongside the historical saving of the Jews seem to merit a deeper examination of the historical records, circumstances, and personalities who helped shape Article 33 as we know it today.

Rabbi Isaac Lewin and the Roots of Non-Refoulement: Article 33

Reading through the commentaries upon Article 33, one is stuck by the discrepancy between the vital importance attributed to this article by the convention drafters in the early 1950s and the deep lacunae in our knowledge regarding the personality and function of its initial drafter – Isaac Lewin. U. Davy, J. Hathaway, A. Grahl-Madsen, and Nehemiah Robinson provide ample thematic information on the drafting process of this article between 1949 and July 1951.[23] All these commentators mention that the draft chosen for consideration by the Ad Hoc Committee was indeed the one tabled by the Agudas Israel World Organization ("Aguda") on February 2, 1950. Weis, who was present during all the Ad Hoc Committee deliberations, goes further than other commentators and quotes a few passages from Lewin's address that day.[24]

Being neither a member-state representative nor part of the UN establishment, one is bound to ask who was Rabbi Isaac Lewin, and how did he come to propose a draft to ECOSOC's Ad Hoc Committee in the first place? How was it that an ultra-orthodox Jewish rabbi, speaking on behalf of an ultra-orthodox Jewish NGO, came to table the bedrock draft for two of the most important clauses of the Refugee Convention: Non-Expulsion and Non-Refoulement?

Rabbi Dr Isaac Lewin was born in 1906 in the city of Lodz in Poland to an illustrious family lineage of orthodox Jewish Talmudic jurists. Lewin's father, Rabbi Aaron Lewin, served as the chief Rabbi of Poland, and as a member of the Polish Parliament representing the Jewish minority in the country.[25] Isaac Lewin received a similar education to other central European middle-class observant Jewish families of his kind. This education consisted of a hybrid of Jewish religious teachings of Talmudic law and an occidental legal training. Lewin was ordained as a rabbi in 1935, and received his legal doctorate at the University of Lodz in 1937.[26] Due to his legal training, Lewin was elected to Lodz City Council in 1936, representing the city's Jewish inhabitants.[27] By the late 1930s, he had already developed a knowledgeable reputation in cases where Jewish law intertwined with other European non-Jewish legal systems, appearing before different European state courts as well as the religious Catholic High Ecclesiastical Court in Naples.[28]

In 1939, upon the German occupation of Poland, Isaac Lewin escaped Lodz and eventually arrived in the US in August 1941, immediately joining the ranks of Aguda there.[29] During World War II, he participated in multi-level efforts on behalf of the organization, which managed to save thousands of European Jews through the provision of Latin American nationalities to them within Nazi-occupied Europe.[30] These efforts consisted mainly of fundraising and the acquisition of foreign citizenships through the Latin American consulates in Switzerland (Geneva and Bern). Once the appropriate travel documents had been issued, Lewin provided the financial means for the voyages of these Jews to Switzerland – and from there on to neutral Portugal and finally, via maritime vessels, to Latin America.[31]

During these years, Lewin became acquainted with other Jewish organizations such as the World Jewish Congress, where Jacob and Nehemiah Robinson and Paul Weis were working at the time.[32] Equally important were his deep acquaintances with senior American foreign service officials such as US Under-secretary of State Summer Wells and the Jewish congressman Sol Bloom, a former chairman of the House Foreign Relations Committee.[33] Lewin's activities also extended to Jewish war-orphaned children, whom he helped rescue through France in coordination with the French Resistance in 1944.[34]

Stefan Troebst has pointed to the disproportionate amount of central European Jewish jurists involved in the making of postwar international legal structures, and of the UN specifically.[35] Jacob and Nehemiah Robinson, Paul Weis, Hersch Lauterpacht, and Raphael Lemkin (initiator of the Genocide Convention) were all central European Jewish jurists who wound up, in one way or another, working for the nascent UN, drafting substantial portions of its early documents and conventions.[36] Recent research points to an additional feature distinguishing this group – namely, the fact that they were all acquainted and interconnected with one another, forming a like-minded network for the promotion of humanitarian values within the newly designed instruments of postwar international treaties.

Lemkin and Lauterpacht had been well acquainted since their early days as students at the University of Lvov – in those days better known by its German name, Lemberg.[37] While the cooperation between Lemkin and Robinson during the Nuremberg trials has already been established, new archive material uncovered at the Israeli Central

Archive in Jerusalem clearly points to the continuation of cooperation between the two men over the promotion of the Genocide Convention in late 1949 and early 1950.[38] Lemkin explicitly solicited Robinson's help in lobbying the various UN member states to ratify the Genocide Convention and securing the required signatures from sufficient member states to make this convention and its ratification binding.[39] The relationships between Jacob and Nehemiah Robinson and Paul Weis have already been proven, as well as those between Robinson and Louis Henkin, the US legal delegate to the Ad Hoc Committee on Statelessness and Related Problems.[40]

It is within this context and in this milieu that one ought to place Rabbi Dr Isaac Lewin. By the late 1940s, Lewin received his tenure as a professor of Jewish History at the Yeshiva University in New York, in parallel with acting as the head of Aguda in the US.[41] At the same time, Lewin secured for Aguda an advisory consultative status to ECOSOC similar to many other accredited NGOs, quite a number of Jewish ones amongst the latter.[42] Following receipt of this status, Lewin began a lifelong engagement with the UN Human Rights Commission, addressing it on issues ranging from children's rights to the prevention of all forms of discrimination and of torture.[43] In 1981, Rabbi Lewin was awarded the UN Medal of Peace in recognition of his lifelong campaign and the final adoption by the UN General Assembly of the Declaration on the Elimination of All Forms of Intolerance and Discrimination Based upon Religion or Belief.

In January 1950, as the Ad Hoc Committee on Statelessness began its work on the draft of what was to become the 1951 Refugee Convention, Lewin was already well acquainted with the UN – and specifically with ECOSOC's working procedures. He had behind him the ample experience of eight hectic years of efforts to save Jewish refugees during and after the Nazi occupation of Europe, mastering the intricacies of consulate travel documents, border crossings, and personal status determinations across much of the European continent. Last but not least, he had trustworthy access to the listening ears of senior US State Department officials, in charge of the negotiations of the Refugee Convention.

On a personal level, Lewin was acquainted with the US delegate to the Ad Hoc Committee Louis Henkin through the latter's father, Rabbi Samuel Henkin, who was among the highest senior authorities on

Talmudic law in the US, teaching at the very same Yeshiva University where Lewin had just received his tenure. In his final, secret report on the proceedings of the Ad Hoc Committee on Statelessness, at the end of its first session in late February 1950, Jacob Robinson explicitly referred to the disproportionate Jewish representation around the Committee's drafting table:

> A few words about the Jewish participation in this Committee: USA was represented by Mr Henkin, who is a son of a Rabbi, an authority in Talmudic family law [...] and he himself is an observant Jew. Formerly the secretary of Supreme Court Justice Frankfurter, he has a sharp Talmudic mind and was very good in drafting. The IRO was represented by Dr Paul Weis (formerly with the World Jewish Congress in London) [...] In addition the Jewish organizations with the so-called consultative status were also present and, as I reported before, two of them, Dr Lewin of Agudath Israel and Dr Perlzweig of the World Jewish Congress addressed the meeting, both without previous consultations with us.[44]

As per their consultative status to ECOSOC, the accredited NGOs could and did request the privilege of addressing the drafters at the Ad Hoc Committee's table, conditioned upon the consent of the committee members, and especially the ECOSOC permanent members. In the case of Isaac Lewin's address, this consent was secured by the formal request of Louis Henkin – the US representative – and tabled and accepted by the committee.[45] His address was scheduled for February 1, 1950 at 11 o'clock in the morning. Lewin focused his address on the problems relating to the expulsion of refugees, and to their turning back into hostile territories (refoulement). Following the end of the morning session, Henkin continued to advocate on Lewin's behalf, requesting as the US representative that the committee discuss in full Lewin's draft, which later became Article 32 and Article 33.

The development of the text of Article 32 has been well documented in the distinguished commentaries by Davy and Weis.[46] The British delegate, Leslie Brass, opted immediately for the draft tabled by Lewin due to its superior structure in comparison to the other versions submitted to the drafting committee. He was immediately supported by

Jacob Robinson from Israel and Henkin for the US, as well as the Canadian chairman of the committee. The Lewin draft was eventually split up into two separate articles through a joint Belgian–American proposal.[47] The first article dealt exclusively with the expulsion of lawfully admitted refugees, and eventually became the Article 32 we know today. The second article, dealing solely with the turning back of refugees, became the well-known Article 33 regarding non-refoulement.

Lewin's draft, reprinted in its entirety in the recent Oxford commentary on the 1951 Refugee Convention, was by no means totally novel.[48] Rather, it was a reworking of elements from the different international instruments existing prior to the Ad Hoc Committee of February 1950 – most notably the 1928, 1933, 1936, and 1938 instruments – in addition to elements from the French and secretariat drafts.[49] As the Ad Hoc Committee adjourned after its second session in August 1950, Article 27 of the proposed refugee convention text relating to non-expulsion read as follows:

1. The Contracting States shall not expel a refugee lawfully in their territory save on grounds of national security or public order.
2. The expulsion of such refugee shall be only in pursuance of a decision reached in accordance with due process of law. The refugee shall have the right to submit evidence to clear himself and to appeal to be represented before competent authority.
3. The Contracting States shall allow such refugees a reasonable period within which to seek legal admission into another country. The Contracting States reserve the right to apply during that period such internal measures as they may deem necessary.[50]

A simple comparative analysis of Article 24 of the IRO draft, prepared by Paul Weis as the Ad Hoc Committee's main working document, along with the previous instruments mentioned above, compared to the Aguda-proposed draft, reveals Lewin's added value to the text. Lewin's addition is, in fact, the second sentence of paragraph 2, above:

> The refugee shall have the right to submit evidence to clear himself and to appeal to be represented before competent authority.

This sentence remained virtually intact all through the excruciating negotiations concerning the articles of non-expulsion and non-refoulement which took place almost a year later at the Conference of Plenipotentiaries in July 1951. To this extent, Lewin's success in providing the working draft for these articles, and in maintaining his provision for a refugee's right for some sort of legal consideration and evidence evaluation, was a considerable diplomatic victory. Seldom did NGOs, let alone ultra-orthodox Jewish ones, get a chance to influence in such a vital way the shape and wording of a first-grade international instrument governing the world order. This success was evident not only to Lewin himself but also to the other delegates participating in the Ad Hoc Committee. After the committee's third week, Jacob Robinson reported to Walter Eytan that:

> During this week some Jewish organizations with consultative status showed up. On Wednesday, February 1st, Dr Lewin (Agudath Israel) addressed the meeting (with long quotations from the book of Amos) on the problem of expulsion and Refoulement and submitted a draft (E/C.2/242 attached herewith) which had certain advantages as compared with the other two drafts (Secretariat and France). At the suggestion of the UK, supported by myself, the Agudath draft was taken as the bar for discussion. Of course the final language of Article 24 differs greatly from the Agudath draft and is the result of long discussions. The Agudath has certainly made most of its "success" [...] All these steps were taken by the organizations without coordination among themselves, and without consultation with us.[51]

Robinson's reports are generally concise and punctilious, similar to the manner in which he drafted UN documents. He hardly wasted words – not least because in many instances the reports themselves were wired via encrypted electronic telex from Geneva, a process which was both time-consuming and costly. Consequently, one must pay special attention to Robinson's talking points in order also to understand sub-textual connotations and meanings in his communiqués. The passage above yields two such issues.

The first one regards the lack of coordination within and among the Jewish NGOs, as well as between them and the State of Israel which

Robinson represented. The above passage was written at the beginning of the 18-month drafting process of the Refugee Convention, a time period which saw considerable "ups and downs" in the convention's draft text and even in its chances of ever being signed and ratified. Robinson's last sentence, concerning the lack of coordination and consultation among the different Jewish representatives, should be read as an explicit request to Jerusalem to "throw its diplomatic weight around," so as to get all the Jewish representatives on board, into one coordinated effort for the sake of the convention's success. By the time of the Conference of Plenipotentiaries, Robinson's calling on this point was already amply answered. In July 1951, he was already coordinating the entire Jewish NGO lobby and the Israeli position in the direction of the enlargement, rather than the limitation, of the convention's scope of refugee protections.[52]

The second point concerns Robinson's view of Lewin's appearance before the Ad Hoc Committee and the reasons for his "success" in making his draft the working document upon which subsequent textual changes would be carried out. Robinson takes the time to communicate to Jerusalem the fact that Lewin extensively quoted from the biblical Book of Amos. To a modern-day reader, this passage is somewhat perplexing as to the relevance of biblical quotations to a concrete and technical international legal instrument such as the Refugee Convention. We know for certain that Robinson held Rabbi Lewin in high intellectual esteem, similarly to the favorable references he made towards Louis Henkin's Talmudic qualities, viewing positively both men's vast knowledge of both Jewish law and European and international legal systems. Being an observant Jew who had received a similar education, dovetailing Talmudic studies with an extensive European legal training, Robinson was referring favorably as much to his own background as to that of his religious Jewish peers at the committee drafting table.[53]

Yet Robinson was writing a secret report to the director general of the Foreign Ministry in Jerusalem. The recipient of this communiqué, Walter Eytan (originally named Ettinghausen), was a vehemently secular German-born Jew. Robinson and Eytan were acquainted well enough for the former to know the director's notoriously punctilious and meticulous character, which had earned him the second most important position in Israeli diplomacy after Foreign Minister Sharett.[54] Robinson would only have mentioned the issue of Lewin's biblical quotations if it had specific and concrete relevance to the diplomatic issues at hand. A glimpse at Lewin's biblical quotation and his added explanatory remarks reveal the diplomatic relevance grasped by Robinson, one which deemed these quotations worth mentioning in his report.

The official UN transcripts of Lewin's address to the Ad Hoc Committee from Wednesday, February 1, 1950 is partial, and does not include any reference to biblical sources.[55] As with most UN records of proceedings, they are a summary of the presentations by the speakers. The transcribers deliver what they see as the main points of importance in the presentation, necessarily omitting points and issues which seem less relevant. Often, the proceedings are edited *post eventum* as per the end result of a certain debate, pointing to the evolution of the main issues through the presentations of the different speakers.

Nevertheless, a reader ought to be intrigued when points publically presented are omitted from the UN records yet repeated in a delegate's report to his superiors at member-state headquarters. The point here, which should attract the attention of any scholar, is the discrepancy between the absences of Lewin's biblical quotations from the UN transcripts and the UNHCR archives, and Robinson's reporting and the importance he vested in them.

Lewin began his address by distinguishing the four different issues which the IRO's draft Article 24 dealt with – expulsion, refoulement, lawful admission, and naturalization – and, while he dissected Article 24, he pointed toward what he saw as the two gravest dangers confronting refugees: expulsion and refoulement. At this stage, Lewin did not completely dissociate these two issues, a process which Jacob Robinson himself undertook a few hours later in the afternoon session of the same day.[56] Lewin proposed that Article 24 be redrafted in its entirety, and provided the following insight:

> Expulsion of a refugee, in the majority of cases, means prolonged agony. It is equivalent to death when he is sent back to his country of origin, and the Draft Convention rightly prohibits this act. In this way it fulfills one of the ethically unsurpassed proscriptions of Jewish law, particularly stressed by the earlier prophets. I have the impression that one of them, Amos, considered the prohibiting of sending refugees back, to be a binding rule of international law of his time. He once said that God would never

> forgive Philistine Gaza and Phoenician Tyre for the crime of expelling the Jewish refugees, who had found asylum in their countries, delivering them to the enemy, the Kingdom of Edom.[57]

Lewin's biblical example is one of refoulement – that is, the returning of refugees back into the hands of their tormentors, and not just a case of expulsion as such. His claim for the early biblical existence of universally binding international laws prohibiting refoulement, applicable to all humankind without exception, lies at the heart of Robinson's reference to headquarters in Jerusalem concerning Lewin's address. In the following paragraph, and before submitting his own draft for the Ad Hoc Committee's consideration, Lewin explained the logic behind his seemingly anachronistic claim for the existence of International legal norms in biblical times:

> It is obvious that since Amos reprimanded Gaza and Tyre, which were not bound by Jewish law; for that sin – he considered their act a violation of international law. We therefore have a precedent for the present convention dating back from the eighth century B.C.E.[58]

Thus, the answer as to the diplomatic relevance of Lewin's biblical quotes lies precisely in the clash between the legal position – which upholds an unlimited and universally binding application of non-refoulement, as advocated by both Lewin and Robinson – and a more limited scope of applicability advocated by selective immigration countries, most notably Australia. This conflict of views, between those opting for an all-encompassing applicability of the refugee convention and those demanding its curbing, manifested itself in the deliberations regarding many of the conventions' articles. Very few issues, if any, were contested more vocally and vociferously at the convention than that of non-refoulement.

From Article 2, to Paragraph 2 Article 33: Non-Refoulement and the Question of National Security

Lewin's draft, which became the base working paper for the discussions underpinning Articles 32 and 33, had not introduced any new language concerning Article 33. Reporting to Eytan in Jerusalem at the end of the second week of the Ad Hoc Committee's work, Jacob Robinson reiterated the fact that the committee's main working document was drafted by the IRO, referring to the credit due to his former employee and protégé, Paul Weis: "the so-called Secretariat's draft which is in fact an IRO draft."[59] [60] Lewin copied the proposed text of Article 33 word for word from the IRO draft written by Paul Weis. The evolution of the text of Article 33, known then as Article 28, at the second session of the Ad Hoc Committee in August 1950 was in all senses a textual development in favor of refugee protection. The IRO draft text concerning non-refoulement, repeated by Lewin and adopted as the working paper on February 2, 1950 by the Ad Hoc Committee, stated:

> Each of the High Contracting Parties undertakes not to expel or in any way turn back refugees to the frontiers of territories where their life or freedom would be threatened on account of their race, religion, nationality or opinions.[61]

Reading the text of Article 33, finally adopted by the Conference of Plenipotentiaries in July 1951, one observes the "ratcheting up" of its forbidding language, further prohibiting the convention signatories from refoulement of refugees:

> No Contracting State shall expel or return ("refouler") a refugee in any manner whatsoever to the frontiers of territories where his life or freedom would be threatened on account of his race, religion, nationality, membership of a particular social group or political opinion.[62]

The first evidence of additional refugee protection can be seen in the words "in any manner whatsoever," precluding interpretive variations which could serve to weaken the negative duty of the article.[63] Seldom have UN treaties used such unequivocal language.

The second strengthening of the text was the reversion to the singular rather than plural, changing the multiple noun "refugees" in the Ad Hoc Committee draft to the singular noun "a refugee" in the final act. As Weis clearly pointed out, the usage of singular rather than plural language pointed to the protection from refoulement as being enjoyed by any refugee *in each and every individual case*. It also means that protection is all the more *a fortiori* in cases where refoulement is being conducted by states against certain groups or categories of refugees rather than simply against individuals.[64]

This change from plural to singular is intimately connected to another strengthening of the text: the addition of a new refugee category, consisting of "a particular social group or political opinion," as meriting protection. The addition of this new category was due to an amendment submitted by the Government of Sweden.[65] Based on inconclusive sources at the Swedish Foreign Ministry archives, Einarsen has posited out that this new category might have possibly referred to refugees fleeing communist regimes behind the Iron Curtain.[66] This hypothesis of Einarsen's is confirmed by two separate and independent sources, thus validating his theory.

The first source is the unrecorded verbal address delivered by Isaac Lewin during the Plenipotentiaries' Conference, which accompanied his submitted amendment (later to be rejected by the conference).[67] In his verbal address, Lewin pleaded for international assistance over a humanitarian crisis which was unfolding in Hungary at exactly the same time (July 1951) as the Conference of Plenipotentiaries was taking place in Geneva. Upon the instigation of the communist regime in Budapest, the deportation had begun of thousands of people deemed "undesirable" by the newly installed communist regime.

As the conference carried on, reports of these mass deportations from Budapest began piling up, eventually triggering a harsh critical response from US secretary of state Dean Acheson, and ultimately meriting a strong condemnation by US President Truman from the White House. As mentioned above, by this time Robinson was coordinating his steps closely with the entire Jewish NGO lobby – possibly even instigating Lewin's address. In the latter, Lewin stressed that the people being expelled from Budapest were first being specifically tagged as members of certain social groups and only then, based upon that membership, being chosen for expulsion:

> The basis upon which the deportation is ordered was stated some time ago in the New York Times by John McCormack, in correspondence from Vienna. He reported that the population of Hungary has been placed in five categories: The top category consists of leading Communists, and class five – of exploiters, the

> Roman Catholic Clergy, Western-minded Protestants, religious Jews, and members of the former middle classes. Class five is being deported "*en masse*" from the larger cities.[68]

The second source confirming Einarsen's theory is a handwritten entry in the file of the UK Board of Trade dealing with the Refugee Convention. The entry was written by H. N. Edwards, who was a legal advisor to the undersecretary of trade, P. J. Mantle, charged with reviewing the draft convention text. Concerning the definition of a refugee and who ought to be included in it, Edwards explicitly referred to the Hungarian dictator Matyas Rakosi and his ideologically instigated mass deportations between 1950 and 1951:

> I think that we should add to the types of refugees suggested by Mrs Wilson in para. 3, Hungarians, Roumanians, and Bulgarians who have left their countries, or leave before the end of this year, because of well founded fear of being a victim of persecution on account of their political opinions or because they are unpopular with the Communist Government e.g. Rightist Social Democrats in Hungary "these old traitors who are finally being unmasked and rendered harmless" – M. Rákosi.[69]

Truman's condemnation of the deportations came virtually on the same day that President Larsen signed the final act in Geneva.[70] The very issue prohibited by the Swedish amendment – refoulement on the grounds of belonging to a certain social or political group – was grotesquely coming to life in Hungary and Romania at exactly the time that the delegates in Geneva were formulating the international tool for remedying such despicable acts. Robinson and Lewin, who by now were closely coordinated, issued a joint press statement highlighting Lewin's address, and Robinson's signing of the convention.[71]

Non-refoulement was no longer an abstract concept in the hands of international lawyers. Lewin had, in effect, just driven the exiled Budapest trains directly onto the marble-paved floors of the Palais Des Nations in Geneva.

Judging from the development of Article 33, one would assume that the whole convention text was moving in the direction of enhancing refugee protections. Yet the textual development of Paragraph 1 of

Article 33 concerning non-refoulement was, unfortunately, the exception to the norm at the Conference of Plenipotentiaries rather than the general trend. In his final report to Foreign Minister Sharett, written three days after the signing of the Final Act on July 28, 1951, Robinson lamented the process of erosion of refugee protections within the final convention text, while reiterating his humanitarian motivations which ran counter to this lowering process. This erosion of the draft – or, as Robinson refers to it, its "de-liberalization" – began at the second session of the Ad Hoc Committee in August 1950, and continued all through the Conference of Plenipotentiaries in July 1951:

> we participated in this conference as in the previous ones, with a sincere desire to get a liberal and well drafted convention. Unfortunately the process of de-liberalization of the substantive provisions of the Conference which started at the second session of the Ad Hoc Committee continued unabatedly during this Conference. The only exception from this tendency was the first Swedish amendment (A/CONF.2/9) extending the criteria of persecution also to "membership of particular social groups".[72]

According to Robinson, this process of the erosion of refugee protections which were attained during the first session of the Ad Hoc Committee was by no means haphazard, and had a distinct logical thread running all through it:

> The most important elements of this de-liberalization were the numerous clauses and references to national security, the reduction of the exemption of reciprocity to legislative reciprocity only and the reduction of certain standards from higher ones to lower ones.[73]

Robinson here provides a first-hand insider testimony of what A. Zimmermann and P. Wennholz had observed – namely, the impact of national-security concerns from member states on the convention draft due to the historical context of Cold War tensions.[74] While the Conference of Plenipotentiaries indeed improved the terms of refugee protections in Paragraph 1 of Article 33 concerning non-refoulement, it nevertheless lowered the general protection scope of non-refoulement as a whole. This lowering of the bar was the direct result of the insertion of a second qualifying paragraph, hitherto nonexistent, into Article 33.

This Paragraph 2 provided exceptions to the generic rule of non-refoulement, explicitly stating the conditions and cases in which this protection *shall not* be provided. As Zimmermann and Wennholz correctly maintain, an unconditional granting of protection from refoulement was something most member states were simply not prepared to accept under any circumstances by July 1951.[75] The Paragraph 2 of Article 33, which was finally adopted, states:

> The benefit of the present provision may not, however, be claimed by a refugee whom there are reasonable grounds for regarding as a danger to the security of the country in which he is, or who, having been convicted by a final judgment of a particularly serious crime, constitutes a danger to the community of that country.[76]

This text which we know today as Paragraph 2 on non-refoulement was originally *not* intended for inclusion in an article instilling a negative duty upon member states against refugee refoulement. Initially proposed by Belgium, and later re-tabled by France, this paragraph was originally intended to serve as a fundamental qualifier to Article 2 of the convention as a whole, concerning the responsibilities of a refugee once admitted.[77] Alarmingly, both the Belgian and French proposed texts envisaged the inscription into the convention text of a mechanism by which asylum seekers were to be *prevented* from obtaining and securing refugee status.

Robinson knew full well the horrendous implications for refugees should a mechanism for the prevention of protection be prominently accepted in the convention text – indeed, in only its second article. Such a measure, if accepted, would almost certainly have nullified a large portion of the protections achieved thus far, since it would provide an *a priori* legal condition which member states wishing not to abide by their obligations and accept refugees could rely upon.

Robinson was also well aware of the situation in Europe, with countries like Belgium and France housing well over a million refugees. He watched from the sidelines as the Belgian Ambassador Plenipotentiary "cornered and pinned" the Australian delegate for attempting to derail the humanitarian standards of the convention on account of 40,000 refugees admitted into Australia. At the same time, Belgium had experienced an influx of 400,000 refugees into a population of approximately 9 million Belgian nationals while still maintaining a higher humanitarian standard than Australia.[78] Yet seeing the dangerous potential of instilling an acceptable mechanism for the revocation of refugee status and correlative protections, Robinson conscripted all the diplomatic pressure he could muster to block this from happening.

Robinson's idea was simple, yet its application demanded something of a "diplomatic tightrope act." By this stage of the Plenipotentiaries' Conference, Robinson knew well enough, as he explained to Sharett (see above), that he could not prevail on all diplomatic fronts. The humanitarian protection standards were going to be lowered whether he liked it or not. Yet what he was able to do was *defer* the discussion concerning the grounds of expulsion to a later subsequent article, which would not be part of the general provisions for the whole convention. This later article could serve to explain what states could do in extreme *abnormal* cases, which were the exceptions rather than the rule – the *esoteric* rather than the mainstream. Explaining the success that he obtained in preventing the lowering of protection standards for refugees, Robinson wrote:

> In three respects, however, I was successful. The Belgian delegation introduced an amendment to Article 2 (General Obligations) according to which (A/CONF.2/10): "'Only such refugees as fulfill their duties towards the country in which they find themselves and in particular conform to its laws and regulations as well as to measures taken for the maintenance of public order, may claim the benefit of this convention". I criticized sharply this amendment (A/CONF.2/SR 3) and the Belgian delegate withdrew it. A French substitute for the Belgian amendment was then introduced (A/CONF.2/18). In plenary meeting (A/CONF.2/SR 4) I asked the French delegate a number of questions to which he tried to reply and took the floor a second time for a procedural suggestion. The subject was turned over to a working group.

The procedural suggestion Robinson refers to here was the working group established during the seventh session of the plenary (A/CONF.2/SR 7) by the convention president, Larsen, consisting of France, the UK, and Israel, and charged with redrafting Article 2.[79] Here he repeated what he had already written in his first, Hebrew-language, secret report to Sharett from the Plenipotentiaries' Conference dated July 8, 1951.[80]

As previously mentioned, Conference President Larsen (Denmark), Robinson (Israel), and the UK's Sir Samuel Hoare were all part of the "Robinson network" of like-minded humanitarian diplomats at the Plenipotentiaries' Conference.[81] President Larsen and Robinson developed a strategy for overcoming the diplomatic "stumbling blocks" at the Plenipotentiaries' Conference, by turning over contentious issues to sub-working committees whose job it was to return to the plenary with an agreed textual version of these contested articles. In creating a working group for Article 2, Larsen, Hoare, and Robinson were merely repeating an already-established working procedure of the Plenipotentiaries' Conference, and nothing out of the ordinary.

However, this seemingly procedural device, a working group for Article 2, masked one of Robinson's greatest defensive diplomatic achievements. It was in this group that he managed to safeguard the textual integrity of Article 2 and prevent any alterations to it, in an admirable exercise of what I have termed "preventive drafting."[82] This was achieved by a diplomatic gambit on Robinson's behalf, as he traded in his consent for a qualifying clause for Article 33 (Non-Refoulement) in exchange for French consent to drop the proposed catastrophic change of Article 2. And thus, Robinson explained to Sharett:

> The subject was turned over to a working group where I persuaded the French delegate to withdraw his amendment – indicating the irony of a document purporting to solve the refugee problem (resulting incidentally from the institution of *déchéance de nationalité*) and introducing the analogous institution of *déchéance de statut de réfugié*...). We settled for a new paragraph (Par. 2) in Article 33 (A/CONF.2/69).[83]

A reading of the UN documents and the Refugee Convention commentaries concerning Paragraph 2 of Article 33 reveals that this qualifying paragraph indeed originated from the amendment known as A/CONF.2/69, submitted jointly by France and the UK, according to the UN archive, on July 11, 1951.[84] [85] In all UN documents, and correspondingly in all later commentaries, A/CONF.2/69 has been referred to as the France–UK amendment on non-refoulement. Nowhere in any UN document, or in any other known record for that matter, do we find any reference whatsoever to the Israeli involvement in the drafting of Paragraph 2 of Article 33. This absence of any clear UN evidence as to Robninson's strong involvement in the drafting of this paragraph poses a methodological challenge – demanding, if possible, some sort of corroborative material to substantiate this new and hitherto unknown information.

Robinson's report to Sharett, crediting himself with managing to secure the retention of Article 2 intact and limiting the damage to the convention text to the second paragraph of Article 33, is only partially validated by other internal Israeli diplomatic sources. All of Robinson's secret reports to Sharett were jointly drafted, corroborated, and confirmed by the other senior Israeli delegate to the Conference of Plenipotentiaries, Dr Menachem Kahany, who was charged with dispatching the interim weekly reports from Geneva via cable back to Jerusalem.[86] Kahany is warmly mentioned and thanked for his help during the three weeks of the Plenipotentiaries' Conference.[87] He was a senior Israeli diplomat, who in 1949 Red Cross signed the 4th Geneva Convention on behalf of the State of Israel.[88] In a later development, unimaginable nowadays given current Israeli–UN relations, Kahany was elected as the chair to the fifth UNHCR advisory council in 1953, his placement lobbied for by France and Belgium.[89] In Jerusalem, these reports were also read by the Israeli high ambassador to the UN in New York, Abba Eban.[90]

It is highly improbable that Robinson would report anything, save the exact and precise channel of events concerning his involvement in the drafting of Paragraph 2 of Article 33, through the creation of UN document A/CONF.2/69. Nevertheless, and as mentioned above, since UN sources apparently do not point to any part whatsoever played by Robinson in drafting of this Paragraph, a second examination of the UN archive documentation and its context seems methodologically imperative.

A careful comparative reading of the UN documents and Robinson's report expose three realms of cross-referencing, which, when accumulated, further substantiate his report to Foreign Minister Sharett. The first of these cross-references concerns the initial exclusive linguistic usage of French for the drafting of Paragraph 2 Article 33. In his aforementioned report to Sharett, Robinson refers very negatively and ironically to the French idea of introducing into the convention text an official structured mechanism for the stripping of refugee status as proposed by France, explicitly mentioning A/CONF.2/18. This amendment was submitted by France at the opening of the Plenipotentiaries' Conference on July 3, 1951.[91] The English text of this French amendment referred to a refugee being "declared to have forfeited the rights pertaining to the status of refugee."[92]

Robinson refers to this in his report, quoting and specifically emphasizing the French wording of *déchéance de statut de réfugié* in the French version of A/CONF.2/18. Robinson's French was impeccable, and we know that he was commissioned by President Larsen to coordinate both the English and French drafts of the convention text.[93] It is safe to assume that any negotiations he would have had with the French delegate, Rochefort, must have been conducted primarily in French. Paul Weis quotes word for word the final text of Paragraph 2 endorsed by the plenary.[94] He explicitly mentions that this original text of Article 33, used during the *travaux préparatoires*, existed in *the French language only in its French version.*[95] If the drafting of Paragraph 2 of Article 33 was indeed a French–UK proposed text, how did it come about that only a French version existed?

It is at least plausible that the reason behind this text existing in French alone, as Weis was convinced it did, was due to it being negotiated in this very language between Rochefort and Robinson, exactly as the latter reports to Foreign Minister Sharett.

The second aspect in the reading of the UN documentation, further substantiating Robinson's involvement in the drafting of Paragraph 2 of Article 33, has to do with an analysis of the sequence of dates of the UN sessions and documents. The UN record places the submission of the French amendment for Article 2 (A/CONF.2/18) concurrent with all the other amendments concerning both Article 2 and Article 3 submitted by other member states and actors during the first week of the Plenipotentiaries' Conference.[96] We also know that working groups were designated to draft Article 2, Article 3, and later Article 6 for the benefit of consideration by the plenary. All these working groups included France, the UK, and the Israeli representatives, with occasional other members in one or more of them.[97]

We know that all three working groups were tasked and designated during the first week of the Plenipotentiaries' Conference (July 2–6, 1951) and that the solution to the highly contentious problem of the drafting of Article 3 was provided for in the week of July 11, 1951, after the Plenipotentiaries' Conference had almost collapsed a day earlier on Tuesday, July 10.[98] The UN archive registrations indicate unequivocally that *both* the English and the French versions of A/CONF.2/69 were submitted and were publically published on July 11, 1951. Weis reports that A/CONF.2/69 initially existed only in French, and it is A/CONF.2/69 which Robinson refers to as his compromise with the French delegate, Rochefort. We know that the conference virtually collapsed on July 10 and was rescued by Robinson the following day with A/CONF.2/72, thanks to his single-handed drafted compromise on Article 3.[99] The availability of yet another compromise – achieved under the triumvirate of Robinson, Samuel Hoare, and Rochefort – concerning yet another one of the most contentious articles in the entire convention, and its publication on the very same day (July 11) makes Robinson's involvement in the drafting of A/CONF.2/69 all the more probable.

However, as convincing as the circumstantial evidence may be concerning Robinson's involvement in the drafting of Article 33 Paragraph 2, his account of the events that transpired differs dramatically from any record we possess as to how this text was drafted. Granted his ingenious "diplomatic trading," Robinson would never have initiated such a risky move on his own. One partner in this diplomatic triangular trade off was missing. Given that A/CONF.2/69 was officially a French/UK-submitted proposal, Robinson must have secured some sort endorsement from the UK delegate, Sir Samuel Hoare.

The UK Drafting of Non-Refoulement and the True Meaning of "National Security"

Robinson's diplomatic trade off, calls for a cross-examination of the UK source material, so as to understand if and how Robinson received Hoare's approval for his "deal" with the French delegate, Rochefort. The sources in the UK archive reveal the extent of the efforts undertaken by the British Government for the sake of a successful endorsement of the 1951 Refugee Convention. This cardinal role played by the UK merits a short explanation of its archive sources, if only because of their vital importance for future legal interpretations of circumstances that, at times, tend to rely heavily on the *travaux préparatoires*.

In contrast to most governments, who tasked their foreign services with the Refugee Convention deliberations, the UK, with its vast experience of refugee absorption before and after the World War II, saw the refugee issue as fundamentally an internal one. Refugees and persecuted people, for whom the UK had habitually served as a safe haven, were first and foremost a matter for consideration by admissions and naturalization authorities. Correspondingly, the Cabinet designated the entire Refugee Convention file to the Home Office rather than the Foreign Office, and entrusted it into the faithful hands of Sir Samuel Hoare, as an undersecretary with ambassadorial prerogatives. Hoare was an old veteran of the Home Office and an expert on refugee issues.[100] Upon receipt of the draft convention text in August 1950, he worked closely with an inter-ministerial taskforce called the International Organizations Committee (IOC), consisting of under-secretaries in different governmental departments. The work of the IOC was coordinated by Hoare so as to yield one single document at each strategic juncture, comprising the amendments and positions of the UK on every single article of the convention text.

While the files containing the preparatory work of the Foreign Office and the Home Office have unfortunately not been found at the National Archives in Kew, the file of the Board of Trade does exist.[101] Of crucial importance are four consecutive Cabinet reports compiled for the IOC, by Hoare, and his team, which came out in printed form after each round of inter-ministerial consultations and the receipt of feedback. These reports demonstrate the evolution of the British positions regarding the Refugee Convention text from September 1950 until after the signing of the final act in Geneva in 1951. The first Cabinet report from September 1950 is 35 pages long.[102] Over three pages of the report are devoted solely to Article 28 (later, Article 33) concerning non-refoulement. The UK, the document argued, must safeguard the right to expel a refugee in cases where he is engaged in severe criminal activity, but this only as "a last resort."[103] Highlighting the importance of a limitation to non-refoulement, the document is unequivocal:

> Unless the Convention is amended in such a way as to provide for these cases, His Majesty's Government will be unable to

> accede to the Convention, and the United Kingdom delegation should make it quite clear at the earliest opportune moment in the discussions.[104]

In simple terms non-refoulement, as it stood, was a "deal breaker" for the UK. If an amendment to Article 36 concerning reservations was unattainable, the document proposed the insertion of a proviso after Paragraph 1 of Article 33, which is the textual ancestor of Paragraph 2 as we know it today. It provided that Article 28 should not apply to:

1. Cases in which the contracting party is satisfied that the refugee is engaging, or is likely to engage, in activities prejudicial to national security; or
2. Refugees who, despite warning persist in conduct prejudicial to good order and government, and who have not been restrained and show no prospect of being restrained from such conduct by the ordinary sanctions of the law; or
3. Refugees who at the time of their presentation for admission are known persons who have been convicted of serious crimes.[105]

While this proviso of last resorts mentions the term "national security," its *raison d'être* is clearly crime-geared, as can be seen in its points 2 and 3 as well as in its explanatory subsequent paragraphs. This focus on criminal activity as suitable grounds which would permit refoulement changed considerably during the following two months. In the next version of the same document, from early November 1950, things took a very different turn. Referring to the problem of non-refoulement, and the previous conditioning of British assent to the convention upon it being limited, the issue at hand was now differently explained:

> The matter has now been further considered, and it is regarded as important that it should be possible *in one type of case, and one only – namely,* where a refugee is engaging in activities prejudicial to national security – for the United Kingdom, *in the last resort*, to return a refugee to his own country even if his life or freedom would be endangered thereby. *There is a serious risk that among refugees will be found some who are prepared to act as secret agents*. This risk is so real, and recent examples of cases in which foreigners

> have abused the hospitality of the country of their residence in this way are so well known (e.g. the Fuchs case), that it should not be difficult to obtain agreement to the proposition that states must reserve their right to get rid of a refugee who engages in such conduct, even, if necessary, by sending him back to his own country [. . .] If it is decided to deal with the matter by way of a proviso to Article 28, the amendment should be on the following lines:
>
> (a) Number present text paragraph 1
> (b) Add a new paragraph 2:-
>
> "2. A contracting state shall not be bound to comply with the provisions of paragraph 1 in the case of a refugee engaging in activities prejudicial to the national security."
>
> It is important to make it clear that *it is only in a very few cases that the use of this power would ever be contemplated*. Although the United Kingdom is very anxious to retain the power to deal with this very limited category of cases, it should not be said in the debate that our adhesion to the Convention is dependent upon our securing an appropriate amendment.[106]

And thus, the meaning behind the term "national security" is exposed. Refoulement could be executed by a convention signatory in one case, *and one case only*: when espionage was involved – and here, too, only as an ultimate last resort. The simplification of the proviso, and the removal of its items 2 and 3 dealing with criminal offences, corresponded to another change in policy. Whether the UK's adhesion to the convention was still being conditioned upon an amendment to Article 28 is debatable. Yet what is certain is the removal of the request to proclaim this conditioning up front, and Hoare's delegation was to "keep a lid" on this conditioning.

As the Conference of Plenipotentiaries approached, the UK further sharpened its definitions for the articles it wished to amend. A week before the conference, the third guideline text prepared by Hoare for the delegation to Geneva was issued for review by Cabinet. The proviso for Paragraph 2, qualifying non-refoulement, was finally formulated to also include those cases where a State suspected refugees of espionage yet could not fully substantiate this. The purely criminal grounds which had triggered the creation of Paragraph 2 in the first place were far less important now. Espionage was the main ground for concern, to which Paragraph 2 now catered:

> This amendment should still be proposed, even if the conference decides to exempt from Article 28 "common criminals" [. . .] The amendment is required because not every refugee whose activities are a danger to security can be charged and convicted of a crime, and also because there have been instances (e.g. 13 Poles who were the subject of a recent statement in the House by the Home Secretary) where foreigners have been in the pay of a foreign government for supplying information relating to their own compatriots and not to security matters, though there is every reason to think that they would, if allowed to remain here, act as agents also for information affecting national security.[107]

In his fourth and final report to the Cabinet two weeks after the convention's signing, Hoare laconically remarked about the now re-numbered Article 33 that, "The second paragraph of the Article was put forward as a joint Anglo–French amendment and was generally accepted."[108] Not a word about Robinson's trade off.

In the absence of further information, one can only hypothesize as to how things unfolded within the working group on Article 2, between Hoare, Robinson, and Rochefort. In his final report, Hoare refers to Robinson's position vis-à-vis Rochefort as follows:

> Mr Robinson, the representative of Israel, made many useful contributions to the debate: he was always ingenious and often convincing, but on several of the main subjects of controversy he remained silent, out of desire not to antagonize the French.[109]

Communicating to Sharett in his final report, Robinson apologetically confirmed Hoare's reading of his somewhat reserved attitude, and his choice not to always fight the trend of the lowering of humanitarian protection standards:

> I would have been lacking in fairness, representing as I was a country which has only a few scores of refugees who may fall under

> the definition of Article 1, had I chosen to fight constantly against the determined will of countries with thousands and tens of thousands of refugees. In some cases I abstained from voting for such de-liberalization of existing standards, in others I even voted against.[110]

We have established already that Paragraph 2 was first drafted by Hoare's team at the Home Office between September 1950 and June 1951. Paragraph 2 is to be seen for what it is – namely, a provision of the grounds for stripping a migrant of their legal refugee status so as to deport them. We now know that Paragraph 2 did not originate with, and indeed was not prepared by, the French; nor was it drafted in the French language, but in pure English – in the UK Home Office. How did it come about that Paul Weis, who was intimately acquainted with the Refugee Convention text after writing much of it himself, came to state in his commentary that only a French version existed of A/CONF.2/69 without any reference to its original English wording? How did someone like Paul Weis get it wrong?

My hypothesis is simple. Ample evidence indicates that towards the end of the conference, most delegates (the UK's included) had a very negative impression of Rochefort's non-diplomatic behavior, culminating in a request to table an appeal against him at the Quai d'Orsay.[111] In all probability, Hoare and Robinson preemptively coordinated the insertion of the UK-prepared text of Paragraph 2 into Article 33. Knowing that Robinson was one of the last delegates still on good terms with Rochefort, Hoare probably asked him to advocate for this Article 33 text with Rochefort, so as to save the convention's Article 2 from the harmful French amendment A/CONF.2/18. If so, then the reason behind this text initially existing in French alone, as Weis claimed, was due to it being negotiated in French in the first place, between Robinson and Rochefort, exactly as the latter reported to Jerusalem.

A Convention for the Protection of Refugees: Drafted by Refugees?

On August 1, 1951, following his signature of the Refugee Convention, Robinson wrote to Foreign Minister Sharett in Jerusalem the following lines, which are corroborated by Hoare's report to the Cabinet in London's Whitehall:

> The Convention is now open for signature until the 31 August 1951, in Geneva. The ceremony took place on Saturday, July 28. While I had my powers, I informed the President that I would not be able to be among the first signers because of Sabbath. My colleagues of the Conference were also informed accordingly. The President expressed his regret that I would not be among the first signers, particularly because I represented, in his view, not only a government, but also morally the refugee as such.[112]

President Larsen's warm words and Robinson's preference for following his Jewish beliefs over the receipt of diplomatic honors echoed loudly in both Jerusalem and London.[113] These words did not refer to Robinson alone. They were meant as a token of respect to all the refugees who took part in the drafting and successful endorsement of the convention. Robinson from Lithuania, Weis from Vienna and Dachau, and Lewin from Lodz were all refugees, who found themselves shaping the international tool for the protection of exiled people just like them. Alongside them was a host of diplomats who, for the most part, labored successfully for a good cause they fundamentally believed in. With this composition at the drafting table, it is no surprise that the convention turned out to be a "Magna Carta for Refugees."[114]

The archive material presented here highlights some major findings concerning the original intentions of the drafters of Article 33 and the principle of non-refoulement. The first finding concerns Paragraph 1 of the Article. Its words "membership of a particular social group or political opinion" were aimed at providing refugee protection for people whose persecution stemmed from the ideological and racist motivations of their persecutors. The protection provided to Hungarian refugees fleeing communism in 1951 could equally be granted to refugees fleeing Pol Pot's Khmer Rouge in 1970s' Cambodia, to South African deportees from District Six in Cape Town in the early 1980s, or to Eritreans fleeing dictatorship nowadays. If one's belonging to a certain social group triggers one's own persecution, then one is entitled to protection from refoulement.

The second insight concerns Paragraph 2, which precludes the protection of Article 33 for refugees who infringe upon the national security of their host country. In the eyes of Sir Samuel Hoare, who drafted this paragraph, refoulement due to national-security considerations was to be invoked on one ground, and one ground only: espionage. The numerous references to the extremity and extraordinary circumstances which would have been required in order for the UK to resort to this application are unequivocal. Hoare and Robinson meant for Paragraph 2 to be used strictly as a *Consultum Ultimum*. "National security" was not meant as a basket clause to be called upon for demographic or political purposes. Nor should it degenerate to the level of including perceived threats stemming from ethnicity, skin color, a different religion, or changes in the demographic composition of one's state.

In reinstating in 2012 the relevance of Article 33 and the extraterritorial applicability of non-refoulement to refugees on the high seas, Judge Pinto de Albuquerque catapulted the debate back to its rightful origins six decades earlier. It is a historical irony that the Supreme Court of Australia still follows the restrictive interpretations of the convention, as advocated by its own delegate in Geneva in 1951. Unfortunately, as the European Court's ruling on Italy recently demonstrated, this restrictive tendency is now commonplace the world over. One ought to see the ruling of Judge Albuquerque for what it is: a return toward the true universal value of protecting a tormented and persecuted refugee wherever he or she may be. It was this ideal which eventually prevailed in 1951 thanks to Hoare, Robinson, Weis, and their colleagues.

Non-Refoulement Revisited at the Israeli–Egyptian Border Six Decades Later

By September 2012, Israel had effectively finished the construction of the 240 km fence along its border with Egypt. In parallel with this construction, the Israeli Army reinforced its patrols along that border, so as to comply with the new anti-infiltration act and its stipulations of immediate incarceration for all illegal border crossers. On September 4 that year, a group of 20 migrants, including women in an advanced state of pregnancy, were observed as they became entangled and trapped between the twin layers of internal and external fences securing the border, just north of the Israeli settlement of Kadesh Barnea.[115] As the Israeli Army spotted these migrants, a patrol was immediately dispatched to ensure they did not cross the fence into Israeli territory. Trapped between the fences in the desert's heat, the IDF soldiers were instructed not to allow the migrants to cross into Israel, yet they provided them through the fence with water, food, and medical supplies.

It is important at this stage to discount the prospective notion that the Israeli authorities might not have known the extent of atrocities, human-rights violations, and torture to which the Eritrean migrants, pleading at the fence near Kadesh Barnea, had been subjected. By early 2013, a watershed of international media reports brought forward by reputable news venues as well as human-rights monitoring groups drew the attention of the international community to the plight of the Eritrean and Sudanese asylum seekers stranded in the Sinai Peninsula.[116] One could still contemplate the benefit of the doubt considering the Israeli authorities' lack of knowledge of the migrants' dire humanitarian plight had it not been for the fact that all the international reports quoted Israeli sources, written in plain Hebrew, by the pro-migrant NGOs who were caring for the tortured Eritrean migrants once they reached Israeli soil.[117] Moreover, many of the Israeli NGO reports upon which the international media base their coverage were submitted to Israeli courts as evidence supporting the asylum requests tabled by the migrants from Eritrea and Sudan, culminating in the acceptance of the Israeli Supreme Court of these pieces of evidence, as quoted by Supreme Court Justice Isaac Amit.[118]

As news of this situation hit the Israeli media, the pro-NGO community began mobilizing its forces in an all-out effort to resolve the issue by forcing the government to allow the entry of this migrant group, under the understanding that they would immediately be jailed. The NGO reasoning was that given the dire medical situation of the group, it was preferable that they receive medical treatment in an Israeli jail facility than die out in the desert. A medical delegation from the NGO Physicians for Human Rights was immediately dispatched to Kadesh Barnea, while the legal NGOs filed a habeas corpus plea at the Israeli Supreme Court, demanding the immediate entry into custody of the migrant group from the border.[119]

Once again the left-wing human-rights-conscious columnists of *Haaretz* newspaper joined hands in an intellectual tour de force, stressing Israel's humanitarian and international obligations in bringing the migrants into Israeli custody and medical care.[120] In a noteworthy op-ed contribution, the Hebrew University history professor, Moshe Zimmermann drew a striking parallel between the Jewish misery during the 1938 Evian Conference, and the current plight of the stranded African migrants. In both cases, Zimmermann recalled, no country on earth had been prepared to help the migrants. In the Jewish case, Zimmermann stressed in his article, the Evian Conference had paved the way for the possibility of the annihilation of the Jews. Zimmermann concluded his article with the rhetorical question as to whether 1938 still remains anywhere within the Israeli psyche, so as to draw upon for the sake of these wretched souls stranded on the border.[121]

Yet Interior Minister Eli Yishai remained firm in his conviction not to allow the migrants stranded between the fences into Israel. Replying to the pleas of the UNHCR representative in Israel, Yishai stressed,

> If we will not be firm in this case, and others we will have one million Africans here, and let's not ask what we will do with one million refugees, excuse my mistake – illegal workers here. We must act very firmly here, apply the blockage of the fence, and incarcerate all the migrants who have already entered Israel. Let their African countries come here and care for them.[122]

The habeas corpus petition to the Israeli Supreme Court was tabled by the pro-migrant NGOs on Wednesday September 5, 2012 and was immediately scheduled for hearing at the first possible instance, which was to be on Sunday September 9 given the intervening weekend. What took place over this weekend in September became characteristic of the new general attitude of the Israeli Government towards the migrants. Moreover, the lack of any public protest or outcry against the new features of governmental treatment of the migrants confirmed and vindicated the fears of the pro-NGO community. Israeli society was becoming numb with apathy towards the suffering of African asylum seekers. Their plight, which had been at the center of public attention in 2010 and which had coerced the government to bury the 2008 anti-migration law, this centrality and public importance was now lost, and channeled to other burning issues perturbing Israeli society at large.

Over that long weekend, as the IDF soldiers prevented the migrants from entering Israeli territory, the latter carried on pleading for their lives, stressing that should they be returned into Egyptian territory they would be jailed and executed by their Bedouin captors. On Sunday morning, as the supreme court hearing went into session, the justices were informed by the State Defense Attorney that the migrant group which was on the border had meanwhile departed over the weekend – splitting so that the pregnant women and the children were let into Israeli territory by the armed forces, while the male members of the group allegedly returned on their own into the Egyptian territory.[123]

As the testimonies of the women in Israeli custody were separately collected, the full extent of the horror became evident. The Israeli Army had crossed into the area in between the Israeli and Egyptian border fences, and actively pushed and shoved the male members of the group back towards the Egyptian side. Most of the male members of the group were in advanced stages of dehydration, and some were already in a coma. The soldiers apparently placed the fatigued male migrants on large pieces of military camouflage material, and hauled them across into Egyptian territory. All the while, the migrants continued pleading for their lives, and asking to be executed by bullet rather than being returned into the hands of their Bedouin tormentors. *Haaretz*' requests for comments regarding the testimonies by the female migrants remained unanswered, with the Prime Minister's office and the army spokesman repeating they had no comments to make on the episode.

Bearing in mind the humane approach of the drafters of the 1951 Refugee Convention, with the Jewish and Israeli representatives at their helm, one cannot avoid positing the question: How did we end up with Israel executing the cruel refoulement of the Eritrean migrants in Kadesh Barnea in 2012? Had the universal origins and motivations which underpinned the work of Jacob Robinson, Paul Weis, Rabbi Lewin, and their peers been consigned to oblivion?[124]

PART II

UNIVERSALISM LOST: ISRAELI GOVERNMENTAL POLICIES TOWARD NON-JEWISH MIGRANTS, 2006–13

CHAPTER 3

THE MODERATENESS OF THE SHARON–OLMERT ADMINISTRATIONS, 2005–8

Broadly speaking, the time period from the beginning of the African migrant influx into Israel (December 2005) until its cessation in 2013 could be broken down into two consecutive periods, in terms of the Israeli governmental policies vis-à-vis these migrants. The first period, from 2005 until 2008, was marked by a lack of any coherent governmental policy with halfhearted measures instigated by the government, which failed to curb the African migrant influx. The second period, between 2009 and 2013, was marked by a visceral contest between the government and pro-migrant Israeli civil-society NGOs over which state measures ought to be administered towards the migrants. While the NGOs won the first round of this battle, the government ultimately prevailed as it managed to push through, against the resistance of both the NGO community and the bureaucratic echelons of parliament, the harsh amendment of the 1954 Anti-Infiltration Act in 2012.

It was during these eight long years of African migration and Israeli political and social contest that Israeli exceptionalism came to prevail over Jewish universalism. At no stage was this contest total or overwhelming. If anything, its main characteristic was the attrition experienced by both parties and ultimately the entire Israeli public, which had by and large lost interest in the African migrant issue towards the end of 2013. Yet bigger processes were set into motion as a result of this eight-year contest between the universalists and the exceptionalists.

As shall be demonstrated in Part III of this book, the appeal to the Israeli Supreme Court by the pro-migrant NGOs triggered judicial and governmental processes far beyond anything initially envisaged by the exceptionalists.

Ariel Sharon's and Ehud Olmert's Move to the Israeli Political Spectrum Center

Assessing the alignment and coordinates of any administration across a given political spectrum is, at best, an exercise in the interpretation of events undertaken in hindsight, using the prism of previous and subsequent administrations for comparison. As to the question of the political alignment of the Sharon Government in 2002, most observers would have claimed it to be one of the most hawkish administrations Israel had ever known. Contrary to Western European or American political spectrums, the Israeli barometer of designated "Left" and "Right" alignments has habitually been tied to positions adopted by the various political actors in government toward the Israeli–Palestinian conflict. Over the years, Israeli political sociologists have amply demonstrated how "hawkish" right-wing governments have tended to be much more social in their economic policies, while the "dovish" left-wing Labor Party all too often promoted what European political economists would coin as "right-wing" lax attitudes towards taxation and free-market economic approaches.[1]

For Israelis, however, the definitions of Left and Right are crystal clear. For the past half-century since the 1967 Six Day War, political alignments have rested first and foremost on one's positions concerning compromise or conflict with the Palestinian people. Those who define themselves as "left wing" implicitly and inherently mean they are prepared for significant Israeli territorial concessions and the removal of Jewish settlements from the Occupied Palestinian Territories (OPT – The "West Bank" and the Gaza Strip) in exchange for a lasting Israeli–Palestinian peace. In contrast, "right wing" constituents are designated precisely by their refusal of territorial compromise and insistence on maintaining and enlarging Jewish territorial presence in the OPT.[2]

With these divisions in mind, there could hardly be any doubt as to the political bearing of the Sharon Government, elected in 2001. The significant pounding of the Palestinians during the second Intifada and the reoccupation by the IDF of all the OPT, hitherto under Palestinian control, effectively nullifying the Oslo Peace Accords, all came to frame the Sharon Government as the epitome of "right wing" thinking.[3]

This view was exacerbated by Sharon's notorious past as the chief architect of Israeli settlement expansion in the OPT since the late 1970s. His diabolical right-wing reputation was consecrated in his singlehanded initiation for the 1982 Lebanon War, and his subsequent removal from office as minister of defense by the Israeli Supreme Court due to his ultimate responsibility for the Sabra and Shatila massacres in West Beirut.[4]

Sharon's long-standing anti-Palestinian attitude and his hawkish image seemed consistent with his government's crackdown on foreign migrant workers. Sharon's deportation campaign in 2002 against the foreign community reduced its numbers to pre-1996 figures, causing over 140,000 migrants to leave the country primarily through the usage of varying degrees of coercion measures.[5] Indicative of the havoc wreaked upon these foreign communities was the destruction of numerous Christian community centers of worship and makeshift churches, thus further undermining the already limited social framework so cherished by such newcomers to foreign lands. To the pro-migrant NGOs and human-rights activists, his administration's actions seemed totally consistent with Sharon's generally upheld extreme right-wing views concerning the Palestinian–Israeli conflict and the continued subjugation of the Palestinian people.[6]

By mid-2003, the Sharon Administration was beginning to receive alarming signs of declining electoral support from the Israeli public, and it is within this context that one ought to understand the recess in the anti-migrant deportations campaign. Almost three years after the beginning of the second Palestinian uprising, and with over two years in office, the Sharon Administration was being politically cornered by the large extreme-right factions within the ruling Likud party. The Israeli public began to question the logic of holding on to the heavily populated Palestinian Gaza Strip, which was drawing so much Israeli soldier attention and casualties.[7]

Into this background came the 2003 massive suicide attack in the migrant neighborhood of Neve Shaanan in Tel Aviv. On Sunday evening of January 6, 2003, Palestinian suicide bombers detonated themselves in the midst of this foreign-workers' neighborhood, killing 23 people and maiming dozens.[8] With Israel fighting virtually on all fronts – in the OPT, as well as against Hezbollah fighters on Israel's northern border with Lebanon – the Israeli electorate just could not see the point in allocating security forces to a deportation campaign against people who were suffering the very same fate as Israelis in suicide bombings.[9] Sharon's slow but consistent movement from right-wing extremism to the political center of Israeli politics is a fascinating lesson in evolutionary politics, which has yet to be studied in detail and is beyond the scope of this book. Evidently, it was during these very months of early 2003 that Sharon began to elaborate what would later be known as his "disengagement plan" from the Palestinians and the consequent unilateral Israeli evacuation of Jewish settlements in the OPT. What began as an initial idea presented by Sharon at an academic policy conference in 2003 gradually evolved into the massive total evacuation and uprooting of all Jewish settlements in the Gaza Strip in 2005.

This unprecedented evacuation of Jewish settlements from the Palestinian lands in Gaza, and the even more important historical uprooting of three settlements in the West Bank, coincided with a colossal redrawing of the Israeli political map. Following on from his own Likud party's rejection of the disengagement and settlement-evacuation plan, Sharon effectively fractured the Likud. He swept up a large group of its MPs, as well as centrist and even moderately left-wing members of the Knesset, to join his newly formed Kadima party.[10]

By 2005, after the Gaza and West Bank settlement evacuations had been completed, the entire Israeli political-party system had been redrawn. The Sharon Administration had moved from the extreme right to the centre of the Israeli political spectrum. By the time the Cairo migrant shootings in front of the UNHCR headquarters took place in December 2005, triggering the arrival of African asylum-seeking migrants into Israel, the political map had totally shifted. What had seemed coherent and feasible for the right-wing Sharon Administration's deportation campaign in 2002 was politically impossible for a realigned, consensus-driven, and politically centered Sharon Administration in late 2005.[11]

In 2006, the Sharon Government saw a change of personnel, with the leadership being handed over to Ehud Olmert due to Sharon's cerebral stroke and incapacitation. Continuing his predecessor's line of political moderation and shift towards the centrist consensus of Israeli politics, Olmert began seeking a remedy for the southern clandestine migration, which by now had become a growing concern. During his entire tenure in office, Olmert was walking a political tightrope, balancing Israel's security needs with what he saw as the ultimate goal of any Israeli leader – the securing of a lasting peace between Israel and the Palestinian people. In retrospect, and based on evidence which emerged much later, we know today that the most far-reaching Israeli proposal for a peace settlement ever was the one proposed by Olmert to the Palestinian leader Mahmud Abbas in Annapolis in 2007.[12] Following the Gaza withdrawal, Olmert had a unique open door with regional Arab leaders, Hosni Mubarak of Egypt and King Abdullah of Jordan.[13]

Thus Olmert began his tenure with the harsh security realities of the second Palestinian uprising (Intifada), coupled with an existing policy of a hard crackdown on foreign migrants inherited from his predecessor (the Barak Administration) back in 2001. By late 2003, as the Israeli public was growing weary of the political dead end of Palestinian–Israeli bloodletting, Sharon began moving to the center of the Israeli political spectrum. In 2004, he went as far as proposing the first ever removal of Israeli settlements from the OPT, in the Gaza Strip and the West Bank, consequently fracturing his own Likud party and resigning from it to create a new, centrist Israeli political force Kadima. By 2004–5, as the African migrants were beginning to make their way across the Israeli southern frontier, the Sharon Administration was already consecrating its newly acquired consensual positioning – right at the centered heart of Israeli politics.[14]

Humanitarianism under Olmert: The Legal Status of Migrant Children

The political centeredness of the Olmert Administration (2006–2009) bore a distinct connection to its own moderate treatment of African migrants, as opposed to the more extreme attitudes of its predecessor – the Sharon Administration of 2001–6. With the Darfur Genocide well known to the Israeli public, governmental treatment of the African asylum seekers came to be seen as the litmus test for political acceptability and attitudes. Humanity and tolerance towards the migrants was seen as a sign of political moderation, which bred political centeredness and ultimate legitimacy.

With Sharon's sudden departure, political centeredness became his successor's main electoral asset, retaining his party's hegemonic position at the heart of the Israeli political consensus. Seeking a reinvigorated electoral mandate in the May 2006 elections, Olmert now ran for office as the head of the Kadima party – the very same breakaway faction from the right-wing Likud, created by Sharon pending his policy of Jewish-settlements removal from the OPT. Olmert refused to risk his image of political centeredness, possibly to be sacrificed on the altar of migration and Israeli demographic fears of "otherness." To this extent, Olmert preferred dealing with the African migration problem through half-hearted measures rather than risk his cherished image of moderation.[15]

The ultimate validation of any governmental policy line lies in its actions, and none more so than the parliamentary legislation it promotes. While different motives and explanations can be given for governmental policy actions and decisions, it is the legislative yardstick which denominates a government in terms of its political orientation and policy direction. In the following pages, I shall demonstrate the Olmert Administration's political moderateness through the analysis of two pieces of legislation proposed in parliament during its tenure. The first law to be examined concerns the legalization and granting of citizenship to African migrant children in 2007. The second is the 2008 version of the Anti-Infiltration Act, which in hindsight turned out to be the most humane version of the preventive legislation aimed at curbing clandestine migration.

As Olmert was preparing for the upcoming elections, he instructed his moderate interior minister, Roni Bar-On, himself an old close confidant of Ariel Sharon, to work on a draft process of legalization and naturalization for children born to non-Jewish migrant families. In early 2005, and largely due to Israeli public-opinion pressures, Sharon had instructed Bar-On as interior minister to commence work on a draft governmental resolution initiating a process of legalization of the status of these children.[16] Two years later, approximately 2,000 migrants became Israeli citizens as a consequence of the legalization of their children, thus breaking new ground in the history of citizenship legalities in Israel. Delving into the intricate mechanics of this naturalization process, one derives a better understanding and visualization of the relative moderation and openness which governed the thoughts and attitudes of the Israeli Interior Minister and his subordinates under the Olmert Administration.

By 2006, approximately 1,500 migrant children were born to foreign migrants and resident workers in Israel. Half of these children were six years of age or older, making them eligible for attendance in the obligatory Israeli state-school system.

As noted by Shahar Ilan of *Haaretz*:

> The older children grew up as any other Israeli child, with Hebrew as their mother tongue and without any acquaintance with their parents' countries of origin. It is this background which has given rise to the outright public demand over the past few years to naturalize and grant citizenship to these children – rather than deport them.[17]

The newly elected Olmert Administration significantly altered the threshold criteria for naturalization of migrant children in comparison with the guidelines of the previous Sharon Administration. While the Sharon Government had held the threshold for eligibility at a minimum of ten years of age, its successor reduced that to six years of age, effectively including almost all children under the scope of the proposed law. While a whole host of other exclusionary criteria of the Sharon Government were abolished, the Olmert Administration retained only the most necessary requirements, in its eyes, so as to enable as much inclusion as possible within the boundaries of the law.

The children had to have been enrolled in the Israeli school system, must have known the language of the country, and neither they nor their parents should have had any criminal record.[18] Of utmost importance was the abolition of the birth criteria, whereby the Olmert Administration revoked Sharon's condition that all children to be naturalized must have been born in Israel, with an Israeli hospital birth certificate issued at their birth and filled in as part of the application process. Instead, the Olmert criteria insisted on a minimum and continuous period of residence in Israel of at least six consecutive years, with the child being under the age of 14 upon application. In the case of full completion of the requirement criteria, the children were granted permanent residence status while their parents were given temporary residence permits conditioned on the residence of the children. Upon completion of compulsory military service in the IDF (which most Israeli citizens undertake – men for a 3-year period, women for 2 years), the children were to receive Israeli nationality, with their parents becoming permanent residents.

Scrutiny of the actions of Interior Minister Bar-On during his ministry's work on the applications for naturalization by the migrant families uncovers even more tolerant policies in favor of migrants. When confronted with marginal cases, Bar-On relaxed the acceptance criteria further, so as to incorporate as many children as possible within the discretionary boundaries of the law.

Along these lines, Bar-On raised the maximum eligible age from 14 to 15 years, and lowered the initiation age from six years to four years, so as to open up the criteria even further. Responding to journalist questions, Bar-On stated:

> It is unthinkable that we should deport children who don't know nor have another culture, and who do not have any mother tongue other than Hebrew. These children are participating in the Zionist ethos and wish to enlist in the army just like their classmates. We have showed the maximum openness possible, and I am especially proud of that, and hope we have concluded and straightened this issue.[19]

Bar-On's actions were commended by his own party, and received acknowledgment from the pro-migrant NGO community as well. Referring to his consistent lowering of the threshold criteria so as to allow for the legalization of residence status for the maximum amount of migrant children, the Center for Aid of the Foreign Workers openly commended the Interior Minister. Anticipating the future, the Center for Aid stressed, however, that it would be better if Bar-On's criteria were to be permanently enshrined in the Israeli legal code, so as to avoid a situation where the future regulation of migrant status relied upon the goodwill of this or that interior minister. Little did they know what was to come in this respect, from the Netanyahu Administration of 2009 and its hard-line ultra-religious interior minister, Eli Yishai.[20]

Humanitarianism under Olmert: The Proposed Anti-Infiltration Act of 2008

On April 1, 2008, the Olmert Government tabled its proposed legislation for the tightening of the border regime and the cross-border activity of African migrants at the southern Israeli frontier with Egypt. As with many other pieces of legislation, the proposed Anti-Infiltration Act of 2008 had just as much to do with internal political considerations as it had with its purported goal of modernizing the legal foundations for stopping cross-border transgression. Olmert's alleged mismanagement of the second Lebanon War, in 2006, and the harsh criticism directed at the government in the Winograd Commission report, which investigated that war in 2007, both portrayed Olmert as "soft" on security issues.[21] By mid-2008, as the African migration issue began to occupy a prominent position in Israeli public perception, its framing had gradually evolved into the main policy area where security concerns and human rights collided. Israel had always perceived itself as a thriving democracy, constantly and existentially threatened by security concerns. Consequently, all legislation concerning security-driven issues had historically been a balancing act between the extensive prerogatives granted to the police and armed forces of the State and the need to safeguard the civil liberties deemed necessary for a functioning democracy.[22]

As previously mentioned, the first ever piece of anti-infiltration legislation passed by the Israeli Knesset was the Anti-Infiltration Act of 1954. This law was primarily enacted to stop Palestinian border crossers within the framework of the end of Israel's 1948 war of independence and its corollary border conflicts of the 1950s until the 1956 Suez Canal crisis.[23] With the Israeli legal system in a perpetual state of emergency since 1948, the 1954 act was legally bound to this declared state of emergency – which, along with a host of legal acts correlating to it, has been renewed every year since 1948 up to the present day. In anticipation of the day when this perpetual state of emergency shall be lifted, Israeli legislators began the trend of replacing all acts based on this state of emergency with permanent legislation independent from the emergency status.[24]

Reading through the official legal explanatory notes to the proposed 2008 Anti-Infiltration Act, the rationale and the ideological background of the legislation immediately shine through. In passing this law, the

Olmert Administration was looking to establish a security platform for the prevention and punishment of infiltration, yet all the while remaining bound to the tolerant humanism it exemplified in its moderate handling of the 2007 naturalization act for migrant children. In addition, the government was looking to adopt a permanent legal tool necessary for the security-based prevention of infiltration in order to revoke the emergency-law status of the 1954 act and to replace it with an orderly and fair (though harsh) legislative platform.

The new 2008 Anti-Infiltration Act set out to accomplish three goals: (a) to provide a new law divorced from the 1948 emergency-powers conditioning; (b) to provide a harsh legal framework for the detention, deportation, and deterrence of security-threatening infiltrators to Israel; and (c) to distinguish between security-threatening infiltrators and the overwhelming majority of African migrants, who were non-threatening border crossers. The legal preface to the proposed law stated:

> In recent years Israel has witnessed a rise in the phenomenon of cross-border infiltration into the country – especially through the Egyptian border, but not via regulated border posts – of trespassers from various countries, including states known to be enemies of Israel. The regulations for dealing with such infiltration had been enshrined in the 1954 Anti-Infiltration Act. Article 34 of this law conditions its validity upon the existence of a state of emergency, which is prolonged each year. Along with the prolongation of this state of emergency, the government strives to replace different legal acts based upon this state of emergency in places where the state of emergency is not deemed necessary [. . .] It is hereby proposed that new regulations be established against infiltration *balancing between human rights and security needs* [. . .] in accordance with the rise in infiltration and considering the judicial rulings on this issue. *This law's point of departure rests upon the sharp distinction between "infiltrators", who pose a security threat to the state, and "trespassers", who do not pose such a threat* [. . .] and who shall be dealt with in accordance with the Law of Entry into Israel (1952) and not this law. It is hereby remarked that as per the overwhelming majority of trespassers into Israel over the last few years, *after examining the grounds of their infiltration, no security threat was associated with their trespassing whatsoever.*[25]

Granted the security background underpinning the rationale of the newly proposed 2008 Anti-Infiltration Act, its stipulations were undoubtedly harsh – and, to a large extent, they contravened Israel's explicit commitments under the 1951 Refugee Convention, which, as we saw earlier, Israel partially drafted.[26] It imposed an immediate jail sentence of five years on any trespasser crossing the borders of the State of Israel illegally rather than through a regulated border crossing.[27] It further imposed an immediate seven-year jail sentence on infiltrators from countries known to be enemies of Israel (including Sudan – and, correspondingly, any Darfur Genocide survivors who reached the Israeli border).[28] It stipulated an arbitrary detention period, without recourse to any judicial process of up to three years, and a 14-day period of administrative detention without recourse to any visiting rights whatsoever, legal representation included.[29]

Yet by far the most alarming part of the law was Article 11 regarding the "hot return" of infiltrators, since they have illegally crossed the border, directly contravening the non-refoulement principle (Article 33) of the 1951 Refugee Convention. In no unclear terms, the proposed law's Article 11 stated,

> Should an authorized officer observe a trespasser recently crossing the border into Israel, he is entitled to command the trespasser's immediate return to the country or area the trespasser came from, as long as this forced return shall be undertaken within 72 hours from the time the officer *intuitively assumed* that this person had entered Israel.[30]

For argument's sake, it is worthwhile repeating here the language of Article 33 of the 1951 Refugee Convention so as to see just how far the above proposed proviso ran counter to it:

> No Contracting State shall expel or return ("refouler") a refugee in any manner whatsoever to the frontiers of territories where his life or freedom would be threatened.[31]

One is tempted to ask whether the legal drafters of the proposed 2008 Anti-Infiltration Act did not deliberately return to the text their forebears had drafted, signed, and ratified – only to directly draft its contravening stipulation in the bluntest of terms. Be the answer to this question as it may, the public outcry and civil-society backlash against the newly proposed legislation followed rapidly.

The public mobilization against the act began almost simultaneously to its governmental tabling before parliament in April 2008, with its first vote of acceptance endorsed by the parliamentary plenary on May 19. Coordinating action against the legislation was the usual coalition of pro-migrant NGOs, spearheaded by the Hotline for Migrant Workers ("The Hotline"), the Aid Organization for Refugees and Asylum Seekers in Israel (ASSAF), and the African Refugee Development Center (ARDC).[32] These NGOs were joined by other service-providing organizations such as Physicians for Human rights (P4HR) and the Worker Hotline – both organizations dedicated to the general assistance of vulnerable communities in Israel. These include, in addition to the African migrants, Palestinian guest workers, victims of human trafficking, and Palestinian residents of the OPT when residing in Israel.[33]

The bill was endorsed by 21 votes to 1, supported by most of the parties spanning the full political spectrum from the extreme right to the far left. The only vote cast against the law was that of MK (Member of Knesset) Dr Dov Hanin, representing the extreme-left "Hadash" joint Arab–Jewish communist party. Alerted in advance by the pro-migrant NGO lobby, MK Hanin was possibly the only MK who had any idea the law was going to be tabled with such harsh measures against migrants. The proposed law would have also included stipulations that could potentially jeopardize the work of aid organizations for the migrants, not to mention its unequivocal contravention of Israel's signed commitments under the 1951 Refugee Convention.[34]

Following the 2008 Anti-Infiltration Act's first endorsement, and as with all Israeli legislation, it was sent to the Knesset standing committee for legislation, in preparation for the final draft to be adopted in the second and third roll-call votes of parliament. It is not out of the ordinary that many pieces of legislation are in fact halted or become "buried" at the table of the standing committee, and to a certain extent this was the wishful thinking of the NGOs. With the Knesset already gearing up, in late 2008, for elections scheduled for March 2009, it was fairly obvious that all first-draft legislation not concluded by the standing committee and voted upon for second and third roll calls would become automatically void and be withdrawn. The only possibility of such legislation enduring was in the specific case where a newly elected parliament extraordinarily decided to positively prolong the consideration of a certain statue from the previous elected chamber – causing it to be carried over into the newly elected house.

And this, to the astonishment of the pro-migrant NGOs, is precisely what took place. Following the election of the new parliament in April 2009, the Knesset approved an automatic procedural continuity act for all tentative legislation from the previous parliament, consequently extending the deadline for the 2008 Anti-Infiltration Act. To the dismay of the NGOs, who assumed that this law's first draft would be abolished with the end of parliamentary term, 95 MKs out of 120 voted for the automatic extension of all previous-parliament legislation. As usual, the only objection to this procedure came from the NGOs, faithful ally in parliament: the implacable Dr Dov Hanin.[35]

Gearing up support for the pro-migrant NGOs, and well aware of the need to mount further political pressure so as to block the new legislation's final endorsement, Hanin set off to orchestrate a full-blown political campaign against it. Communicating with fellow activists during the strategic preparation of the law's final parliamentary plenary session, the MK did not mince his words:

> A law which casts a jail sentence on any Israeli aiding a "trespasser" from Darfur is an omen of shame for our parliament and Israeli society. This law shall prove to be a black stain in our legal codex and all who pertain to a rightful conscience must mobilize in order to block it. The lessons of our Jewish and world history can not coincide with draconic punishment of refugees and asylum seekers.[36]

During the summer of 2009, the pro-migrant NGO lobby, in coordination with Hanin, elaborated a strategy and subsequent plan of action against the new anti-migrant legislation. Anticipating the commencement of the Knesset's winter term in October 2009, just after the Jewish Day of Atonement (Yom Kippur) and the festival of Sukkoth, the NGO lobby fleshed out two courses for action. On the advocacy level, the pro-migrant organizations were required to break out of their habitual political marginalization and team up with bigger and stronger "players" on the Israeli NGO scene. At the parliamentary level, support for the migrants needed to be generated from all strands of the Israeli political spectrum, where each political party – left or right, religious or secular – was to be provided with the arguments as to why support for the African migrants was conducive to and coherent with that party's respective political goals and electorate.[37]

Since the early 1970s, one of the strongest nongovernmental actors in Israeli civil society has been the libertarian pro-human rights and freedoms Association for Civil Rights in Israel (ACRI). Winner of the Israel Prize for contribution to the State, the ACRI has habitually been headed by former presidents of the supreme court who resigned from the bench at the compulsory age of 70. The ACRI enjoys an unsurpassed legal reputation, and has been viewed as a paragon of civil-rights defense while retaining the respect of the Israeli military and security establishment – against whom a large portion of the ACRI's work is aimed.[38] In virtually all cases over the past 40 years where infringement on civil liberties has been contemplated, the ACRI has maintained the toughest stance against the security and military establishments.[39]

The ACRI's unique standing within the high echelons of the Israeli legal system – and specifically the Supreme Court – has often acted as a significant deterrent for the enactment of anti-libertarian measures. The security establishment, suffering several defeats over the years over its hard-line legislative views, has duly turned cautious towards the ACRI. This has often brought a rethinking of harsh legislation proposals by the establishment, proposals which might well be deemed unconstitutional and overruled by the high court given the chances of prospective potential appeals by ACRI arguing for unconstitutional grounds.

It was precisely with the "security vs. civil liberties" theme that the migrant-NGO forum approached the ACRI. Consequently, the forum managed to conscript the ACRI to spearhead its legal campaign against the 2008 Anti-Infiltration legislation with the new law's security agenda as the primary target for attack. As early as 2003, the Israeli Attorney General voiced his contention with the State's claim of security concerns resulting from cases of African clandestine migration, stressing their civilian nature. Elyakim Rubinstein (later a Supreme Court judge) had instructed all security agencies, following an initial assessment of security threats, to treat all African migrants approaching Israel's southern border with Egypt in accordance with the legally more lenient stipulations of the 1952 Law of Entry into Israel, rather than the harsh 1954 Anti-Infiltration Act. Rubinstein's successor, Menachem Mazuz, continued this stipulation as he entered office in 2007.[40]

The 2008 Anti-Infiltration Act was deliberately framed so as to contravene this legal directive of the Attorney General. In its opening explanatory part, the law specifically stipulated:

> all trespassers shall initially be held according to this Anti-Infiltration Act, and once their circumstances have been dully ascertained, they shall be transferred for further processing and treatment under the stipulation so for the 1952 law of entry into Israel.[41]

Furthermore, as per the security-based agenda of the new 2008 act, its responsible governmental authority was to be the Israeli minister of defense, as opposed to the 1952 Law of Entry into Israel where governmental oversight is civilian by its nature and therefore under the purview of the Interior Ministry. Correspondingly, governmental oversight over the new 2008 act was to be initially administered in the field by the Israeli Army (IDF) before turning suspects over to the police and civilian immigration authority officials. This is in direct contrast to the 1952 Law of Entry into Israel, wherein the coercive governmental agencies who executed overriding authority over all other governmental organs (the IDF included) were the Israeli Police and Interior Ministry immigration officers.

For its part, the ACRI was in any case already engaged in bitter legal sparring with the Ministry of Defense concerning a similar continuity procedure which overwhelmed the pro-migrant NGO forum. In this case, the association was alarmed by the proposed creation and usage of a biometric database for security agencies, which the ACRI rightly feared would consign Israelis to an informational tyranny orchestrated by the State's security agencies. For the ACRI to combine its legal motions against both the 2008 Anti-Infiltration Act and the 2008 biometric database legislation made all the more sense, seeing as both constituted infringements upon civil liberties by the same security establishment.[42]

In parallel with the legal front, being now handled by a professional "heavyweight" in the form of the ACRI, the pro-migrant NGO forum concluded it needed some external credible international voices to supplement its claims against the 2008 Anti-Infiltration Act. Depicting the dangers of the proposed legislation in no uncertain terms, the NGOs secured the formal and official endorsement of Amnesty International, both morally and financially, for their campaign. Supplementing this support from Amnesty International, the forum crucially secured the tacit endorsement of the United Nations High Commissioner for Refugees' regional office, which meant that the NGOs now had vital access to UNHCR's databases (albeit unofficially). The coordination of dates of publication of source materials by the NGOs, using UNHCR data, with the dates of planned parliamentary debates leaves little room for speculation as to the ample cooperation between the NGOs and the UN in this case.[43]

With the strategy now in place, with the partners in the campaign all aligned, and with the objective clear, the NGOs proceeded toward generating as much public pressure as possible so as to reverse the tide on the 2008 Anti-Infiltration Act. First to be targeted were all the Knesset members who had voted affirmatively and endorsed the law's first draft. Second to be targeted were those MKs who had endorsed the application of the continuity principle to this legislation in April 2009, preventing its procedural downfall between parliaments. Third to be targeted were remaining Knesset members, who came under a "bombardment" of advocacy pleas, explanatory materials, and position papers detailing the dangers, misinformation, and outright deceit abounding in the official governmental explanatory notes to the 2008 Anti-Infiltration Act.[44]

As the Knesset winter term unfolded, the NGOs increased their pressure – shaming, blaming, and naming MKs who had voted affirmatively for the 2008 Act, on public radio; on television, during daily shows; and in the newspapers. Reporting from the front line, NGO activists praised the IDF for its humanitarian actions towards the migrants. The activists made it a point to specifically mention the adamant and positive execution of orders to the letter by the Israeli Army in accordance with the 1952 Law of Entry into Israel, as stipulated to the army by the State Attorney General, reiterating these orders when examined by the State Comptroller.[45]

By February 2010, at the height of the Knesset winter term, as the parliamentary legislative committee began its sessions concerning the preparation for final voting over the 2008 Anti-Infiltration Act, parliamentary support for the law began to wane. With public perceptions swaying in favor of the migrants, the electoral ground was beginning to shake beneath the politicians' feet. "Out of the woodwork" suddenly appeared the left-wing members of the Labor Party, claiming they were overburdened with legislation following the new elections, and had simply and mistakenly overlooked the true implications of the proposed 2008 Anti-Infiltration Act when they endorsed it during the first roll call.[46]

As the Knesset's winter term came to a close, it became clear that public opinion had mobilized against the 2008 Anti-Infiltration Act. Youth movements and pupil associations began questioning the validity of the law, both on moral and on Jewish religious grounds. The ACRI secured the endorsement of the Israeli Bar Association for its legal positions. The NGOs also managed to secure the help and support of Yad Vashem, the Israeli Holocaust memorial, with the faithful Yehuda Bauer coming to their aid. On July 28, 2010, as the Knesset members were leaving for their summer holidays, the Netanyahu Government officially informed the parliamentary registrar that it had decided to withdraw in its entirety the 2008 Anti-Infiltration Act.[47]"

The Interim Ascent of Universalism

The defeat of the 2008 Anti-Infiltration Act and its removal from the agenda of the Knesset was first and foremost a victory for the pro-migrant Israeli NGOs and their parliamentary allies. They were the ones who had mobilized, lobbied, and even bullied for it, at times coercively arm-twisting and badgering Israeli legislators to strike down that proposed law. Most parliamentarians eventually caved in to the lobbying pressure inflicted upon them by the NGO campaigners. And they probably did so from fear of being politically tagged as inhumane extremists, thus losing some support with their respective electorates.

In all probability, some of those parliamentarians who bowed to the NGOs' public pressure and media campaign did so as a result of aroused humanitarian convictions; some probably did so out of sheer political expediency. Be their motivations as they were, one conclusion seems likely: in their subjective perceptions, Israeli society was more aligned with universalist humanitarian values, as represented by the NGOs, than with the proposed hard-handed anti-migrant legislation championed by the government, which entailed the arbitrary incarceration of African asylum seekers. After all, the 2008 Anti-Infiltration Act had not been sent to the Knesset floor by some group of backbenchers, nor as an independent piece of legislation from a single MK. Rather, it was a governmentally proposed law, articulated over many months within the corridors of government – primarily through the auspices of the Ministry of Justice. The normal chain of events would have been for the parliamentary majority-led coalition to simply vote affirmatively for its own piece of proposed legislation, and for the parliamentarians to vote in accordance with their coalition whips, who executed the governmentally required discipline. This "normal" anticipated chain of events did not require coalition parliamentarians to go out of their way and second-guess governmental policy lines. Like so many thousands of laws and decrees, the 2008 Anti-Infiltration Act could have been endorsed by the Knesset in a "business as usual" manner.

The active overturning and striking down of the 2008 Anti-Infiltration Act demanded something overwhelmingly different. It demanded that parliamentarians take up the initiative *against their own government's policy line*. Appropriating the Burkeian maxim that "All it takes for evil to triumph is for good men to *do nothing*" (my emphasis), the Israeli MKs *did something*. The procedural banality with which the 2008 Anti-Infiltration Act was almost *unintentionally* endorsed, by parliamentarians who claimed they did not pay attention to what they were voting on, was *intentionally* overturned. By striking down the 2008 Anti-Infiltration Act, the Knesset opted for a universalist approach toward the African migrants rather than resorting to the habitus of Israeli exceptionalism. Had the legislation gone through, Israel would already in 2008 have drifted away from prevalent international norms enshrined in the 1951 Refugee Convention. Indeed, when Israeli legislators did finally undertake a similar departure from the international universalist norm – with the 2012 Anti-Infiltration Act, and again with its 2014 successor – both of these laws were eventually revoked by the Supreme Court, which realigned Israeli policy back on to the universalist track and away from exceptionalism.

In this context, the actions of the Sharon–Olmert administrations' interior minister, Roni Bar-On, stand out as a shining, positive example of a synthesis of Israel's exceptionalist ethos and its universalist tendencies, with Bar-On heavily leaning towards the latter of these ideological poles. The conservative interior minister was, however, politically distant from left-wing parliamentarians associated with the pro-migrant NGO lobby, such as Dr Dov Hanin. His decision to legalize the status of non-Jewish migrant children through their naturalization stemmed first and foremost from his emphasis upon the Jewish Hebrew-speaking character of Israeli society as he understood it. For Bar-On, it was the Hebrew-speaking character of these non-Jewish children, coupled with their identification with the Israeli State as manifested though their wish to undergo military service, which demarked them as part of Israeli society. Once they were born in Israel and had been acquainted with Israeli society to a much greater degree than with the cultures of their ancestral countries of origin, they merited naturalization. To this extent, Bar-On had resorted here to a classical *jus soli* type of reasoning, inherently universal in character.

Much of the same reasoning goes for the 2008 Anti-Infiltration Act as proposed. The explicit separation between trespassers, who posed no security threat (and therefore were to be dealt with under the provision of the 1952 Law of Entry into Israel), and those posing a threat (to whom the 2008 Act applied), even granted the harshness enshrined in this legislation, denotes a universalist criterion. State security is a legitimate concern shared by all countries. Israel's enhanced security threats – given the geopolitical realities of a vehemently hostile Middle Eastern environment, as opposed to the situation of other Western countries, challenged by clandestine immigration – rendered the security rational of the 2008 Anti-Infiltration Act acceptable. The exclusion of migrants who posed no security threat from that law's purview merely denotes this aspect of the legislation. State security, while a legitimate universal concern, was not to be extended and applied automatically to all.

Yet "state security" is not an *idée fixe*. So long as the numbers of illegal African migrants could be viewed as tolerable, security concerns remained confined to threats of cross-border terrorism. By 2011, as the migrants were crossing into Israel at the rate of 1,000 people per month, imagined threats to Jewish demographic supremacy began to fester. "National security" was no longer limited to immediate terrorist threats, but would gradually be extended so as to safeguard against "demographic threats" – real or imagined.

CHAPTER 4

THE RISE OF THE ISRAELI EXTREME RIGHT, 2009–12

The following pages cover the time period from the coming to power of the Netanyahu Administration in 2009, along with its "extremization" of Israeli politics, up until the partial electoral shift back towards the center of the political spectrum in January 2013. This period poses an intellectual challenge in the search for an explanation of the radical shift in public attitudes towards the African migrants – from the tolerant policies under Olmert to the harsh governmental legislation under the Netanyahu Government (the 2012 amendment of the 1954 Anti-Infiltration Act), which was mirrored by xenophobic arson attacks and a significant rise in physical and verbal violence against the migrants. It was during this period that the exceptionalist tendencies within Israeli politics came to prevail over universalist ones. One vital component to which I attribute this shift is the political and electoral rise of an ethnocentric, nationalistic Israeli extreme right, which resembled (if not copied) xenophobic anti-migrant movements well known from the rise of European extreme-right parties with strong anti-migrant xenophobic agendas.

As with many European examples, the newly proposed, harsh anti-migrant Israeli legislation of 2012 was not, in fact, the result of legislative efforts undertaken and pushed for by the extreme-right parties. Rather, the main motor behind the new and "beefed up" legislation was the government itself, represented by its senior bureaucratic legal experts from the Israeli Ministry of Justice and followed up by its delegate inside the legislating Knesset Interior Committee (KIC). As the new, harsh legislation came into being, it was parliamentary legal experts (as opposed to governmental ones), and other legislators, who pointedly voiced their objections and concerns regarding the inhumane features of this newly presented anti-migrant legislation. Indeed, many of the parliamentary criticisms of the proposed legislation, voiced during its endorsement process as it was pushed and advocated for by the government through the parliamentary channels, were ultimately reiterated by the high court at a later stage.

The legislative process within the KIC is fascinating, in that it exhibits all the different strata of the Israeli political establishment as well as the interactions between government and parliament, often exposing significant political rifts and inconsistencies – even within a single political party (SHAS being a case in point, as explained below).

By July 2010, the public NGO campaign against the Knesset's proposed 2008 Anti-Infiltration Act had rendered the latter void, and it was officially withdrawn by the government from the agenda. Yet, in a strikingly contrasting manner, 18 months later – between December 2011 and January 2012 – a much harsher piece of anti-infiltration legislation was rapidly adopted, overshadowing the 2008 bill in its severity, scope, and procedural legislative implications. Rather than being a newly proposed piece of legislation, as the 2008 Act had been, the 2012 Anti-Infiltration Act was an adaptation and significant revamping of a notorious, and bitterly contested, military law five decades old: the 1954 Anti-Infiltration Act.

The "Extremization" of Israeli Society

In the following pages, I shall attempt firstly to reconstruct the political and social contexts within which this far-reaching anti-migrant amendment of the 1954 Anti-Infiltration Act took place. My underlying rationale here is to set this legislative process in the more general context of the increasing extremism in Israeli society at large, as it veered toward more ethnocentric and radical religious positions during these years. The fundamental point stressed here is that one should see the abrupt shift of Israeli immigration policies – from the moderate acceptance of migrants under Olmert to their harsh, subhuman treatment under Benjamin Netanyahu – as part of the general pattern of extremism which Israel society underwent between 2011 and 2013, and *not* as something specific to this wave of African migrants. Though different analysts and social scientists have provided a full spectrum of answers as to *why* this move towards the religious ethnocentric right happened in the first place, there is hardly any doubt that it did indeed take place. While a full account of this radicalization process is well beyond the scope of the present volume, some examples in this regard are important – especially those concerning the electoral and political aspects.

Gauging the extent to which a certain society has moved towards an extreme position is not a straightforward or simple task, least of all when one is dealing with the realm of current affairs. The fact that one sees (and is convinced) that an accumulated collection of events is the result of societal extremization is still not a measure of proof in and of itself.[1] The process of grounded proof and the validation of a correct hypothesis, granted the strong "gut feeling" which one evidently has, often becomes the main challenge of any well-grounded societal research. In essence, it is no more than the difference in Plato's *Meno* between "True Belief" and "Knowledge."[2] In order to validate the general claim of extremization, one specific feature of which was (as I argue) the anti-migrant onslaught, one would need to obtain generic indicators of societal extremization as such. In short, we are looking for indicators which would validate the claim that Israeli society indeed had become more extreme during the time period from 2011 to 2013.

It is thanks to the late George L. Mosse, an expert in the processes of societal radicalization, that we have today at our disposal a set of sociological indicators with which to gauge when a society becomes radicalized and moves towards an extreme. A first, and vital, indicator of a society's radicalization is measured though a close observation of its attitudes towards three distinct, vulnerable human groups: homosexuals; ethnic minorities; and, most importantly, women (with a concomitant rise in misogyny).[3]

That Israeli society had undergone a significant "extremizing" process, shifting societal beliefs and practices heavily towards the ethnocentric religious right wing, can be observed through the continued process of social erosion and disfranchisement experienced by homosexuals, Israeli Arabs, and, particularly, women in Israel between 2009 and 2013. The Jewish–American intellectual Leon Wieseltier amply captured Israel's societal development concerning this consistent and dangerous shift towards the extreme. Writing as the adoption of the harsh anti-migrant legislation was in full sway, Wieseltier openly linked the recent, and hitherto unheard of, misogynistic tendencies in the country and the radicalization of Israeli society:

> "The list of controversies grows weekly," Ethan Bronner and Isabel Kershner, filing from Jerusalem, write in the *New York Times*. "Organizers of a conference last week on women's health and Jewish law barred women from speaking from the podium, leading at least eight speakers to cancel; ultra-Orthodox men spit on an eight-year-old girl whom they deemed immodestly dressed; the chief rabbi of the air force resigned his post because the army declined to excuse ultra-Orthodox soldiers from attending events where female singers perform; protesters depicted the Jerusalem police commander as Hitler on posters because he instructed public bus lines with mixed-sex seating to drive through ultra-Orthodox neighborhoods; vandals blacked out women's faces on Jerusalem billboards." And a distinguished professor of pediatrics whose book won an award from the Ministry of Health was instructed that she could not sit with her husband at the ceremony and that a male colleague would accept her prize for her because women were forbidden from the stage. Bronner's and Kershner's report provoked widespread revulsion [. . .] The odious misogyny of the ultra-Orthodox is certainly not typical of Israeli life [. . .] But more needs to be said. There has occurred a renaissance of Jewish fanaticism in the Netanyahu years.[4]

As Wieseltier had pungently pointed out, the onslaught against women was orchestrated first and foremost by Jewish ultra-religious circles. While this attack on women – Mosse's major socially vulnerable indicator group – was embraced by all ultra-orthodox strata in Israeli society, the onslaught against members of the second of Mosse's indicator groups, homosexuals, was specifically claimed by the Sephardic ultra-religious party SHAS, with its fanatic leader, Eli Yishai. Representing between 10 and 15 percent of the Israeli electorate, SHAS had made a point of distinguishing itself as the alleged guardian of traditional Jewish, and specifically Sephardic, values. The party's acronym literally translates as "The Torah Guardians – Sephardic," designating both its ultra-religious affiliation and the constituencies it represents.

SHAS' role as an instigator and orchestrator of the onslaught against the African migrants is crucial in explaining the governmental policy shift from moderate humanitarianism under Olmert to the harsh policies under Netanyahu. George L. Mosse's logic of tracing sentiments against vulnerable groups as an indicator of a certain society's extremizing was further reinforced by SHAS' assault on its next societal "punch bag." Mosse's methodological litmus test crystallized as SHAS became the most ardent opponent of, and posed the greatest political threat to, homosexuals in Israel from the party's electoral zenith in the 1999 elections until after the lethal anti-gay shootings of 2009.

SHAS' open attacks on the gay community can be traced back as early as 2001, when MK Nissim Zeev assailed the pro-human-rights MK Yael Dayan, and referred to homosexuals as "sick people who have a serious defect, who do not recognize their own malaise and who deserve mental treatment." Zeev's words were soon translated into action, when homophobic graffiti were sprayed on the walls of MK Dayan's house that very same night.[5]

In 2003, Zeev continued his onslaught on the gay community when the liberal anti-religious interior minister, Abraham Poraz, chose to appoint an openly gay candidate as his chief of staff. MK Zeev accused Poraz of deliberately appointing a homosexual to this post so as to bar the ultra religious from attending ministerial meetings, knowing full well that SHAS delegates would refrain from any contact with this official since he was, as Zeev maintained, "far worse than a beast."[6] In 2006, SHAS' attacks against homosexuals went even further, reaching governmental ministerial levels, when the head of the party and then-minister of health, Eli Yishai, reiterated the words of fellow MK Zeev, stating that, "homosexuals are sick people who deserve medical treatment, and I hope they are cured from this illness. Though a remedy and medication has yet to be found for this illness, I hope such a medication will be found soon."[7]

In 2008, SHAS' verbal assaults on the gay community began drifting towards support for physical violence. The request of the gay community to hold a gay-pride parade in Jerusalem was viewed by the ultra religious as a direct act of sacrilege aimed at the holy character of this divine city. In a failed legislative attempt to bar the parade from taking place, MK Zeev raised his anti-homophobic attacks one notch higher, claiming that "homosexuals should be treated in the same way as the Ministry of Health had treated vermin stricken chickens with bird flu."[8] In his complaint to the Knesset ethics committee, the chair of the homo-lesbian association, Mike Hammel, strikingly predicted the immediate future, asking rhetorically, "if this is not incitement for murder and an open call for killing homosexuals, what is?"[9]

It was not long before Hammel's prediction came painfully true – albeit on criminal, rather than ideological grounds. On August 1, 2009, a masked man dressed in black entered the gay community's youth club in central Tel Aviv and opened fire on the teenagers and the educational staff at the center, leaving two dead and 15 severely wounded – some maimed for life.[10] Though not in any way connected to SHAS' statements, at the time – and as the case remained unresolved – most analysts agreed that the main suspects were assumed to be ideologically motivated, with the police not ruling out the possibility of the incident being a hate crime (a notion later reversed as further evidence of a more criminal nature began to surface).

The public backlash against the SHAS MKs came almost immediately after the attack. In no uncertain terms, gay speakers directly and, as it turned out, mistakenly linked the shootings to the inflammatory rhetoric of the SHAS parliamentarians. Non-partisan commentators stressed the responsibility borne by MK Zeev and Minister Yishai for their years-long hate campaign which had seemed to culminate in these killings. On the electoral defensive, ultra-religious SHAS dignitaries issued stern condemnations to the killings, qualified only by MK Zeev's assertion that the shooter and/or perpetrators generally might well be in some way associated with the gay community itself.[11] With the Israeli president, Shimon Peres, at the crime scene and Prime Minister Netanyahu appalled (saying his own adolescent children could have been possible victims as well), SHAS officials were quick to comprehend the public-relations disaster they possibly faced. SHAS' habitual societal "punch bag" was now lost in the realms of national grief and pan-Israeli empathy. SHAS' extreme-right leader, Eli Yishai, grew desperate for a new "punch bag" now that the gay community as his target of choice was publically lost.

Of Mosse's vulnerable social groups susceptible to harm during the rise of social extremism, it was the Arab ethnic minority in Israel and the consequent attacks upon it which were most expected to correlate with the hostile sentiments voiced against the African migrants. As a rival ethnic minority alongside a Jewish majority, the Arab–Israeli community had often been subject to coercive treatment and racial discrimination. That said, most scholars agree that between 2009 and 2013, during the tenure of the eighteenth Knesset, an unprecedented racial and ethnic onslaught was carried out by the Israeli right wing against the Arab–Israeli community.[12]

At the governmental level, this onslaught manifested itself through an unprecedented string of legislative acts, proposed and mostly endorsed, with the objective of infringing upon Arab civil, cultural, and religious liberties. In the field of cultural rights and free speech, these legal acts included the "Nakba Law," prohibiting public protest against the Israeli Independence Day through highlighting the Palestinian refugee catastrophe (*Nakba*) which coincided with Israel's creation in 1948. In the field of religious freedoms, the "anti-mosques law" ordered the silencing of Muslim public calls for prayer over loudspeakers (by traditional *muezzins*) in ethnically mixed areas, hence also silencing a well-known feature and an integral part of the Israeli religious experience and landscape. At the societal level, equality was further eroded through the "reception committees' law," establishing the role of citizens' committees in villages and neighborhoods, vested with the right to prevent Arab families from either buying or renting houses in predominately Jewish areas.[13]

These legislative acts were often accompanied by public and civil-society actions targeted at the country's Arab population. Thus, for example, the "reception committees' law" was immediately followed by a public pamphleteer's statement, published and signed by over 300 rabbis associated with the extreme right wing, calling upon all Israelis to neither rent nor sell any apartments, houses or real-estate property to Arabs.[14] Another example, this time from the field of popular culture, saw a manifestation of anti-Arab sentiment on the soccer field, carried forward by the notoriously right-wing Betar Jerusalem football club. Though "death to the Arabs" was a habitually routine slogan sung by Betar Jerusalem's fans, its anti-Arab sentiments were grotesquely exposed when the team's management decided to purchase a Muslim

Chechen international footballer so as to improve its spearhead and scoring squad. In a perverse display of idiosyncrasies, some fanatical Betar Jerusalem fans left the stadium precisely when their very own team scored and went into the lead, merely because the scorer on their own behalf was Muslim.[15]

It was against this backdrop of the extremizing of Israeli society, that the flows of African migrants began arriving in ever-growing numbers. In contrast to the reality of the mid-2000s under the Sharon–Olmert administrations, by 2011–12 significant portions of Israeli society began to perform as a hotbed for extremist tendencies, ranging from misogynistic and anti-gay sentiments to blunt hatred against Arabs. The spillover into hostility against African migrants should be seen as a final step within this more general trend of extremization. Setting Israel's extremization in direct contrast to the humanistic tendencies of world Jewry, the well-known Hebrew University historian Daniel Blatman, a successor to Yehuda Bauer and Jacob Robinson at the same Institute for Contemporary Jewry, called out to American Jews to save Israeli society from the dangerous road upon which it was embarking. Recalling the historical support for human rights advocated by Jewish leaders on behalf of the civil-rights movements in the US and South Africa, Blatman wrote:

> If I were an American Jew who held Israel dear, I would view the crisis afflicting the greatest Jewish dream in modern times with despair. When sitting down to Shabbat dinner with my adult children, I would hear that Israel no longer represents the values on which they were raised: human dignity, equal rights, a pluralistic society, and the obligation to fight for the weak and the persecuted [. . .] If I were an American Jew I would recall that Jews made up 30 percent of civil rights activists in the US South in the 1950s and '60s. Rabbis such as Julian Feibelman in New Orleans, Ira Sanders in Arkansas, Perry Nussbaum in Mississippi, and Jacob Rothschild in Atlanta opened their synagogues to black activists and supported the movement openly and fearlessly [. . .] If I were an American Jew I would recall that during the historic march from Selma to Montgomery, Alabama, in March 1965, Rabbi Abraham Joshua Heschel marched alongside Martin Luther King [. . .] if the vision of an open, egalitarian and peace-loving Israel is

> important to Jews around the world, they cannot leave the chances of fulfilling it in the hands of Israelis alone. The racist cancer [. . .] has spread deep into Israeli society. World Jewry must help Israel to be cured of it. It must speak out and act. It must come out openly and sever any economic, cultural, or political ties with any person or organization that promotes turning Israel into a racist apartheid state, whether a settler, a rabbi who preaches violence, or a politician who promotes racist legislation.[16]

The Changing of the Electoral Landscape

The electoral composition of the seventeenth Knesset (2006–9) under the Olmert Government was roughly split along the line between center-left and center-right parties, in common with most Israeli parliaments over the past three decades. The eighteenth Knesset (2009–13), on the other hand, was arguably one of the most right-wing parliaments in the history of the Israeli state, in terms both of the numerical majority of elected MPs from right-wing parties and the projected policies it advocated. Within this general pattern, several important political actors came to play a crucial role in the reintroduction of harsh anti-migrant legislation, in the form of the 2012 Anti-Infiltration Act.

The first important actor who influenced governmental policies towards the African migration to Israel was the right-wing Yisrael Beyteynu party, headed by the former Russian Jewish immigrant Avigdor Lieberman. During its first tenure in the fifteenth Knesset in 2002, Yisrael Beyteynu managed to secure five seats (out of a total of 120), representing roughly 4 percent of the Israeli electorate. During the seventeenth Knesset elections in 2006, it had already doubled its power to ten seats, representing almost 10 percent of Israeli voters. By the eighteenth Knesset in 2009, Yisrael Beyteynu had consolidated an even more considerable standing in Israeli politics, securing 15 parliamentary seats and becoming the second largest partner in Netanyahu's governing coalition, with Lieberman as Israel's foreign minister. The party's political orientation positioned it to the right of the large center-right Likud party on issues of foreign policy and attitudes vis-à-vis the Palestinian–Israeli conflict.

Most of Yisrael Beyteynu's MKs were former Russian immigrants, quite a number of whom had become Israeli settlers in the OPT.[17]

In addition to this core of Jews of Russian origin, the party "embellished" its top echelons with retired senior security officials, corresponding to its declared "security first" political agenda. This enabled the party to project itself as the primary political player advocating Israel's security, dovetailed by an appealing representation of native Israelis in tandem with new Jewish immigrants.

The two other important political actors who ultimately exercised influence on the new Israeli Government's policies towards the African migrants were SHAS and the extreme-right National Unity (Haichud Haleumi) party. One further significant factor regarding the composition of the eighteenth Knesset worth mentioning was the clear electoral stagnation of both these radical political actors – SHAS and Haichud Haleumi.

SHAS reached its electoral zenith in the 1999 elections with 18 MKs, sharply declining in the 2001 elections, and consolidating its electoral standing in both the 2006 and the 2009 elections at around 11 seats in parliament (corresponding to approximately 10 percent of Israeli voters). By the eighteenth Knesset, many commentators pointed to a certain electoral fatigue with SHAS and its policies, not least due to the overtly low public esteem for its then leader, Eli Yishai. This general voter fatigue towards SHAS, coupled with the party leader's public weakness, later served as the primary drivers in its extremization on migrant issues.

If the case of SHAS was one of electoral fatigue, the condition of the extreme-right Haichud Haleumi was one of explicit electoral free fall. This process took place consistently from the 2003 elections, when the party received seven seats in parliament, down to six KMs in 2006, reducing again to four KMs in 2009 and ultimately nullifying the party, and ousting its KMs from parliament, in the 2013 elections.

In contrast to Haichud Haleumi's hard-right positions, which produced a somewhat monolithic and vehemently oppositional attitude towards the African migrants, the example of SHAS provides a much more nuanced and multifaceted approach vis-à-vis the issue of non-Jewish African migration. This nuanced character was primarily the result of conflicting views within the party about the interpretation of Jewish religious attitudes and religious jurisprudence concerning non-Jewish migrants in general. Adhering to its ultra-religious ethos, SHAS' contradictory attitudes mirrored the age-old Jewish dichotomy between assimilation and connection to the world (*Or Lagoyim*) on the one hand,

and an introverted resignation to Jewish seclusion (*Am Levadad Yishcon* – literally: "a nation reigning alone") on the other. This dichotomy was clearly manifested in the different political strata within the SHAS party, as individual SHAS MKs came to voice diametrically opposing views regarding the very same issue of non-Jewish African migration – especially during the various legislative stages which eventually resulted in the endorsement of the 2012 Anti-Infiltration Act.

In terms of this legislative process, discussions concerning the 2012 act took place at the Knesset Interior Committee (the KIC), chaired by SHAS' well-respected MK, Amnon Cohen. As with all Knesset committees, the KIC exhibited an electoral mirroring of the parliamentary "division of forces" between the different Knesset parties. As per the internal division of labor within those parties, each MK was assigned to the committee dealing with issues closest to his or her concerns. Knowing full well that most of the "heavyweight" legislative work would be carried out at the KIC, most of the later protagonists in the public street-level onslaught against the African migrants saw to it in advance that they were appointed as their party representatives to the early discussions and drafting processes of the newly proposed legislation. Thus, for example, MK Michael Ben-Ari from the extreme-right Haichud Haleumi party was present at all four KIC hearings at which the draft Anti-Infiltration Act was discussed, between August and December 2011.[18] At the opposite end of the political spectrum, and almost as adamant as MK Ben-Ari, stood the implacable MK Dr Dov Hanin representing the extreme-left socialist party, Hadash. Being the MK who most aided the 2008 NGO campaign against the then-proposed anti-migrant law, MK Hanin was also active in trying to prevent the adoption of the harsh anti-migrant law of 2012 through his countless motions for changes in the wording of the proposed legislative text.

CHAPTER 5

THE LEGISLATIVE PROCESS AND MODERN ADAPTATION OF THE 1954 ANTI-INFILTRATION ACT

By July 2011, with the proposed 2008 Anti-Infiltration Act having been "buried" by the pro-migrant NGO lobby, African asylum-seeker numbers were clearly on the rise. Exactly when the Netanyahu Administration began to contemplate the enactment of the extreme legal measure that became the 2012 Anti-Infiltration Act is not completely clear. The governmentally proposed legislation number 577, as it was known then, was initially internally circulated between the different governmental ministries of Justice, Defense, Interior, and Health, probably at the beginning of January 2011. Given that the first official publically accessible draft of the act was dated March 28, 2011, it is safe to assume that the elaboration of this legislation took place somewhere between December 2010 and January 2011.[1]

Chronology is important here. It validates the fact that, contrary to the sense of victory and perhaps even slight gloating on the side of the pro-migrant NGO lobby, governmental efforts were nevertheless well underway to find a swift and all-encompassing substitute for the defeated 2008 legislation, withdrawn by the government merely eight months earlier. On December 26, 2010, and as part of general efforts toward governmental legislative transparency, an initial draft version of the revised 1954 Infiltration Act was posted on the official governmental media website coupled with publications in the newspapers, requesting public participation and inputs concerning the newly proposed legislation.[2]

The governmental decision to promote the proposed anti-infiltration legislation through an adaptation of an existing harsh emergency law, which dated back to the existential war circumstances of 1954, was anything but accidental. The legal logic behind this course of action was clear to both supporters and opponents of government-proposed legislation number 577. The dramatic rise in numbers, and ever-growing influx of African migrants crossing the southern Israeli border demanded a heightened sense of urgency – or so it seemed to government officials. Emergency legislation under immediate parliamentary decree, initially for a limited period of three years, seemed a swift and immediate legal remedy, proportional to the dramatic rise in African migrant numbers. By the time legislation number 577 had landed on the table of the KIC, the governmental rationale for this specific legislative course of action (adopting a form of emergency legislation) had already become part and parcel of the proposed legal act.

The Choice of the 1954 Anti-Infiltration Act as the Legislative Platform for 2012

As with most legislation (save on issues of national security, where the debates are confidential and held behind closed doors), the main bulk of the wording and drafting of governmentally proposed legislation number 577 took place in four open consecutive sessions of the KIC. These debates opened a fascinating window onto the thoughts and challenges which faced Israeli policy makers with regard to the new wave of clandestine African migration. Often, the debates portray contradicting views between the humane tendencies and the harsh, publically advocated policies of certain MKs. Overall, one can definitely identify at these committee hearings most of the societal precursors that were later to erupt at "street level" across the spectrum of Israeli society – from tolerant attitudes to hard-line, almost subhuman policies; from egalitarian acceptance to xenophobic and racial slandering.

The first KIC session where legislation number 577 was discussed took place on August 10, 2011. At the meeting, only two of the committee's 11 MKs were present: the chairman, SHAS' MK Amnon Cohen, and the extreme-right MK from Haichud Haleumi, Michael Ben Ari. In contrast to the overt parliamentary absences from the meeting, a considerable representation of the pro-migrant NGO lobby was present, including all the legal advisors to the various civil-society bodies engaged with aid to the African migrants in Israel. A third, large group of participants in this session comprised the governmental bureaucrats, mainly legal advisors of the different departments of the Israeli executive branch. As per Montesquieu's classical distinction between the executive and legislative organs of the State, a fourth group – of legal advisors whose task it was to advise parliament as the legislator – were also present.[3]

The problem of adapting the 1954 Anti-Infiltration Act to the needs of 2011, as planned by legislation number 577, was immediately evident to all the participants as a divisive and bitterly contested legal approach. The greatest point of legal contention regarding the new law concerned its enactment as an extension of existing, if outdated, emergency legislation enacted over 50 years earlier. While the government's best course of action envisaged an adaptation of the age-old harsh 1954 act, parliamentary legal advisors were heavily leaning towards the carving out of a new law, either by revisiting the defeated 2008 proposal or by adapting the general 1952 Law of Entry into Israel so as to accommodate the new migratory realities. In his opening statement, Chairman Amnon Cohen gently pointed out this problem, providing an early clue as to his preferred course of action, which was diametrically opposed to that of his own party within the ruling government of which he was a part:

> the KIC already held a preliminarily discussion concerning this law. The goal was to hear about the proposed legislation. We heard the agencies and NGOs who appeared here. At this point we will pose a basic fundamental question to the governmental ministry of Justice, and then we will proceed towards discussions about the proposed legislation. From a professional or rather a procedural manner, I understand that the legal framework for this law belongs somewhere else. The legal advisors to this parliamentary committee will enlighten us on this regard. We shall see if this is the right legal framework for this law, or whether it fits somewhere else. After this we shall know how to proceed with this proposed act.[4]

In his lengthily and authoritative review of the issues at stake, the parliamentary legal advisor stressed the grave legal difficulties in applying the 1954 Anti-Infiltration Act to the problem of African migrants in 2011. The fundamental difference lay between the war-like nature of the 1954 infiltrators, who back then directly threatened the security of the nascent State of Israel, and the current African migrants, who posed no security danger whatsoever to the State and who were, by and large, to be treated as cases in need of humanitarian assistance:

> The explicit objective of this proposed legislation is to provide a legal mechanism for dealing with people illegally entering Israel, mainly for work or a better life, whereas the government does not claim that they pose any threat to national security [...] the overwhelming majority of those crossing Israel's southern border do not have any intention whatsoever to harm or infringe upon the security of the State. We know this from the mere fact that they cross the border and wait to be "picked up" by the army, not trying to escape or run in any sort of way. The 1954 Anti-Infiltration Act was legislated against the *Fada'ayun* terrorists whose only goal was to infiltrate in order to kill Israeli civilians and security personnel, and as such the penalties stipulated in that law, and the legal practices stipulated in it, are amongst the harshest of the Israeli penal code [...] We are of opinion that a discussion ought to be held as to the applicability of this legal framework and whether it is the correct one to deal with the phenomenon of border crossing into Israel we are lately witnessing.[5]

As we shall see below, the issue of which legal platform was best suited for the new and much-needed anti-infiltration measures was to perturb the heart of the African migration issue, and would be ultimately examined by the Israeli Supreme Court. An indicative prelude as to the government's more general line of thought vis-à-vis the growing influx of the African migrants could already be detected in its reaction to Chairman Cohen's ponderings regarding the suitable legal framework for the new law, and the possibly contested usage of the harsh 1954 Anti-Infiltration Act as its legal bedrock. The representation of the government's position was entrusted to the director of the legislative department within the Israeli Justice Ministry, Advocate Avital Sternberg.

A long-standing civil servant with a highly respectable record and a sharp legal mind, the Harvard-educated Sternberg came to personify the impossibly contradictory nature of the legal framework she was instructed to defend on her government's behalf. Drawing an initial distinction between refugees and other aliens, in line with the stipulations of Article 6 of the 1951 Refugee Convention, Sternberg vociferously advocated the need to use the contentious and legally problematic 1954 Anti-Infiltration legal platform as a form of deterrence to African voluntary migrant laborers. In her address to the KIC as she replied to the parliamentary legal counselor, Sternberg unequivocally defended the government's position – opting for the usage of the 1954 platform:

> concerning the legal contention voiced by the committee's legal advisor I wish to repeat what I have already reiterated previously. This proposed legislation is not intended for the treatment of refugees, which is why a Refugee Status Determination (RSD) procedure will be conducted for all cross border trespassers, including Sudanese and Eritrean nationals [. . .] the question whether to use the general legal platform of the 1952 Law of Entry into Israel, or the 1954 Anti-Infiltration Act, this point was considered and deliberated upon by the government. At the end of the day the government took a deliberate and conscious choice to use the 1954 Anti-Infiltration Act, so as to deliberately project a message of harshness towards those who are not refugees. Thus we requested to use in this law the overall responsibility of the Minister of Defense . . . we therefore insist upon the point that the legal framing shall be specifically and deliberately carried out under the framework of the Anti-Infiltration Act".[6]

During the first protocol session of the KIC, much of the remaining discussions centered around the most basic questions of applying the newly proposed legislation to Israel's obligations under the 1951 Refugee Convention. In her explanations of the various articles of the new law, Advocate Sternberg clearly pointed to her inclusion of a specific reference to the principle of non-refoulement, embedded in the new draft legislation under its Article 3.[7] A further protection referred to by Advocate Sternberg came in her explicit assertion concerning non-expulsion, as per Article 32 (Non Expulsion) of the 1951 Refugee Convention:

> Before an expulsion order is issued and executed, we will need to verify that no danger awaits the person being expelled from Israel. This is explicitly stated in the explanatory notes to the law: it is underscored here that the proposed new legislation shall be implemented in accordance with the obligations of the state of Israel under international conventions, including the principle of *Non Refoulement* enshrined in the Refugee Convention [. . .] the State of Israel is obligated, both according to her internal legislation, as well as according to her obligations under international treaties, not to return a human being to a place where his life or freedom is in danger due to the reasons mentioned in the convention [i.e. the 1951 Refugee Convention].[8]

Sternberg's explanations and qualifications of the grounds upon which the Israeli state may exercise expulsion orders, as well as her unequivocal upholding of the principle of non-refoulement as enshrined in the UN 1951 Refugee Convention, did not go unnoticed or unanswered by the extreme right-wing MK, Michael Ben Ari. Directing his blunt criticism directly at Sternberg, Ben Ari asserted that "as for Israel's international obligations, Israel also has an obligation to itself and has a right to exist." Ben Ari was clearly referring to what he perceived as an imminent demographic danger should hoards of African migrants overrun the southern Israeli border, allegedly threatening Israel's fragile Jewish demographic majority. All through the protocol discussion, Ben Ari continued to badger Sternberg on issues concerning Israel's obligations under the 1951 Refugee Convention – from the switching of burden of proof for the Refugee Determination Status onto the migrant, to the imposition of financial penalties on migrants so as to ensure their departure.[9]

The KIC was by no means working in laboratory conditions. As the number of African migrants continued to grow rapidly, governmental policy seemed to exhibit a certain paralysis when confronted with the new demographic realities caused by this human influx. Referring to the new, large communities of African migrants concentrated in the poorest areas of south Tel Aviv, Chairman Cohen exposed his concerns regarding the gravity of this new situation. Referring to a visit he had conducted to south Tel Aviv, Cohen reiterated that as chairman of the KIC he was receiving pleas from mayors all over the country expressing the urgency and acuteness of the new reality whereby the numbers of African migrants in poor areas of Israeli towns was growing daily. Cohen skillfully presented a balanced approach, stressing on the one hand the fear and anxiety of Israeli residents confronted by large populations of unemployed homeless Africans while on the other maintaining Israel's humanitarian responsibilities, according to its international treaty obligations in addition to the humanitarian stipulations of Jewish law.[10] Summarizing his opening statement, Cohen explained how he was being torn between his wish to halt the African migration and his humanitarian convictions:

> There is a real and tough problem because on the one hand we want to remedy and take care of the migration problem, and from the other hand these are human beings and we ought to give them whatever assistance we can. There are also international treaties, and as a Jewish state, we have morals which must be applied.[11]

The deliberations over the correct legal framework for the new anti-migrant law masked a deeper schism within the KIC, and mirrored the rift between the governmental and parliamentary legal bureaucratic branches. Using the government-supported 1954 Anti-Infiltration Act meant *ipso facto* adherence to a security-based approach, thus overriding humanitarian values. The proposed alternative advocated by the Knesset legal advisor, opting as he did for a legal framework underpinned by the 1952 Law of Entry into Israel, was diametrically opposed to the government's policy line in that it advocated a "humanitarianism-first" approach. This conundrum was epitomized by the KIC chairman. As we shall see below, Amnon Cohen's Judaism-based humanitarian concerns, which brought him to oppose his government's "security first" approach, were to be reiterated and relied upon by the Israeli Supreme Court in its revocation of the 2012 Anti-Infiltration Act, precisely on these very same religious Jewish-law grounds.

The Knesset Legal Advisor's Objection to the Use of the 1954 Legislation

As pressure from the government grew for the immediate enacting of the new anti-migrant legislation, so did the pressure upon Chairman Cohen and the KIC members. Government and parliament, NGOs and anti migrant campaigners – all began to gear up for the KIC's two final sessions in December, before the newly proposed legislation was sent to the Knesset floor. As the stakes rose, so did the participation of MKs in these last two sittings on December 13 and 19, 2011. Contrary to the previous low attendance rate, on these final two occasions the committee was full, with all its members present alongside the legal advisors of both government and parliament in addition to the NGO community. In a rare occurence, the UNHCR chief of mission to Israel, Ambassador William Toll, also took part in these final proceedings.

With the law now officially being tabled for parliament's consideration as an amendment of the 1954 Anti-Infiltration Act, the Knesset's chief legal counsel decided to launch an appeal of last resort, urging the KIC to reconsider its problematic legal choice. A long-standing civil servant and Sternberg's former colleague at the Justice Ministry, Advocate Eyal Yinon, voiced his deep alarm at this legal course of action during the KIC's third session, on December 13, 2012:

> *Chairman Cohen:* [...] during the meeting on the 10th August, the legal advisors examined the legislative platform of the proposed law [i.e. the problematic usage of the 1954 amendment of the Anti-Infiltration Act] [...] I supported our legal counselors in their proposal [i.e. NOT to use the 1954 platform but rather the 2008 defeated proposal] and I have pleaded with the government to take our course of action. Unfortunately the government has tabled this law to the KIC, and I want to thank the Knesset's chief legal counsel – advocate Eyal Yinon for delving deep into this issue.
>
> *Eyal Yinon:* Thank you Mr Chairman. The legal proposal discussed on today's agenda of the KICs, is exceptionally irregular by any standard with regard to its social, financial and security implications. It is due to this extremity that I have come here today to appear before this committee, and explain the extreme legal difficulties I see in this proposed legislation. There can be no question that the African cross border migration is a deeply disturbing problem, and that we as a country with all our governmental systems must provide an adequate systematic response to it. From all the different legislative solutions, we as legal advisors to the KIC have brought forward, the government

has unfortunately decided to present to you the proposal you are discussing today.

What does this governmental proposal entail?

The bulk of it envisages an interim decree stipulating *the immediate incarceration of migrants under order, for an indefinite period of time*, through an administrative decree, yet without that migrant being either prosecuted, or judged and sentenced by a court of law. This decree is highly extreme and is an anomaly, since today in Israel it is legally impossible to keep a human being incarcerated indefinitely, and to strip him of his liberty without him being convicted by a court of law and sentenced to a jail term, after being found guilty in a due judicial process. The only administrative detention possible in Israel today is limited in time and is due exclusively to national security threats, and even those detentions are subject to stringent judicial supervision and oversight.[12]

The Knesset's legal advisor's words left little room for interpretation. At the heart of the matter stood the most basic of human liberties in any society – the right to freedom and judicial due process before the law. In a very unusual press intervention, and contrary to his habitual non-disclosure, Yinon publically voiced his view that the newly amended 1954 Anti-Infiltration Act was well beyond the limits of constitutionality, due to its indefinite infringement on human liberty.[13] Eighteen months later, Yinon received the ultimate vindication which confirmed his legal concerns. On September 16, 2013, the Israeli Supreme Court revoked the newly adapted 2012 Anti-Infiltration Act, precisely on the legal grounds he had so vociferously highlighted.[14]

Many of the dilemmas and personalities present during the deliberations over the 2012 Anti-Infiltration Act within the KIC continued to play a crucial role in the unfolding of the African migration challenge throughout the period between 2011 and 2013.[15] MK Hanin, from the socialist left, and his extreme-right nemesis, MK Ben Ari, continued their roles on opposite sides of the divide over the new legislation as the main arena of contestation shifted to the public sphere of mass demonstrations and street violence. Reading through the KIC's protocols, one is struck by just how many of its issues and personalities came to play a part in the subsequent public debates and events concerning the African migrant challenge, and how prescient these KIC deliberations really were.

One of the prescient elements present in the early KIC deliberations was the issue of unlimited incarceration as stipulated in the new act, and as advocated by governmental officials and supported by the committee's extreme-right MKs. As their stern opponent, MK Hanin correctly and prophetically envisaged its grave constitutional implications for all incoming African migrants, and the public outcry which was sure to follow. As he tabled his long series of legal objections to the proposed law, Hanin warned the government that, should it continue unabatedly its legislative line:

> I would like to stress that the legal concept proposed by the Knesset's legal advisors, makes much more sense than that of the government [. . .] and here I arrive at the constitutional legal question as just presented by the Knesset Chief legal Counsel [. . .] *we are speaking here about a real possibility of indefinite incarceration. That is why my fellow MKs, this law is simply unconstitutional*. I am saying this here to the governmental representatives: please see my objections as a friendly suggestion to prevent you from legislating a grave fault [. . .] you will produce here a law which will be chastised in Israel and internationally and ultimately will be legally revoked and rendered illegal and invalid by the High Court. So why go down this route? I know the government likes doing things the hard way, but I urge you this time to reconsider your position.[16]

Hanin's prescient objection to the unconstitutionality of the proposed amendment of the 1954 Anti-Infiltration Act also highlighted other trains of thought in the KIC's legal proceedings, which recurred as the African migration challenge continued to evolve. One of these trains of thought concerned Israel's Holocaust heritage, and its application toward the African migrants notwithstanding the multiple challenges they pose to Israeli society. As with Israel's involvement in the making of the 1951 Refuge Convention, adherence to the Holocaust's heritage was present as early as 2006, with Yehuda Bauer's appeal to the supreme court in defense of Sudanese refugees from genocide-stricken Darfur. Following Bauer's predicament, Hanin also drew heavily on the history of the Jewish people and their suffering as a result of being tagged as the primordial "alien" through the ages. Evoking Jewish suffering and its corresponding moral implications, Hanin stated his ethical position. In one of those rare instances where law makers break away from the daily technical wording of drafted articles and paragraphs, Hanin provided an insight into the new ethical challenges tugging at the soul of Israeli society:

> My third reservation is a moral one and I voice it here up front. The problem is difficult and I as a Jew, as a son to a people who so many times had been tagged as a problem, as a menace, as the source of all evils within the peoples we dwelled in, I as Jew have a problem with this pattern of looking for the enemies from within, a pattern that demarcates the foreigners, that stipulates that those different to us in religion, or in their skin color are the source of our problems. Too many times in our history have we been in this situation. I suggest we be cautions even when the situation is undoubtedly hard and the deficiencies deep, we must not fall to this evil.[17]

The perplexing paradoxes between the will to protect Israel from unwanted foreign ethnic migration on the one hand, and the need to maintain humanitarian values and international commitments on the other, were bound to come to a head once the Anti-Infiltration Act received final parliamentary approval. The impossibility of the situation was amply demonstrated when MK Ben Ari, who moved his headquarters into the midst of the south Tel Aviv area, revealed that he at times found himself aiding the African migrants, pointing to a case where he delivered a lost African child to the hands of the Israeli Police so as to be returned to its mother. Arguing against the criminalization of humanitarian help which was still present in the original 1954 Anti-Infiltration Act, MK Hanin pointed out that Ben Ari would have in effect broken the law and faced a jail sentence had he executed the humanitarian act he had just performed with the African child he helped. The KIC's discussion began to border on political irony, when the extreme right-wing MK Ben Ari himself requested a non-criminalization clause so as to protect Israelis aiding migrants on humanitarian grounds from prosecution or criminal intent. Finding himself in the odd political position of humanitarian agreement with his extreme political left-wing rival, MK Hanin sardonically turned to the government capturing the absurdity of the current situation:

> Representatives of the government, as supposedly moderate right wingers: you have come to the fantastic situation in this Knesset where you are to the right of the extreme right MK Ben Ari.[18]

MK Hanin's remarks found an echo as Chairman Cohen took the decision to halt and freeze all discussions concerning the governmentally initiated Anti-Infiltration Act until the government's legal advisors "did their homework."[19] The existence of legal anomalies within the proposed text was the result of a patchwork mixture of clauses from the 1954 Act, coupled with newly amended clauses, which made a consistent reading of the entire legislation virtually impossible.

The temporary suspension of the discussions by Chairman Cohen on December 13, 2011 coincided with his direct criticism of the governmental legal advisors represented by Advocate Sternberg, who demanded – to no avail – the continuation of proceedings that day. To this extent, the coming of the African migrants and the government's attempt to deal with them in the urgent format of the reapplication of the 1954 Anti-Infiltration Act pitted the administrative powers of the Israeli state against each other. Chairman Amnon Cohen, heading the legislative authority, came into direct conflict with the executive power represented by Advocate Sternberg from the Israeli Ministry of Justice.[20]

Both representatives were officials highly respected for their professionalism and intellectual integrity. Both exhibited an honest, unquestioned desire to balance the demographic cross-border threat with humanitarian values that they believed ought to underpin Israeli legislation and policies. Furthermore, with Cohen belonging to the SHAS political party which formed part of the Netnayahu governmental coalition, and Sternberg being a senior governmental official, both felt at times constrained vis-à-vis harsher elements *within* their own administration. Their clear halfheartedness regarding the harsh governmental measure proposed in the new anti-infiltration act evoked a reluctant acceptance of a governmental policy line that both Cohen and Sternberg were bound to execute, despite their own criticisms thereof.

Ultimately, both found ways to assuage their concerns. For Sternberg, the solution lay in the nebulous distinction between refugees, asylum seekers, and other aliens – all of whom were supposed to undergo an RSD process performed by the State. For Cohen, the solution was simply to accept and execute his own party and governmental line, albeit that on numerous occasions he vocally stressed his discontent and open disagreement with the line he was legislating. Ultimately, the NGOs were the ones who exposed the conundrum, challenging both Cohen's and Sternberg's halfhearted legislation at the supreme court, exposing the impossible inconsistencies of the new law. By the time the new anti-migrant legislation came into force in February 2012, Israel had already experienced over six years of government inaction concerning the absorption and accommodation of the newly arriving Africans. As evidence of the strain upon municipal authorities rose – as they were left alone to deal with this national new wave of migration – so social tensions boiled over.

Violence Erupts in South Tel Aviv

No municipality bore this brunt more harshly than that of Tel Aviv. As the Israeli economic powerhouse, and its main employment hub, over half of the newly arrived migrants began concentrating themselves in the most poverty-stricken neighborhoods of south Tel Aviv. Habitually home to non-Jewish migrant communities since the early 1990s, the neighborhoods of Hatikva, Neve Shaanan, and Shapira had become a hotbed for tension between their already underprivileged Jewish inhabitants and the non-Jewish, ethnically different newcomers. This explosive sociological cocktail, of governmentally neglected neighborhoods and their inhabitants, coupled with a steep rise of a foreign poverty-stricken newly arrived population, was bound to cause social frictions and tensions.

On the night of Israeli Independence Day, in early April 2012, a 15-year-old Jewish Israeli girl was violently attacked, and her male companion was beaten while witnessing his girlfriend being gang-raped in front of his eyes.[21] Following a police debriefing and DNA tests, which confirmed the rape victim's complaint, the Israeli Police immediately applied and executed a court order restraining any press coverage of the event so as not to hamper the investigation. Being fully aware of the potentially violent social unrest that could be unleashed, the Israeli Police assembled a team of over 30 investigators who clamped down on virtually all migrant neighborhoods and localities, in an attempt to find the suspects before word got out – igniting the imminently lurking social unrest. As the police arrested three African migrants charged with the Independence Day rape case, two additional rape incidents had come to the public's attention, setting in motion the local mobilization for strong anti-migrant protests.[22] Meanwhile, sporadic violent action began erupting, carried out primarily by criminal Israeli elements stepping in and taking action against random migrant targets.[23]

On April 27, several Molotov cocktails were thrown through the windows of ground-floor apartments inhabited by African migrants in the Shapira and Hatikva neighborhoods. The next day, another Molotov cocktail was thrown into a kindergarten administered by the African migrant community.[24] From late March 2012, local groups of Israeli vigilante militia-like gangs began patrolling the streets of Hatikva and Shapira, attacking and severely beating people of African origin.[25] As the dry season of the Israeli summer months approached, public opinion was being mobilized for a hot, violent onslaught against the newly arrived African migrants, orchestrated by the underprivileged inhabitants of the southern Tel Aviv neighborhoods, amongst whom the bulk of the new immigrants were now dwelling. On May 6, the Israeli pro-migrant NGO Mesila received its first death threats, compelling the Tel Aviv municipality to install a 24-hour security presence near the Mesila clinic in the South Tel Aviv area.[26]

May 2012 saw this string of rape cases, carried out by African migrants against Israeli women, become public knowledge. The swift and determined actions of the Israeli Police bore fruit, and the rape suspects were arrested during the first week of May and immediately indicted by the Israeli prosecution, with positive DNA-tested results backing the charges. As the charges were tabled to the district court of Tel Aviv, the judicial legal ground underpinning the media ban over these crimes was lifted, given the end of the police investigation and the bringing of the suspects into custody. On May 16, the Israeli interior minister, Eli Yishai, reacted to the recent involvement of African migrants in criminal offences. Speaking on national public radio, Yishai called for the immediate incarceration and later deportation of all African migrants and their families.[27] In reaction to Minister Yishai's words, Mesila – the center for aid of the foreign community in Tel Aviv – released a press statement accusing Yishai of xenophobic racism:

> It is saddening that a minister in the government of Israel chooses to instrumentalize the current situation in order to release his weekly racist statement. The crimes of individuals are no reason for the incarceration of an entire community. The application of a collective punishment on the basis of religion or skin color, implies a habitus belonging to dark historical periods.[28]

The harsh exchange of words between Interior Minister Yishai and this pro-migrant NGO, which took place on national public radio in mid-May 2013 and which echoed throughout the Israeli printed media, incorporated many of the components of the broader public debate concerning the challenges African migration posed for Israeli society. The protagonists in this drama had come to crystallize and distill their positions, or so it seemed. In one corner of this "societal boxing ring" stood reactionary religious and xenophobic forces, embodied by the ultra-orthodox Eli Yishai. In the opposing corner stood the defenders of human rights, the so-called Enlightenment-values-driven pro-migrant NGOs. The boxing ring itself was the Israeli media and press, across whose newspaper pages and radio airwaves the contest was being played out. On the sidelines of this contest stood the rest of Israeli society, at this stage more a spectator than an active actor in the debate.

With the benefit of hindsight, one is left with the impression that at the heart of the KIC deliberations regarding the transformation of the 1954 anti-migrant legislation into its new reincarnation as the 2012 Anti-Infiltration Act stood *both* exeptionalist and universalist tendencies. The end result, whereby the exceptionalist strata gained ascendancy over the universalist one was by no means deterministically self-evident – or at least not to the people involved in this legislation's creation.

One key factor which tilted the legislative pendulum towards the exceptionalist pole was the increasing involvement of Israeli governmental state structures, primarily the Attorney General's office and the Justice Ministry bureaucrats. These actively promoted and advocated for the very problematic legislative course of re-amendment of the 1954 Act over the initiation of new legislation or, better still, the revival of the defeated 2008 Anti-Infiltration Act. There is hardly any question as to the clear motivations underpinning the actions of these ministerial bureaucrats. These were primarily instigated by a Weberian outlook, regarding what they saw as a real and viable possibility by the State to legislate a harsh – and, indeed, inhumane – legal tool, which would then be applied strictly within the positivist boundaries of the law. Yet by the time these very same bureaucrats were called upon to defend their own government's policies, which stemmed from the punitive legislation they had helped create, the Golem had already struck its creator. Once the State had obtained a harshly coercive legal tool in the shape of the 2012 Anti-Infiltration Act, the chances that it would *not* pursue this tool to its ultimate conclusion were slim indeed. The motivations of Chairman Cohen, who was bound to the humanitarian precepts of Jewish Law, were clearly not sufficient to deter the State from moving towards the mass incarceration of African migrants. Once the State had legal justification to act harshly – it did so unabatedly.

CHAPTER 6

THE ISRAELI EXTREME RIGHT'S ANTI-MIGRANT ONSLAUGHT

This chapter traces the evolution of the African migrant challenge, from the outbreak of violence in late May 2012 until the national elections of January 2013. This eight-month period began with the public onslaught and violent racial riots which targeted African migrants, involving unprecedented lethal attacks against them – predominantly in Tel Aviv and Jerusalem. It dovetailed with a steep rise in inflammatory political rhetoric voiced by both right-wing and extreme right-wing MKs, rhetoric which in turn exacerbated the street violence against the migrants, especially in the south Tel Aviv neighborhoods of Hatikva and Shapira. By late June 2012, this inflammatory rhetoric and the violent attacks on migrants began to alarm moderate government ministers, who began the process of calming both the rhetoric of the MKs and the Israeli public. As campaigning for the upcoming 2013 elections began in October 2012, the politicians involved in the inflammatory discourse began channeling their energies towards re-election, utilizing their demonstrated onslaught on the African migrants as electoral currency so as to score what they falsely presumed were points in their favor. As the electoral results unfolded, it became clear that the Israeli public had decided to punish these MKs by ousting them from parliament or positions of power, thus significantly reducing the support for the ones remaining in the Knesset.

The main question perplexing the researcher here is one of *political motivation*. What was the motivation behind the onslaught of the different parliamentarians on the African migrants?

Governmental Rhetoric and the Framing of Native–Migrant Social Tensions

As the rape crimes became public knowledge due to the apprehension of suspects and the compulsory lifting of the judicial media ban, the mass mobilization of anti-migrant inhabitants of the south Tel Aviv neighborhoods began. In a joint meeting on May 6, 2012, the action committee for south Tel Aviv neighborhood representatives took a strategic decision to organize a day of nationwide anti-migrant demonstrations on May 23. This action committee was chaired by Shlomo Maslawi, the Likud representative on the Tel Aviv municipality city council.[1] As the local representative of the national Knesset ruling party, Maslawi coordinated his efforts with his senior representatives at the national legislator, MKs Miri Regev and Dani Danon – the very same representatives who had taken part in the deliberations of the KIC, and who held even more extreme views than those of the far-right MKs. Ten days before the orchestrated anti-migrant demonstrations, journalistic attention was being channeled towards the issue of African migrants. As the violent rape crimes were exposed in the press, a deliberate media buildup was heavily underway, overriding other pressing issues such as Iranian nuclear capabilities, peace with the Palestinians, or the steep rise in the cost of living which had led to mass public riots just a few months earlier.

As the working week began on Sunday May 20, three days prior to the mass anti-migrant demonstrations, Prime Minister Netanyahu decided to relay his views regarding the African migrant problem to the Israeli public. As he opened the weekly government session, Netanyahu set out to frame the issue of the migrants in demographic–ethnic terms, as he stressed that Jewish demographic supremacy was being threatened:

> The phenomenon of illegal African infiltrators is very severe, and threatens Israeli society, its security and its national identity. The problem began 7 years ago, and with the establishment of the current administration three years ago, we decided to treat this problem immediately and with regard to all its facets [. . .] if we will not stop this problem, sixty thousand infiltrators may become six hundred thousand, thus bringing the annihilation of the State of Israel as a Jewish and democratic state.[2]

The fact that the Prime Minister chose to televise his opening statement from the weekly cabinet session merely confirmed the point that the media had become the current playing field upon which the societal contest between divergent Israeli social views regarding the African migrant challenge was being played out. Yet Netanyahu added another, far more ideologically explosive, component to the debate, urging and awakening the deepest of all Jewish-Israeli existential phobias: the threat of ceding demographic Jewish supremacy.

A detailed extrapolation of the primordial Israeli fear of being demographically overridden is far beyond the scope of this research. Suffice it to say for our purposes here that ethnic homogeneity, and the retention of Judaism through abstention from interreligious mixed marriages, has been a consistent Jewish historical challenge. The growth of the Jewish population in Palestine, and subsequently in the State of Israel ever since the rise of Zionism in late nineteenth century, was always perceived to be endangered by the mere existence of the Palestinian people in the same land. The eternal Israeli anguish over the prospected loss of the Jewish majority in Israel – through the necessity of including the occupied Palestinian people into Israel, and due to historically higher Arab birth rates – was now being fed with a new set of "sociological raw materials." As Netanyahu toyed with the idea of a possible demographic flooding of Israel by "one million Africans waiting on the other side of the Egyptian border," the prime minister irresponsibly unleashed the most visceral of Israeli existential fears, and pointed them in the direction of the African migrants.

Surprisingly though, at the very same time that Netanyahu was releasing the demographic genie out of the bottle, the most senior ranks of the Israeli security establishment began voicing inversely opposite opinions, calling for calm and for the adoption of tension-reduction policies. Following a late-night patrol with his senior officers in south Tel Aviv, the chief Israeli police commissioner, Yochanan Danino, broke ranks with his elected superiors by demanding that the African migrants be granted working permits immediately:

> We have here tens of thousands of existing migrants. Once you do not generate working places for these people, this will drive them immediately over the line towards crime. The migrants who are

> already here, as long as they are here, we need to verify that we do not block their employment in sectors they can really be employed in.[3]

Chief Danino's words were echoed by his deputy and police commander of the Tel Aviv area, Aharon Eksol, as he appeared in front of a special session of the Knesset parliamentary committee for foreign workers. Eksol was subpoenaed by the committee to provide explanations regarding the rise in crime and rape cases committed by African migrants, following the lifting of the judicial media ban and public exposure of these crimes. Replying coolheadedly to inflammatory statements by Likud MK Dani Danon, Eksol reiterated the official position of the Israeli Police forces condoning the employment of African migrants. Speaking a mere day before all hell broke loose in the anti-migrant demonstrations, Eksol's words seemed almost prophetic:

> We have identified a stark rise in crime rates of migrants over the past few months. We see a rise of a few dozen percentages in crimes of violence and rape. I suppose this is no surprise to anybody here. The sharp rise of tension between the Israeli local inhabitants and the migrants in the South Tel Aviv area is dangerous and complicated. This phenomenon is just in its beginning. If we do not act immediately, the situation might further deteriorate. We the police do not come with a political agenda, but only with the agenda of crime reduction. We fundamentally believe that these migrants are performing what we in professional terms call "survival crime," we are unequivocally stating that the employment of migrants in one way or another will indeed alleviate the tension itself.[4]

"Migrants – The Cancer in the Body of our Nation"

On the afternoon of Wednesday May 23, 2012, a day after the police chiefs had warned about upcoming public violence against the African migrants, the anticipated violence erupted. A pre-orchestrated nationwide series of anti-migrant demonstrations in the cities of Eilat, Ashdod, Bnei Brak, Jerusalem, and Tel Aviv resulted in violent overtures against the migrants and inflammatory rhetoric hitherto unheard of. At the epicenter of the demonstrations stood the south Tel Aviv neighborhood of Hatikva. As the demonstrations gathered force, anti-migrant members of parliament began taking their turns in rhetorically inflaming the protesters, reciprocally exacerbating one anothers' statements, to the ever-growing cheers of the exited crowds. Likud MKs Dani Danon and Yariv Lewin demanded the swift and immediate deportation of all African migrants back to their countries of origin. Danon claimed that immediate incarceration and subsequent deportation were the only viable solutions to the inter-societal tensions which had surfaced in the south Tel Aviv area where the main demonstration was being held.

By far the most inflammatory statements heard at the May 23 demonstrations belonged to the newly elected Likud MK, Miri Regev. A former spokesperson for the IDF, Regev's statements were to prove a major turning point in Israeli attitudes towards African migrants. Speaking from a raised podium, Regev embarked on a xenophobic rant. Referring specifically to South Sudanese migrants whose legal clearance for deportation had been recently provided for by the Israeli Attorney General and Foreign Ministry, Regev remarked:

> The Sudanese infiltrators are a cancer in our body and in our state. We will do everything in our powers to return these people to their places of origin, and we will not permit these people to seek employment in Israel. We shall first provide for the poor in our country. All the "left wing activists" who have been appealing to the Supreme Court should be ashamed of themselves – they alone are preventing the deportation.[5]

As the MKs concluded their inflammatory speeches, the angry crowd embarked on its violent onslaught against migrant dwellings, stores, and passersby. Several dozen shops belonging to migrants were broken into and looted, while other stores were set on fire. As the arson continued, the crowd began stopping public-transport vehicles and searching them for people of African origin to be beaten and lynched. As violence levels climbed further, the Israeli Police began intervening with overwhelming force, arresting 17 suspects charged with throwing rocks, metal bars, and two fire grenades at the police themselves.[6]

As the Israeli riot police continued its containment of the anti-migrant violence, its special investigative branch apprehended 11 suspects charged with running a clandestine gang that beat, harassed, and extorted migrants for ransom money. The judicial arrest warrants against these 11 suspects were issued by the Lower Court of Tel Aviv on the exact same day of the planned anti-migrant demonstrations, as the prosecution had amassed sufficient evidence for the judicial authorities to warrant the arrests. Yet in a very unorthodox manner, the lower court also issued a temporary media-ban gagging order based on the fact that it had authorized the prosecution's request for the arrests that very same day.

Judicial media bans and gag orders are not uncommon in the Israeli legal system; however, they are treated with great care both by the prosecution that demands them and by the courts, should they decide to ultimately issue them. With the Israeli press "deliciously free," in the words of Leon Wieseltier, most Israeli news outlets are able to override any media ban by quoting foreign international news sources over a certain story. Since the courts are well aware of this, and primarily due to the overwhelming importance ascribed to a free press in Israel, a tacit agreement exists between the press corps and the courts. In short, media bans are acceptable to the press in extreme cases – but even in those instances, only for a limited period of time. Serious breaches of national security, which could directly harm Israelis, are deemed an acceptable cause by the press, albeit always checked and balanced to verify no abuse by the State of the media ban. Strict media bans are upheld for long periods by the press when family matters and the well-being of children are involved (in cases of child abuse, forced removal of children from families, etc.), yet these are always coordinated by the family courts.

The last remaining ground upon which this tacit agreement exists between the press corps and the courts concerns cases where the court is convinced that the release of certain information to the public could ignite immediate violence, resulting in bodily harm. Classic examples of such cases include the arrest of Muslim clerics on charges of incitement. Since both the courts and the press are well aware that an arrest of clerical authorities from the Muslim ethnic minority could immediately ignite demonstrations with the potential to rapidly descend into bloodshed, arrest orders for police questioning in such cases (limited to a few hours) will be media-banned. Thus, the suspects' arrests only become public knowledge once they have already been released from police questioning, and do not trigger immediate civil unrest.

It was this ground of civil unrest – not by any ethnic minority group but rather due to the probable severe public reaction to the arrests in the south Tel Aviv area, concurrent with the mass anti-migrant demonstrations – which prompted the courts to issue a media-ban gag order over these arrests. The courts' concern for the eruption of violence against vulnerable African migrants, instigated by Jewish-Israeli inhabitants of south Tel Aviv, was shared by the chiefs of police, who pleaded for the ban so as not to stretch police capacities even further. The fact that the press corps accepted this reasoning by the police and courts meant that they too "bought into" the explosive potential of these arrests, and a possible descent into violent anti-migrant attacks.[7] The mass anti-migrant demonstrations of May 23, 2012 marked the second of three peaks of physical violence unleashed against African migrants in Israel, the first having been the torching of the migrant kindergarten in the Shapira neighborhood one month earlier.[8] On June 4, physical violence against the migrants took another turn, as a migrant apartment in Jerusalem was torched with a Molotov cocktail, seriously injuring four Africans.[9]

The outbreak of anti-migrant attacks in the heart of Jerusalem confirmed some of the worst fears of the Israeli Police, Justice Ministry and Attorney General officials. Should the police not manage to curb this wave of attacks immediately, then, before long, the Israeli security establishment was going to be faced with cross-country attacks on migrants. The absurdity of the situation crystallized as it gradually became clear that Israeli politicians were the main source of the inflammatory rhetoric which risked further exacerbating the anti-migrant violence. The day after the Jerusalem attack, the minister of internal security overseeing the Israeli Police, Yizhak Aharonovich (himself a former police commissioner), did not mince his words. In his annual speech for fallen Israeli policemen, Aharonovich openly accused members of the Knesset of inciting and exacerbating the anti-migrant violence so as to cover up their inaptitude and their "do-nothing and get paid" ethos, as they deliberately manipulated an explosive situation for their own electoral benefit:

> The Israeli Police force has many challenges ahead of it. These include the coming of migrant infiltrators through our borders and the growing crime rate of these migrants, but to no lesser a

> degree of severity – to deal with the implications of the rhetoric of elected officials. These officials cannot restrain their words, and are trying to camouflage their inaction and inaptitude over many years by inciting this popular wave of violence. Their words can bring us all unneeded violence, as we have witnessed yesterday in Jerusalem.[10]

The physical onslaught against the migrants had now begun to spread fear and anxiety within the migrant communities. Migrant schoolchildren began reporting violent attacks on them on their way to and from school, ranging from racial slurs to physical abuse by Israelis.[11] The clear distinction of the victims due to their dark skin color, an aspect of what is known in migrant-anthropological literature as "migrant visibility," came to play a crucial role in the heightened potential for targeting this specific group in contrast to other migrants in the south Tel Aviv area (most notably Filipinos and former Soviet-bloc inhabitants).[12]

Eli Yishai and the Application of Anti-Migrant Policies by the Interior Ministry

On June 3, 2012, the government decided to begin the implementation of its new 2012 Anti-Infiltration Act by rounding up and deporting South Sudanese migrants.[13] As if by accident, the unexpected court ruling authorizing this deportation seemed to coincide with anti-migrant demonstrations.[14] Simultaneously, the onslaught of violent arson attacks against migrant dwellings, and rising levels of incitement by senior governmental officials, continued.[15]

The court ruling permitting the deportation of South Sudanese migrants traced a legal opinion condoning the action, tabled by Attorney General Yehuda Weinstein to the Prime Minister on the very same night of the violent anti-migrant demonstrations of May 23.[16] Based upon an assessment by the Foreign Ministry regarding the conditions in South Sudan after its new accession to UN membership, the government began distinguishing between South Sudanese migrants and those from Eritrea and Darfur – the latter two groups still receiving collective protection status. A closer examination of the events of May–June 2012 confirms what was already well known to the Israeli pro-migrant NGO actors on the ground: the "top down" government campaign against African migration as a whole was in full swing.

No Israeli official was as closely identified with, or as committed to, the anti-African-migrant onslaught as the Interior Minister. While Yishai was always clear and specific regarding his anti-African views and attitudes, he conspicuously *did not* maintain these same views vis-à-vis other non-Jewish migrant groups. Yishai was the leader of the third-largest political party in the Israeli Parliament – the ultra-orthodox Sephardic party, SHAS. Originally moderately positioned in the center of the Israeli political spectrum, SHAS emerged in the 1990s as the kingmaker in Israeli politics, joining governments from both left and right with the explicit aim of promoting a religious Jewish socially driven agenda.[17]

Under its brilliantly charismatic leader, Arye Deri, the party grew in power, controlling at its zenith over 15 percent of the Israeli legislature (in the 1999 elections), from an initial 3 percent in the 1988 elections. This ascendancy was first and foremost a result of the political moderation exemplified by the SHAS leadership under Deri. In contrast with other religious Knesset parties, who were on the extreme right in terms of their views on the Palestinian–Israeli conflict and their attitudes toward the Arab minority within Israel, SHAS was a supporter of the Oslo peace process. Moreover, SHAS under Deri came to personify just and equal treatment of the underprivileged Arab minority in Israel, which was habitually discriminated against in terms of budgetary allocations by the interior ministry and affirmative-action infrastructure projects.[18]

Deri's resignation from the SHAS leadership marked a radical right-wing turn under its new leader, Eli Yishai. Economically, the party became more and more attuned to capitalist interests at the expense of its socially driven agenda, while promoting a vehemently hawkish line in security and foreign-policy matters.[19]

SHAS was by no means a coherent party adhering to one worldview, not least with regard to the issue of African migrants. While MK Nisim Zeev and the party leader, Eli Yishai, shared strong anti-migrant views, SHAS' senior MK and KIC chairman, Amnon Cohen, was diametrically opposed to these views, stressing what he saw as the need to provide humanitarian assistance while blocking further waves of cross-border trespassers from entering the country. As Israeli politics shifted toward the right, the party line represented by the hawkish Yishai prevailed over the more moderate elements within SHAS, such as KIC Chairman Cohen and Deri's protégés, Ariel Atias and Itzik Sudry. Yishai's unprecedented attacks and incitement against African migrants ought to be seen within this context as the precursor to SHAS' general veering towards the right within the Israeli political spectrum.

Yishai's anti-migrant incitement traced back to the beginning of his tenure at the Interior Ministry in early 2009, and was probably also influenced by right-wing militaristic research literature which was circulating in government circles at the time.[20] Referring to reports from the Health Ministry concerning the particular need to vaccinate African children against meningitis and measles due to the lack of sufficient immunization facilities in Sudan and Eritrea, Yishai remarked:

> if hundreds of thousands of foreign workers come rushing here, they will bring with them a multitude of diseases: hepatitis, measles, tuberculosis, AIDS, and the usage of narcotics and drugs. With all due respect – is this not threatening the Zionist enterprise and the State of Israel?[21]

Three years after this statement, both the political landscape and the number of African migrants had radically changed. While Yishai received ample criticism for his words back in 2009, after the sporadic criminal actions performed by migrants and the mass anti-migrant demonstrations of May 23, it seemed as though public opinion had softened towards Yishai's racist views. A week before the demonstration, with reference to the few sporadic criminal offences carried out by African migrants against Israelis, Yishai advocated the mass incarceration and immediate deportation of all African migrants from Israel back to their countries of origin.[22] On May 20, three days before the mass demonstrations, Israeli NGO activists filed a police complaint against the Interior Minister, accusing Yishai of needlessly jeopardizing their safety and well-being due to his public claim on Israeli radio that the NGO activists were "pacifists who are immediately threatening the Zionist enterprise."[23] Yishai did not reserve his criticism only for soft-spoken pacifists but bluntly attacked the state security establishment, referring to Police Chief Danino as a "softy." Replying to the Israeli

Police Commissioner's recommendation to allow some sort of employment for the African migrants, so as to avoid what the security establishment came to term as "survival crime," Yishai commented:

> I am tired of the pacifist niceties of some people and politicians too. Employment places will root them here, they will breed children and the Police chief's idea of allowing them employment will only bring further hundreds of thousands of them to come here. We must lock all of them up and deport them all with a monetary departure bonus payment. The minute we lock them all up, they will not be coming here anymore.[24]

Granting an exclusive interview to the weekend supplement of the Israeli daily newspaper *Maariv*, Yishai carried his incitement one step further as he began to target not only the African migrants but also the Israeli NGO employees who were providing voluntary support to the African migrant community. As Shalom Yerushalmi reported:

> The minister of Interior is at ease nowadays. The man who first came out vehemently against the African migration back in 2009, and paid a dear public price for his hard-line views, received wide-ranging support in the recent demonstrations. In South Tel Aviv last week, Yishai was by far the most popular politician.[25]

Following the anti-migrant demonstrations of May 23, as the government began implementing the deportation of South Sudanese migrants, SHAS leader's views concerning the risks posed to Israeli society seemed to be vindicated. His next step was to move the government further in the direction of mass incarceration of the migrants, based upon the newly enacted 2012 Anti-Infiltration Act. Yishai began escalating his inflammatory rhetoric, gearing the public toward what it had hitherto refused to condone in 2009 and 2010: across-the-board jailing of all African migrants. To this end, he reverted to some of his old rhetorical flourishes such as the disease-bearing nature of the migrants and the demographic threats to Israeli society, along with his continuously reiterated vocal call for their mass incarceration. In the weekend interview in *Maariv* following the May 23 demonstrations, Yishai displayed a mixture of new and old arguments, all supporting his overt policy of mass jailing. His line of incitement reached its peak in severity and hatefulness as the government prepared for the implementation of mass jailing stipulated in the newly legislated 2012 Anti-Infiltration Act:

> South Tel Aviv has become Israel's sewage cesspit. To all those pacifists who are speaking against me, I recommend they house some of these migrants in their own affluent neighborhoods, and let's see how they enjoy their children playing with these African kids. Yesterday I received a call from a woman who was chased down the street by two migrants in Jerusalem who wanted to rape her. Do you know that a lot of women in Tel Aviv have been raped and are afraid to report it from the fear of being stigmatized as sick with AIDS? [...] the first thing we need to do is mass jailing. Any migrant crossing the border needs to be incarcerated immediately, without any exception. From this Sunday onwards things will change and these orders will begin to be implemented. All border crossers will be jailed for a minimum of three years. You can quote me on this, and let the migrants read this in the paper loud and clear, from Sunday onwards everybody goes to jail, no one will arrive in Tel Aviv. We have diplomatic relations with Eritrea, and we can deport 90 percent of their migrants back to their home country immediately. Currently our international commitments and treaties do not allow us to deport and incarcerate, yet it is not important what the world will say, it is important what we will do. Our country is dearer to us than any UN condemnation.[26]

Lo and behold, on June 3, 2012 the Israeli Government officially announced, to the dismay and indignation of NGO activists and human-rights groups, a new policy of mass incarceration for all new trespassers across the southern Israeli–Egyptian frontier.[27] While the respected Israeli daily newspaper *Haaretz* referred to this new administrative detention measure as "dark and inhumanly cruel," and as the pro-migrant NGOs pleaded that it contravened Israel's obligations under the 1951 Refugee Convention, Yishai was already working towards his next policy goal. With the newcomers now sent immediately to jail, the next step was to begin mass incarceration of the roughly 70,000 existing African migrants already residing in Israel.

Seasoned Israeli political observers have pointed out that once the left-wing human rights-conscientious columnists of *Haaretz* newspaper jointly deplore a certain Israeli governmental phenomenon, it is usually the ultimate vindication that yet another piece of Israel's shrinking free political space has been lost to the growing anti-humanist non-democratic right-wing electoral majority. The outpouring of articles by renowned humanist voices such as Gideon Levy and Yossi Sarid, not to mention the editorial column of *Haaretz* newspaper itself, were the ultimate proof of Yishai's and the anti-migrant lobby's victory over the pro-migrant NGO community.[28] Summarizing a week of violence against the migrants, as the government began jailing new arrivals, Gideon Levy wrote;

> Israel is the most racist and most innocent Western Country. Racist because in no other country could politicians refer in such words to migrants and continue their tenure. Innocent because it is only now that she acknowledges that for years she is a highly developed country of the first world. Only in Israel can a parliament member from the ruling party call migrants "cancer", and far worse, only in Israel does she utter these words knowing full well that her deplorable racism will only win her electoral support.[29]

Levy correctly pointed to the public backing enjoyed by migrant-bashing parliamentarians, yet this support was to be short-lived – overridden by other concerns perturbing the Israeli public in that hot summer of 2012. Mass anti-capitalist demonstrations began to alert the ruling Likud party to the prospect that the Israeli electorate could significantly alter the composition of its parliament during the upcoming elections of 2013.[30] As electoral priorities shifted toward the economic woes of the Israeli middle class, the anti-migrant lobby began dovetailing its racist demographic arguments with false economic claims concerning jobs and welfare benefits, which were allegedly being hijacked by the African migrant community. At the end of August 2012, Interior Minister Yishai made the national headlines again, as he declared the official start of the mass incarceration of all African migrants in Israel, to begin by mid-October that year.[31]

Electoral Apathy and the Descent of the Migrant Issue into Public Non-Relevance

By mid-October 2012, as the Israeli electoral campaign was already in full swing, the political parties began flexing their communication muscles so as to make headlines and grab the public's attention through the country's vibrant media. Capitalizing on the coverage he had received following the anti-migrant demonstrations of late May, Eli Yishai sharpened his messages further. In early October, his media advisors began issuing official statements, pinning October 15 as the due date for the beginning of the mass incarceration of all African migrants.[32] Following his statements, the coalition of pro-migrant NGOs and the UNHCR's Envoy to Israel appealed to the supreme court against the minister's newly declared initiative. In its statement to the court, UNHCR added that Israel would be bitterly contravening its own legal obligations, as a signatory of the 1951 UN Refugee Convention, should it apply such steps against Sudanese and Eritrean asylum seekers who had received UN collective-protection status.[33]

To the astonishment of the plaintiffs, the Attorney General's mandatory reply to the supreme court directly contradicted the Interior Minister's statements. In fact, no governmental decision whatsoever had been taken to incarcerate all migrants:

> the interior minister has not instructed the director of population affairs, nor anybody else in the department of population affairs for that matter, to begin incarcerating Sudanese nationals currently in Israel forcefully and coercively, as of the 15th October. The department of population affairs assures the High Court that it shall take no such measures without an ample, explicit and specific order from the government.[34]

Given this extreme situation, whereby a state bureaucrat contradicted his own ministerial superior in the government's response to the supreme court, Israeli media outlets issued multiple requests for comments from the Interior Minister's chambers. In the late afternoon of October 25, Yishai's media advisors issued a laconic statement stressing that:

> The Minister is disappointed by the response of the Attorney General to the High Court, after a ministerial team had already concluded a decision on the issue. The Minister's position is well known, that all illegal migrants must return to their countries of origin, so as to retain the Jewish character of the Israeli State.[35]

The day after the statements from the Interior Minister's chambers were released, the full extent of the media "hit" that Yishai had suffered became evident. The next morning, the radio talk shows came to question Yishai's motives for his repeated onslaught against the African migrants. The hosts of these shows began grilling him, as they uncovered the fact that his arch-rival and electoral nemesis in SHAS, Arye Deri, had returned to politics and had been chosen to lead the party in the upcoming elections alongside him. Was Yishai increasing his pressure on the defenseless African migrants so as to project a more hard-line public appearance in order to better his appeal in the eyes of his constituents?

November 2012 proved to be yet another point of escalation on the Interior Minister's agenda – albeit this time involving lashing out against Israel's primordial rivals, the Palestinians. Following months of rocket and mortar attacks launched from Gaza into Israeli sovereign territory, the Israeli government launched a massive 10-day air and artillery offensive codenamed "Operation Pillar of Defense," targeting the Palestinian-Islamist controlled area of the Gaza Strip.[36] Between November 14 and 21, 2012, some several hundreds of artillery shells were fired reciprocally between the IDF and Palestinian militant forces in Gaza, killing over 100 and wounding more than 1,000 Palestinians and Israelis.[37]

While the Israeli public reacted moderately to the violence on the Gaza front, Eli Yishai threw a tantrum, demanding a heavy-handed response against the Palestinians through a substantial ground assault in the heavily populated Gaza Strip. On public radio and TV talk shows, and in the internet blogosphere, Yishai demanded the mass pounding of Gaza, with a deliberate retaliation against civilians and non-military targets so as to project a punitive message against the public support underpinning the Palestinian militant attacks. This alarming message was being carried forward in the media by Yishai, whose responsibilities included those of deputy prime minister in addition to his Interior

Ministry role. He would be first in line to take charge of the government in the event of the Prime Minister being incapacitated or unable to fulfill his duties. This was no "pie in the sky" scenario but rather a recent Israeli reality, given Sharon's cerebral stroke, and Olmert's ascendance to power in 2006 following the former's health-related incapacitation. Ringing public alarm bells on this issue, *Haaretz'* editorial of November 20 warned the Israeli public against its elected deputy prime minister:

> While the public discourse on operation "Pillar of Defense" is evolving more moderately than in previous similar military operations, pointing to a maturity and moderation of Israeli society, the Deputy Prime Minister and Interior Minister stands out in his shame. Over the last few days, the Minister did not miss any chance to infuriate and exacerbate the public [...] Yishai is speaking out this way for the sole purpose of catering to his voters. He has always done so. Deceiving and manipulating, instilling fear and hatred, against African migrants, homosexuals and other social minorities. Israeli society ought to have ousted Yishai long ago. The Prime Minister is responsible too: he should have kept his Deputy Prime Minister at bay. Yishai is the voice of the government and the State of Israel. Since 1948 Gaza is a disaster stricken zone. Poverty, refugeeness and misery depict the lives of its inhabitants, in addition to previous Israeli occupation, a maritime quarantine and rupture from the West Bank. Hitting the civilians and their infrastructure is not only inhuman – it is a war crime [...] he who suggests "bombarding Gaza back to the Middle Ages" is a disgusting politician, and an evil councilor.[38]

The importance of the above-quoted editorial lay not only in its quality of "speaking truth to power," a character trait that has been synonymous with *Haaretz* for almost a century since its founding in 1915. The editorial of November 20 stressed for the first time in crystal-clear terms the fact that incitement had become a generic consistent trait of the Israeli Interior Minister, drawing the precise sequential line between the different groups against whom Yishai had incited (Arabs, homosexuals, and African migrants). It was the key media outlet which associated Yishai's incitement with his underlying electoral strategy of harassing the vulnerable social elements within Israeli society, and thus catering to right-wing voters with the hope of securing their electoral support so as to enlarge his voter base.

By December 2012, it had already become clear that the African migrants were no longer a pivotal issue in the upcoming general elections. The electorate was now primarily focused on Israel's considerable economic disparities (the widest of any country in the OECD – the Organisation for Economic Co-operation and Development) and ever-growing living costs. These economic concerns dovetailed with the habitual Israeli security concerns: about Hamas in Gaza, the Iranian nuclear threat, and the never-ending stalemate of the Palestinian occupation in the West Bank. Several thousand African fugitives residing in south Tel Aviv, whom most Israelis actually never came across, were simply a "non-issue."[39]

In mid-December, Yishai made a "last ditch attempt" to electorally capitalize on the African migrant agenda. Ten days earlier, an elderly single woman in south Tel Aviv had been violently raped by a young Eritrean migrant with a previous criminal record of petty crime and theft. Following the woman's immediate hospitalization, the Tel Aviv Police launched a massive manhunt to capture the suspect, identified through security cameras in the area, along with an immediate request for an interim media-ban gag order, which was duly issued by the Tel Aviv District Court. On December 31, 2012, the prime suspect in the case was arrested, with his DNA matching that found at the crime scene.[40]

Following the arrest, Justice Dorit Reich-Shapiro moved to lift the media-ban gag order she had issued a week earlier, thus releasing the information to the public. With the newspapers stressing the suspect's origin as an African migrant, Justice Reich-Shapiro reprimanded the police for releasing this specific detail. Stressing the dangers to public safety, due to the potential for anti-migrant riots to erupt in south Tel Aviv as a result of this rape case, Justice Reich-Shapiro commented,

> The Police investigative branch should know better. It ought to give due consideration and thought to the dangers to public peace and safety, when exposing details from the police investigation, providing the African origin of the suspect, even before charges have been pressed.[41]

As in most cases of this sort, the media outlets knew early on both of the violent rape case and of the stringent media ban issued upon it, including a media halt over reporting the ban decree itself.[42] Following the lifting of the ban, the Israeli daily *Maariv* explicitly stated the media ban's primary objective, as being a measure of public restraint aimed to prevent another violent onslaught against African migrants:

> Though the case happened ten days ago, the police decided, in a very unusual step, to prevent any public knowledge of this rape case, fearing mass violent attacks against African migrants [by] south Tel Aviv residents. This is why the case was subject to a total media ban, which included even the mere mentioning of this judicial decree itself.[43]

Not surprisingly, it was none other than the interior minister, Eli Yishai, who first commented on the recent rape case following the lifting of the media-ban restriction. Issuing immediate statements to all the daily newspapers, Yishai stressed his conviction and determination to incarcerate all migrants, and eventually deport them all back to their African countries of origin. On the evening of December 31, following the media exposure of the rape case, some minor demonstrations and sporadic attacks against migrants were organized, partially orchestrated by the extreme right-wing Knesset member Michael Ben Ari. As the morning radio talk shows began on January 1, 2013, it was Yishai again who was stressing in front of any available microphone his stern conviction to cleanse Israel of all African elements.[44]

Interestingly, a few hours before Yishai's morning radio interviews, electoral images hitherto unseen in SHAS' campaign, explicitly targeting the African migrant issue, began appearing in the Israeli blogosphere, with internet web-links to Yishai's website and Facebook page.[45] Along with slogans and announcing that "SHAS is our home, Sudan is theirs," a well-prepared 6-minute film clip was aired, pointing to the alleged demographic disaster awaiting Israel due to the coming of African migrants.[46] The clip depicted Eli Yishai, surrounded by military personnel, climbing out of an Israeli Air Force helicopter hovering over the southern Israeli desert and the newly constructed double-deck fence built to prevent unlawful entry into Israel from Egypt. Simultaneously, full-size posters depicting Yishai alongside the slogan "Only a strong

SHAS will stop the Infiltrators" began appearing on billboards along main highways and high-volume traffic routes.[47] The Israeli daily newspaper *Yedioth Aharonot* quoted unnamed sources close to the Interior Minister's cabinet who explicitly stated that the new anti-migrant campaign had been prepared long before the most recent rape case, of late December 2012. The idea behind its preparation, according to the quoted sources, was its use as a "Doomsday electoral weapon" in the event of a drastic decline in the electoral polls or in case of an internal rivalry dispute, with SHAS' rank and file split between Eli Yishai and his returned archrival, Arye Deri. It was calculated that this campaign could result in three additional electoral seats in the 120-seat Israeli Parliament.[48] At least, this was how it seemed to Eli Yishai's advisors.

Electoral Punishment, Political Manipulation, and Anti-Migrant Convictions

As the election campaign evolved, the breadth and depth of the electoral shift awaiting the upcoming parliament became clear. In total, 53 out of 120 Knesset members found themselves exchanged for new candidates. The political map, while maintaining its left–right divide over security and foreign-policy issues, changed dramatically over the course of election night 2013. While most political commentators dreaded the prospects of yet another right-wing ultra-religious government coalition, even they did not see the rise of the centrist power block represented by the Yesh Atid party.

The Likud, which began the elections by joining forces with the right-wing Israel Beyteynu party, lost over 25 percent of its electorate, being reduced from 42 to 31 seats in the house of representatives. Rather than lurching to extremes, the Israeli electorate defied all expectations with its moderation and its rational choice of reinstating centrist politics at the top of the country's power system. Consequently, all extreme right-wing parties were ousted from parliament, having failed to clear the minimal electoral threshold.

As for SHAS, it clawed its way through the electoral turmoil that characterized the nineteenth Knesset elections, maintaining its powerbase at 11 seats out of 120. Yet under the triumvirate of Yishai–Deri–Atias, the party failed in its coalition negotiations and did not make it into the government. For almost 20 years, and through

10 coalitions out of 12, SHAS had been part of the Israeli governmental establishment. During all this time, it had enjoyed privileged access to generous government funding in both left- and right-wing administrations, as well as a strong influence in all spheres of Israeli policy through its cabinet-minister votes. The severing of the party from these positions of political power and its march into the opposition were rightfully seen as a colossal leadership failure, primarily attributed to the party's leader – Eli Yishai.

At a deeper level of political analysis, Yishai's failure, as well as those of the extreme right-wing MKs Ben-Ari and Eldad, was intimately connected to the general downfall of the Israeli extreme right wing in the nienteenth Knesset. Leading a hard line during the campaign and deliberately lashing out against secular portions of Israeli society, the Arab minority in Israel, and the African migrants, Yishai, Ben-Ari, and Eldad lost touch with their own electorate, who veered towards the diametrically opposed political pole. Arye Deri's last-ditch attempt to scrap the hard-line elements of the SHAS campaign were countered by Yishai's repeatedly obtrusive media remarks. These included lashing out against Russian Jews, as he questioned their Judaism, along with his extreme views on the Palestinian–Israeli conflict. Ben Ari's and Eldad's attempts to reignite anti-migrant violence in south Tel Aviv were notable by the simple lack of participants in their organized demonstrations – an omen of the public indifference toward the African migrant question.

It is within these parameters that one ought to understand the public disdain felt towards Yishai, Eldad, and Ben-Ari as they continued their anti-migrant onslaught long after the Israeli public had lost interest in the issue. Yishai's unleashing of his alleged electoral "doomsday weapon," in the form of his anti-migrant campaign, backfired and severely harmed his political career. All three politicians came to be perceived as public manipulators who attempted to gain votes on the backs of migrants, Russians, and Palestinians – in short, through exacerbating the differences tugging at the fragile Israeli social fabric. On the other hand, their supporters rightfully claimed that their views benefited from a unique level of political consistency, mostly absent in the crudely opportunistic Israeli political landscape. Indeed, when one examines Yishai's, Ben Ari's, and Eldad's positions, they do come across as politically reliable and consistent with their extreme-right attitudes against African migrants, which could be traced back to early 2009.

On the first week of January 2013, two weeks before election day, the Knesset Chairman decided to relieve the parliament's senior researcher on migration issues, Dr Gilad Nathan, from his position due to a vicious media campaign launched against him by fanatical, extreme right-wing media outlets.[49] A graduate of the Hebrew University, Dr Nathan had worked in the Knesset research authority for eight years, acquiring a unique level of knowledge and intellectual authority on issues involving migration to Israel – especially concerning the recent African migration.[50] Respected for his in-depth research and impeccable reporting, Dr Nathan was nominated as the senior Israeli expert to the OECD task force on migration in 2010, a position he held until his forceful removal from office.[51] Nathan's dismissal was the result of a targeted campaign by an extreme right-wing media-monitoring NGO named MIDA, which was affiliated to and funded by the political sponsors of the Knesset's extreme-right factions.

Reading Dr Nathan's reports on the African migrant issue, MIDA became concerned with his comparative positioning of Israel's migration challenges alongside those of European, North Atlantic, and other developed countries. Remaining truthful to his findings, Dr Nathan continuously chose to highlight the relatively limited scope of Israel's clandestine African migrant problem when compared with the situation in other developed countries. In addition, and as per his duties as a parliament-employed civil servant, Nathan continued to reiterate Israel's legal obligations towards asylum seekers and refugees in accordance with Israeli law and the UN treaties the country had signed and ratified, the original copies of which were stored down the corridor from his own office in the Knesset building.

As the radio and television talk shows assembled voices condoning Nathan as a trusted researcher and army-reserve noncommissioned officer, Israeli newspapers began back-tracking his reports, demanding an external oversight committee to investigate the validity of his reporting. A week after his removal, the external, independent oversight committee concluded that neither flaws nor information gaps were to be found in Dr Nathan's work, further establishing the credibility of his reporting. Upon requests for comment from the media, a Knesset spokesman admitted that the research papers drafted by Dr Nathan had been "without any factual flaw and highly commendable for their professionalism and trustworthiness."[52]

This archival investigation into Dr Nathan's employment enabled a thorough, if unintended, public examination of information accumulated for and distributed to public policy makers. Unintentionally, it also exposed their deliberate manipulation of the research data to suit their political needs. Thus it turned out that, in 2010, the then-chairman of the Knesset committee on foreign workers had deliberately suppressed one of Dr Nathan's reports. The main research finding thereby withheld concerned the moderate and negligible effects of the new African migration upon Israeli society in comparison to such measurable effects in similar situations in Western European countries – most notably, France and the UK. The decision to suppress Dr Nathan's report could possibly have been intended so as to avoid a contradiction with the statements of Prime Minister Netanyahu regarding a "tidal wave of one million African migrants threatening to swarm Israel from the Egyptian side of the border," uttered just a few weeks earlier.[53]

The depth of the contradictions between Interior Minister Eli Yishai's arguments for Jewish demographic purity and his mass-issuance of residence permits to non-Jewish migrants provides further insights into the contradictions between his rhetoric and his executed policies. As someone who vocally identified himself with the protection of a solid Jewish majority in Israel, Yishai's insistence on the mass deportation of African migrants was logically consistent with his declared ideological standpoint regarding the need for Jewish demographical supremacy. As someone who had constantly waved the Jewish demographic flag from as early as 2009, one would expect him to be a consistent advocate of limiting all non-Jewish immigration to Israel. As the interior minister, Yishai was the sole and ultimate governmental authority concerning all immigrants entering the country, Jewish and non-Jewish alike. From the beginning of his tenure at the Interior Ministry, all working visas to Israel for non-Jews were to be issued exclusively in the ministry and overseen by Yishai himself. Furthermore, SHAS had exercised full control over non-Jewish working permits even prior to 2009 – indeed, as far back as the years 2000/2001. The following chart shows the numbers of government-issued work permits for non-Jewish residents. The graph shows each year, within the twelve year time period from 2000 to 2012, with the respective political party who controlled the permit-authorizing ministry during that period:[54]

For most of the period between 2000 and 2008, SHAS was in control of the Ministry of Industrial Development and Labor, the government body in charge of issuing foreign-worker permits in Israel at the time. In 2009, the governmental prerogative for the issuance of these permits was turned over to the Interior Ministry, again under the direct control of SHAS and Eli Yishai. Thus for 13 years, with a three-year interval from 2003 to 2005, SHAS effectively controlled all non-Jewish immigration into Israel, executing direct oversight over all entry permits for non-Jews into the country.

The statistical data concerning the alien working permits provides some alarming conclusions. Yishai himself, while lashing out against African migrants on the ideological grounds of Jewish demographic purity, broke every record for residence-permit issuance to non-Jewish aliens. While journalists had pointed out this record-breaking tendency by Yishai, they did not highlight the *accumulative effect* of around 13 years of SHAS ministerial leadership on migration. In total, SHAS issued over 1 million working permits to aliens entering Israel, a number equivalent to approximately 18 percent of the total population of the country, in average, during this period.[55]

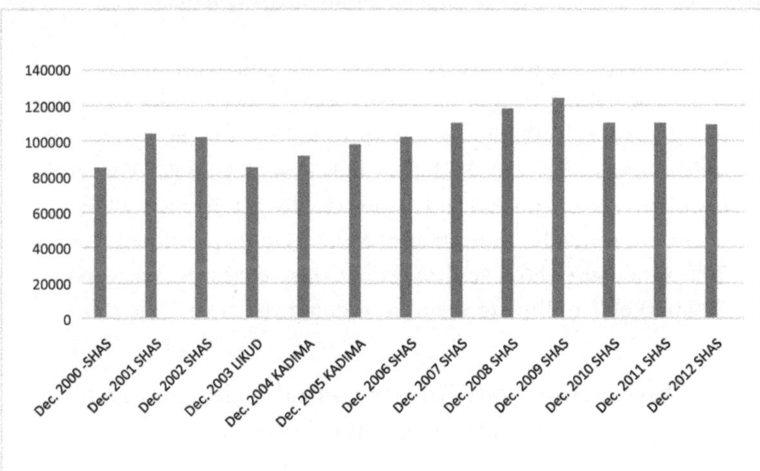

Graph 7.1 Working permits issued to non-Jewish residents in Israel, 2000–12. Data Sources: Israeli Central Board of Statistics, *Haaretz*, *YNET* News Agency, *Maariv*, Knesset Research Unit, the Israeli population and immigration authority (Israeli Interior Ministry).

One explanation, provided by SHAS officials, for the stark discrepancy between their rhetoric of demographic purity and their actions of massively importing foreign workers into Israel centered on the needs of specific economic sectors that these workers were brought in to service. SHAS officials have explained that most of them were brought in to serve the medical sector, and specifically geared toward geriatric assistance to elderly people. In addition, officials have acknowledged that most other permits were issued either in the agricultural sector (as simple "working hands") or in construction as daily, unskilled labor aimed at substituting for Palestinian workers from the OPT, which were under Israeli military curfew or closure at the time.[56]

When confronted with the question as to the logic behind importing more foreign labor rather than providing working permits to existent African migrants, most officials have stressed their unequivocal objection to allowing African migrants legal employment. The argument repeated in interviews was that providing existent illegal migrants from Africa with working permits would only entice and enhance the will of other migrants to attempt the crossing of the Egyptian desert so as to arrive at the employment-providing "promised land" of Tel Aviv.[57] As one official eloquently explained:

> the issuance of a working permit to a Filipino woman coming to Israel and taking care of an elderly man, cannot bring the entire population of the Philippine Islands to walk across the waters of the Indian Ocean up the Red Sea and into Tel Aviv. The entire population of Eritrea and Sudan can actually get up and walk not on water, but through the desert and swarm us in their millions. Look at 70,000 of them who have already done this, so what prevents another 700,000 or 7 million of them from doing the exact same thing?[58]

Assessing Israeli Governmental Policy towards African Migrants, 2005–12

While these explanations as to the alien-permits conundrum do carry a certain logical validity, the *accumulative* nature of Yishai's anti-migrant actions and rhetoric point to the deep-rooted fanatical intentions which underpinned his policies. No government body held more power regarding immigration policies than the Interior Ministry.

The importance of the role of Deputy Prime Minister and Interior Minister Eli Yishai was the single most vital factor in determining the future of the African migrants. Just like his predecessor, Roni Bar-On, Yishai had total control over the fate of the African migrants already in-country. In Israel, with a strong military and security apparatus, with total control over its borders and inhabitants, the role of the Interior Minister and his control of the border regimes of the State cannot be overstated. While Bar-On had vouched to ameliorate the conditions of the African migrants, Yishai saw them as an imminent threat that needed curtailing. In his defense, one must emphasize that Yishai was faced with the reality of hundreds of daily illegal border crossers, which Bar-On never dealt with. On the other hand, Bar-On never "spiced up" his policy choices with the kind of media manipulation which Yishai undertook.

Within the public perception, Yishai remained the manipulative, cunning, and right-wing religious fanatic who did all he could, fair or manipulatively unfair, to toughen Israeli government policies with the end objective of reversing the African migrant wave. Contrary to the simplistic portrayal of Yishai as an opportunist racist,[59] it seems as though his actions genuinely were creed-based, as he fundamentally believed that African migration posed an acute danger to Israeli society. One could ask whether motives matter at all where politics are concerned. Yet when policy is administered and legislation is applied, as was the case with the 2012 Anti-Infiltration Act, motives do matter. At the most fundamental level, the difference between Yishai and his predecessor Bar-On lay in a difference in motivation. As a secular well-educated corporate lawyer, Bar-On had been inclined to adhere to a Western, humanistic set of values, which affected his judgment positively towards the plight of the African migrants facing him as Interior Minister. Yishai, on the other hand, was primarily driven by religious, Jewish exclusionary sentiments which bred his concern and anguish vis-à-vis the coming of the African Muslim, or Christian "other."[60]

Yishai secured public support when his views seemed to cater to the needs of the Israeli population of south Tel Aviv as they were faced with a rise in violent crime by a small non-representative portion of African migrants. Yishai's extremely negative views of the African migrants were no doubt enhanced by the fact that many of the crimes were sexually orientated, some entailing extremely violent rape cases. The impact of the image of an African non-Jew raping and violently penetrating a Caucasian Jewish female left an unprecedented and appallingly negative imprint in the Israeli media.

Yet it was precisely here that Yishai also lost his electoral support, primarily due to his meddling in manipulative politics, which, when exposed by the harsh Israeli media, served to portray him as an opportunist of the lowest character. His *ad hominem* attacks on faithful and trustworthy civil servants like Chief of Police Danino, the Attorney General's staff, and Dr Gilad Nathan all served to turn the public against him. His political demise ultimately surfaced as he cynically used the rape crimes committed against Israeli females as a political linchpin for his anti-migrant attacks.

At a deeper level, Yishai's failure, and the failure of the whole cohort of extreme right-wing Knesset members such as Michael Ben-Ari and Arye Eldad, was due to a miscalculated sense of political timing. By July 2012, the Israeli public had begun to turn an apathetic "blind eye" toward the African migrants, as evident in the public lack of interest vis-à-vis the incident of the migrants stranded between the fences on the Israeli–Egyptian border in early September 2012.[61] If, for Yishai, the African migrant question remained a creed-based issue, for the Israeli public it was no longer pertinent. Yishai and other extreme right-wing Knesset members failed to sense the Israeli public's disengagement from the African migrant issue, as they detached themselves from the acute troubles of the economy, the cost of living, and the security issue which bothered their electorates. Yishai's misguided electoral "doomsday weapon" in the form of his campaign against the African migrants, already a non-relevant issue for most Israelis, merely served to prove just how detached he was. By the time Arye Deri managed to shelve this campaign, SHAS' electoral efforts were already in vain, and Yishai would ultimately pay the political price for this.

What took place between January 2012 and the elections of January 2013 was a classic case of a mistakenly assumed political opportunity, falsely manipulated by extreme-right politicians who thought of capitalising upon ill-perceived demographic fears among their own electorate. Ben-Ari, Eldad, and Interior Minister Eli Yishai "turbocharged" the anti-migrant riots with extreme-right nationalistic rhetoric.

Yet rather than exacerbating the onslaught and violence against the migrants, their actions were generally received with public disdain, given the African migrant issue's dwindling in the public's interest toward a level of political non-relevance. Yishai's ill-conceived political opportunity effectively backfired. The majority of the Israeli electorate was no longer interested in the migrant issue, so artificially pushed to the forefront of the political agenda by these extreme right-wing politicians. The electorate consequently shifted its votes toward other parties and actors.

PART III

UNIVERSALISM REGAINED: THE ISRAELI JUDICIARY AND THE AFRICAN MIGRATION CHALLENGE

CHAPTER 7

THE REVOCATION OF THE 2012 AND 2013 ANTI-INFILTRATION ACTS

On September 16, 2013, the Israeli Government experienced what amounted to a major political earthquake. The exceptionally enlarged nine-judge chamber of the Israeli Supreme Court, which included both the President and the court's Deputy President, unanimously revoked the 2012 Anti-Infiltration Act due to its unconstitutional stipulation of unlimited incarceration for African asylum seekers. The law's overt contradiction with the principles of human dignity and freedom, as enshrined in Israel's Basic Law (subtitled "Human Dignity and Liberty"), merited its removal.

In its forceful and unequivocal revocation of the 2012 Anti-Infiltration Act, the supreme court effectively reinstated and revived the universalist elements within the Israeli ethos, in this case concerning Israeli migrant policies. This reinstatement of universalism was undertaken through the employment of *both* international laws and universalist elements existent in ancient Jewish Law. The State reacted to the supreme court's action by hastily legislating some minor revisions within the very same law, and securing its rapid parliamentary approval. This second version of the 2012 Anti-Infiltration Act was also revoked by the supreme court, this time with six judges endorsing the revocation and three (including the court's President) dissenting from the majority opinion of their peers. Recalling the experience of other Western countries, the Israeli Government then opted for the expulsion of the

African migrants to two underdeveloped African countries, Rwanda and Uganda, with whom Israel then concluded dubious and legally questionable third-party asylum agreements.

The Israeli Supreme Court: A Short Overview

The Israeli legal system is the hybrid result of an attempted synthesis between the occidental legal traditions of English Common Law and the Jewish Hebrew Law, both of which serve as its two-pillar foundation. Upon the creation of the Israeli state in 1948, the legal system of the British Mandate in Palestine continued to serve as the legal basis of the State. Yet almost from its inception, the Israeli legal system slowly and gradually came to introduce significant elements from Hebrew Jewish law and jurisprudence, *Hamishpat Ha'ivri*, into the public legal system. Developed over 2,000 years and compiled in the *Halacha* (which includes the Jewish Torah, the Talmud, and Rabbinical decrees and jurisprudence), the Jewish legal code has over the years evolved into the second pillar of the Israeli legal system.[1] With the growing influx of African migrants and their pleas to the Israeli Supreme Court, both pillars, along with significant influences from public international law, have been invoked by the court to justify their protection from harsh government measures. The conditions of urgency during the Israeli war of independence in 1948 as the legal system was being created, the absence of an all-encompassing Israeli constitution, and the hybrid patchwork of legal traditions could have all played towards a weakened and politically dependant judiciary and supreme court. Yet the complete opposite is true.

From the moment of its inception, the Israeli Supreme Court enjoyed a unique position within the Israeli state, respected and revered by politicians who understood full well the uncompromising support it enjoyed from Israeli public opinion. The court was established in July 1948 during one of the cease-fires between the Israeli Army and the Arab armies who declared war upon the nascent state following UN resolution 181 for the partition of Palestine in November 1947. It was the first national-government institution to be deliberately based in Jerusalem, preceding the Knesset and the executive-branch governmental offices. It initially comprised five judges, most of whom had been presiding judges appointed under the British Mandate, and thus continued the

English legal tradition of the impartiality of the judiciary in common law. From its very beginning, the supreme court already reflected the hybrid legal legacy outlined above. One of the five first supreme court judges, Justice Simcha Asaf had been a rabbinical luminary in Hebrew jurisprudence, and was appointed to the bench with the consent of all parties.[2] Though not a lawyer, but rather a professor of Jewish religious thought at the Hebrew University, Justice Asaf's lack of formal legal training did not prevent his appointment to the high bench. It is striking to note that this legacy of appointing judges who had hitherto not been part of the judiciary has been continued, with the Hebrew Law element becoming a formative consideration in the court's application of the law, down to the present day.

Over the years, and markedly since the mid-1970s, the Israeli Supreme Court has become a beacon of stability and resilience in the face of government coercion, perceived with the highest respect by the overwhelming majority of the Israeli public and body politic.[3] The growing involvement of the Israeli Supreme Court in policy making and policy execution is by no means unique, and should be seen within the general trend of quite a number of Western democracies who, over the past two decades, have experienced what Roger Cohen has coined the "juridification of political processes."[4]

The appointment of formidable jurists, considered impartial and apolitical, together with a strong sense of almost ascetic humility, granted the court immediate respect from the political sphere and the public alike. The perceived continuation of the British Mandate legal heritage, along with the strong international backgrounds of the presiding judges, granted the court much-needed independence from the overbearing influence of the founding fathers of the State – foremost among them, David Ben-Gurion. The importing and implementation of the idea of *Rechtsstaat* and legal positivism by the German judges of the court meant that any hint of personal political preference within the judicial science would be regarded as tantamount to sacrilege. An overwhelming number of the court's judges during its first 20 years of operation were either German or Anglo-Saxon natives who had earned their legal education in German, British, or American universities.[5] The German judges' importation of *Rechtsstaat* dovetailed with the Anglo-Saxon concept of the "Rule of Law," imported from the US legal tradition and embodied by another chief justice, Simon Agranat, himself a native of Kentucky.[6]

Thus, virtually from its inception, the Israeli Supreme Court incorporated within its judicial ranks certain judges who were visibly identified with universalism (like Justices Chaim Cohn and Simon Agranat), while other judges – many of whom were religious, like Justice Asaf and, later, Justice Mencahem Eylon – came to personify the exceptionalist strata within Judaism.

Befitting its ascetic nature, the court was housed on the top floor of the Russian Provoslav Monastery in central Jerusalem, with the government leasing the space from the Russian Orthodox Church. The unassuming simplicity and locality of these Jerusalemite chambers were a stark contrast to the worldly, profound, and erudite character of its new occupants. This was all the more evident to Israeli visitors to the court as they listened to the heavy German and English accents of the judges' spoken Hebrew, which contrasted with the impeccable biblical written Hebrew adorning the court's judgments.

From the outset, the supreme court demonstrated independence and a deep obligation toward checking and balancing the actions of the executive arm of government. In 1953, Justice Agranat overturned the government's decision to close the communist newspaper *Kol Haam*, curtailing for the first time an interior minister's decision and founding the Israeli free-speech precedent. The year 1965 saw the first instance of a political party being barred from participating in the elections due to its electoral platform, which denied the existence of the State from a communist–anarchist perspective – a precedent repeated in the 1980s, with the barring of the extreme-right Kach party due to its racist and xenophobic ideologies.

In its role as inquisitor on government-appointed inquiry committees, the court had effectively toppled two governments: that of Golda Meir, via its investigation into the Yom Kippur War in 1974 (the Agranat Commission), and that of Menachem Begin and Ariel Sharon in 1983 due to the latter's ultimate responsibility for the Sabra and Shatilla massacres in Beirut (the Kahn Commission).[7]

The 1990s brought the zenith of the courts' power, ultimately testing the limitations of its own tendency to intervene in strictly executive roles of government. The "judicial activism" endorsed by Chief Justice Aharon Barak led the court to unprecedented interventions in the workings of government. Justice Barak's approach ultimately brought about some erosion of the court's stature in the eyes of certain segments of Israeli society, most notably the religious right wing and the settler communities in the OPT.

The first decade of the new millennium saw a string of public figures and politicians being tried by the Israeli judicial system on penal charges. These charges ranged from bribery (Ministers Arye Deri, Yair Levi, and Shlomo Benizri) to fraud (Prime Minister Olmert), and ultimately rape, as in the case of President Katzav – found guilty by the district court, and whose appeal to the supreme court brought a severe toughening of his own sentence. Public disillusionment and anger at so many senior politicians being put on trial has, nevertheless, only served to strengthen the public's perception of the supreme court as impartial and untainted.

In 2011, *Haaretz* newspaper interviewed five leading jurists, requesting them to lay out their image of a utopian court in a perfect world. Avigdor Feldman, the paragon of human and civil rights law for well over 40 years, stunned the readers by his claim, that rather than theoretical and utopian, he himself had indeed actually experienced this ideal court in real life:

> My ideal Supreme Court indeed existed at the Russian Compound in Jerusalem. Warmth resided in the chamber emanating from electrical heaters sporadically cast around, and halved by the brown attorney table, overflowing with warmth and benevolence. On the bench were seated Justices Chaim Cohn, Justice Landau and Justice Asher. My plea was scheduled for that day, probably concerning land expropriation. It was the end of the 1970s and the land expropriating giant was only beginning his way, treading carefully between the Palestinian localities in the Occupied Palestinian Territories of the West Bank.
>
> Pending my plea, a few smaller pleas were scheduled that day, so as to grant ample time for mine. One of these concerned a certain issue of governmental agricultural quotas if I recall correctly. The plaintiff was not represented by a lawyer, and was speech impaired. Justice Cohn invited him from the court room to be seated at the attorney table. As he began to plea his words were heavy and his speech inconsistent. "Approach us", said Justice Landau accompanying his words with an inviting

> hand gesture. The plaintiff crossed the table and stepped into the "no man's land" between the attorney's table and the Justice bench.
>
> The court bailiff, instinctively wanting to bar him from this "forbidden" territory, was calmed with a hand gesture by Justice Cohn. The man spoke heavily as if he was imprinting his work-shoes in the heavy muddy earth, and the judges listened patiently. Occasionally Justices Landau and Cohn would repeat the words of the plaintive that seemed like heavy rocks extracted from the earth, and would exchange them for polished legal jargon. Upon conclusion, Justice Landau addressed the state prosecutor. "The man is right", said the judge, "he is entitled to the state assistance and the Court's protection he has asked for" [. . .] The state prosecutor fell silent, brushing agitatedly through the affidavits in her file. Finally she replied: "Yes, your honor is right, indeed he is entitled to the requested state assistance", and the flittering of angel wings was heard from above in Jerusalem.[8]

Feldman's recollected experience demonstrates a unique feature of the Israeli High Court, operating in its capacity as the Supreme Court of Justice. In this capacity, it is entrusted with administrating justice and legal assistance in cases of an abuse of power by the State or any of its organs against an individual citizen. It is noteworthy that this function of the court has existed since its inception in 1948 and, as such, preceded the legislative foundations of the court itself, which were only finalized three decades later in the Basic Law of the Judiciary 1980. Though initially restricted to habeas corpus appeals against arbitrary detention, the right of appeals swiftly gained ground on all issues where judicial protection was required to check and qualify the coercive powers of the State.

In essence, the Israeli High Court's function as a supreme court of justice does not differ from that of other Western of procedural legal systems. Yet the circumventive character of the Israeli High Court, leapfrogging the whole legal system so as to receive one's "day in court," in front of the highest legal instance of the land, is indeed unique and unparalleled when compared globally. Most legal systems – the British, US, and many continental European examples among them – require a tabling of motions, including that of habeas corpus, to the lower courts, initiating the long process of judicial decisions and appeals until one reaches the high court of the land. The circumventive nature of pleas being tabled directly to the high court in the Israeli case have often pitted the supreme court directly against the government. The circumvention of all lower judicial instances has often granted swift retribution retaliation to the State's coercion. Since it is the ultimate judicial authority, the State is thus deprived of its habitual tendency for procrastination and dragging out of legal processes, at times wearing down the plaintive, through a series of seemingly never-ending court procedures and judicial processes.

The court's accessibility to the public, including the unparalleled option of a citizen pleading his or her own case without legal representation, has retained a positive proximity between it and the Israeli public, thwarting government attempts to limit the court's jurisdiction through legislation.

The *a priori* right of a plaintiff to stand in front of the court has also undergone considerable development over the years. Initially reserved for Israeli citizens only, this entitlement was enlarged to include non-Israeli citizens following the occupation of the Palestinian territories of the West Bank and the Gaza Strip in 1967, granting this right to the occupied population there.[9] A further development in the 1990s was the opening up of this right to NGOs and claims which had public importance. In the case of African migration to Israel, the right to stand in court for non-citizens and for NGOs has played a fundamental role in the conflict between governmental limitations against the migrants and NGO actions in their favor.[10]

It is against the background of this widening of the right to appeal, against governmental policy, on issues of public interest that one should understand the somewhat special position acquired by the NGO coalition for the defense of the rights of the African migrants. Organizations such as the legal clinic for migrant's rights at the Tel Aviv University Law Faculty, in cooperation with the ACRI; the "Hotline for Migrant workers," and ASSAF (the Aid Organization for Refugees and Asylum Seekers in Israel) were all active as early as 2007/8, with ever-growing influence over government policies. A prime aspect of their effectiveness in wielding public and legal power against the State was their ability to plead to the high court, forcing the government to succumb to judicial oversight.

In the year 2000, and following unprecedented strain on the supreme court due to the sheer volume of legal cases brought to its doorstep, the government, in consultation with the high court, created procedural courts within the district courts with the aim of alleviating some of the burden from the high court. These procedural courts, referred to as the "Mini Supreme Court," perform as the delegated arm of the supreme court, and deal mostly with civil legal cases concerning executive governmental coercion. The legislature has maintained for these lower courts the same powers previously consecrated in legal jurisprudence concerning the right to stand and the immediacy of aid availability which the high court administers.

The importance of the supreme court in qualifying the governmental executive has been seen in recent years through the ever-growing reference by all parties to "The Supreme Court test" (*Mivchan Bagaz*), which has become a common Hebrew proverb frequently heard on political talk shows, in newspapers, and in the media generally. The term is usually followed by a question or exclamation mark – will a certain issue stand "The Supreme Court test"? – or evokes an ontological statement that this or that action shall or shall not stand the test.

An Overview of the Israeli Supreme Court Ruling Revoking the 2012 Anti-Infiltration Act

Looking back at the deliberations of the Knesset Interior Committee (KIC) during the last months of 2011, as it prepared legislation for the 2012 Anti-Infiltration Act, one is struck by the farsightedness of two of its members: the chairman, Amnon Cohen, and MK Dov Hanin. While Cohen repeatedly expressed his concern as to the incorrect constitutional framing of the new legislation, Hanin's prediction that the Supreme Court would invalidate and revoke the new act when appeals against the latter were brought before it seemed naïve to some observers, an exercise in wishful thinking to others:

> you will produce here a law which will be chastised in Israel and internationally and at the end will be legally revoked and rendered illegal and invalid. So why go down this route? I know the government likes doing things the hard way, but I urge you this time to reconsider your position.[11]

To most seasoned observers, Hanin's conviction that the high court would revoke this government legislation simply ran counter to the prevailing tendencies of the court's rulings ever since its newly appointed conservative president, Asher Gronis, had been sworn in, succeeding the overtly human-rights-minded previous president, Dorit Beinish.

Confirming their positive surprise as to the unequivocal and unanimous vote by the extended supreme court bench, *Haaretz*' editorial board expressed its satisfaction with the court's decision, seeing it as a fundamental shift in judicial policy:

> After several severe disappointments in the field of Human Rights in recent years – such as the ruling that upheld the discriminatory Citizenship Law and the ruling [that] the Hours of Work and Rest Law doesn't apply to home caregivers – it must be hoped that the current ruling, whose main conclusions were handed down unanimously, heralds a renewed commitment on the Court's part to defending human rights.[12]

Most people in Israel did not believe the court would overturn the governmental legislation concerning African migrants, however immoral the court might have thought it to be. Even within the minority of Israelis, like MK Hanin, who honestly believed the court would indeed revoke the law in some way or other, none had anticipated a unanimous decision by the extended bench of all nine judges. Moreover, no one foresaw the harsh criticisms of government anti-migrant policies expressed within the concurring opinions of the members of the bench.

Ruling number 7146/2012 of the Israeli High Court of Justice was originally tabled as a habeas corpus plea for the release from custody of five Eritrean nationals, indefinitely incarcerated with an initial prison term of three years following the introduction of the newly legislated Anti-Infiltration Act of January 2012, which came into force in June of that year.[13] In addition, the motion contained a secondary, procedural plea tabled on behalf of five different pro-migrant NGOs, in which they stressed the unconstitutional character of the new legislation as it contradicted Israel's Basic Law of Human Dignity and Liberty. In January 2013, the high court incorporated into the plea additional appeals against expulsion orders, decreed by the District Court of Beer Sheva, against five additional Eritrean and Sudanese plaintiffs.

Interestingly enough – and by no coincidence – thanks to the work of the pro-migrant NGOs, two of the new plaintiffs were the very same women who had been caught stranded at the Israeli frontier with Egypt back in September 2012, drawing extensive media attention to their humanitarian condition.[14]

The ruling began with an extensive survey of the factual circumstances referred to by the pleading attorneys and the Israeli Attorney General, who represented the State.[15] The court set the African clandestine migration into Israel within the more general context of world refugee migrations from the underdeveloped South towards Western, developed countries.[16] It then surveyed in detail the critical human-rights conditions in both Sudan and Eritrea, these being the plaintiffs' countries of origin, and quoted extensively from UN Human Rights Council reports on both countries and their oppressive regimes.[17]

Two pages of the ruling were dedicated to Israel's signing and ratification of the 1951 Refugee Convention and the implications thereof. Of considerable importance was the court's reference to non-refoulement as enshrined in the convention's Article 33.[18] The court explicitly drew attention to two separate legal implications of non-refoulement. In the first instance, it examined the non-refoulement principle in so far as it applied to people who had already undergone a Refugee Status Determination (RSD) procedure and had succeeded in receiving refugee status.[19] The second application of the non-refoulement principle by the court concerned people who had not yet officially secured refugee status, their precarious position earning them the designation "asylum seekers":

> Beyond the ample protections provided to refugees, international law has come to accept an extra overarching protection from being expelled back to one's country of origin, due to the overriding principle of non returning (Non-Refoulement), which means that the state of Israel shall not expel a human being to any place where his life of freedom are under threat. This principle has also been recognized by internal Israeli law, which recognizes the value and sanctity of human life. *Therefore, even a person who is not recognized as refugees as such, according to the definitions of the Refugee Convention, it may well be that his return to his country of origin may not be possible due to Non-Refoulement as a principle.*[20]

This position of the court is of vital importance in understanding its dramatic decision to overrule government legislation. Once non-refoulement had been internalized into domestic Israeli law, and once it had been coupled with the general principle of non-arbitrary detention, non-refoulement effectively became a stipulation for freedom. The general part of the ruling culminated with a review of the African migration phenomenon into Israel since 2005, detailing the government actions that had been undertaken to halt it.[21] Three areas of government action came under scrutiny: the construction of a physical barrier on the Egyptian–Israeli border, the resettlement efforts of the Israeli government vis-à-vis third-party African governments, and legislation as enacted in the Anti-Infiltration Act of 2012.[22] Following this general introduction, the court detailed the arguments of the plaintiffs and subsequently those of the defending Attorney General.

The plaintiffs' arguments were clear and straightforward. The court was requested to invalidate and revoke in full form the Israeli anti-infiltration act due to its unconstitutional character. This far-reaching claim was substantiated through the evocation of one single legal ground: given the complete halt of the influx of African migrants due to the erection of the Israeli–Egyptian border fence, the incarceration of African migrants already in Israel served one purpose and one only – *deterrence*. The sole purpose of the indefinite incarceration of existing migrants, who had not been convicted of any crime, was to deter other migrants from attempting to cross the border into the country. The State was therefore harming African migrants already in Israel not because of their own actions, but as a tool to prevent the actions of others. This, according to the plaintiffs, ran counter to basic constitutional rights to freedom, bestowed upon any human being, as per both Israeli and International law.[23]

In its reply, the State did not refute the deterrence rationale referred to by the plaintiffs. On the contrary, it came to justify it. In his defense, the Attorney General opted for two lines of argument: the geographic exceptionalism of the Israeli case, and the concerns for state security. Israel was the only Western developed country with a long territorial border accessible to Africa over ground. Given the ineffective legal situation prior to the new legislation of the 2012 Anti-Infiltration Act, the State did not possess an adequate legal framework to deal with the massive influx of African migrants that had been experienced in

2011–12. The Attorney General urged the court to consider these special – indeed, exceptional – circumstances. The stark income disparities between Israel and those African nations in its proximity served as the primary driver for even more migrants to enter Israeli territory clandestinely. These migrants, knowing full well that they would be released from incarceration after a short period, had to be deterred. The new legal framework provided for such deterrence.[24]

The State also claimed that the migrants were a threat to national security and public order, due to the rise in criminal acts performed by the incoming African migrants. As proof of the necessity of the 2012 Anti-Infiltration Act, the State pointed to the sharp decline in the number of African migrants who had entered Israel since its coming into force, and attributed this decline directly to the deterrence effect of the legislation rather than to the construction of an insurmountable barrier along the Egyptian–Israeli border.

Following both presentations, from the plaintiffs and from the State, the court delivered its verdict. Justice Edna Arbel commenced her concurring opinion on the court's behalf, with a critical cautionary self-reminder of the limitations and care required from the high court as it came to consider the overturning of parliamentary legislation. The court could only do so in cases where that legislation contradicted one of Israel's basic laws, which together served as the material constitution of the State. The revocation of legislation by the court meant nothing less than an obstruction of the will of the people in a democracy, since the elected parliamentarians, in their legislative actions, serve as the direct and immediate arm of the people: parliamentarians were elected, judges were not.[25]

Justice Arbel then proceeded with a two-staged examination of the Anti-Infiltration Act. The first stage of examination inquired into the question of whether or not the rights of liberty and freedom of movement had indeed been infringed upon by the State. The second stage of the judicial inquiry examined whether this infringement was justified, as per the qualifying clauses on national security and "reasons of State" of the Israeli Basic Law of Human Dignity and Liberty. Following an extensive survey of the legal precedents applicable to the case, Justice Arbel concluded that the Anti-Infiltration Act indeed harmed significantly both the right to liberty and the right to freedom of movement of the migrants – a conclusion uncontested either by the plaintiffs or by the State's defense attorneys.[26]

Justice Arbel then began to examine the qualifying clauses of the Basic Law of Human Dignity and Liberty, and it is here that the crux of the rift between the plaintiffs and the State attorneys exposed itself most strongly. The State declared that the 2012 Anti-Infiltration Act had two clear and explicit goals: to prevent the African migrants from striking roots in Israel, and to halt their incoming via deterrence. Justice Arbel concluded that while the goal of prevention of residence indeed stood the test of "legal worthiness," the second goal, that of deterrence, could not be upheld. Thus, the court continued its investigation of proportionality only with regard to the first goal explicated by the State – that of the prevention of permanent residence by clandestine African migrants in Israel.[27]

After an extensive review of the proportionality between the goal of prevention of residence and the harsh implications of a three-year incarceration period (which could be prolonged indefinitely), Justice Arbel concluded that the grounds for the legislation of the 2012 Anti-Infiltration Act were unjustifiable. This merited both its revocation and the immediate release from incarceration of the detained plaintiffs and all other migrants in custody due to the same legal grounds. In her concluding statements, Justice Arbel chose to revert to the Jewish legal code and tradition as she cited extensively from the various religious Jewish legal sources which underpinned her concurring opinion.[28] The remaining pages were dedicated to the legal opinions of the other eight judges who had presided alongside Justice Arbel in this ruling.

The Failure of the Argument for the Securitization of the African Migration Issue

The revocation of the 2012 Anti-Infiltration Act was first and foremost the result of the supreme court's fundamental rejection of the national security rationale which underpinned that law. In the deepest of senses, the court could not accept a security-based argument if it were to be applied to people who – despite the sporadic criminal actions executed by some individual migrants – had never posed any security threat toward the Israeli state. In essence, the defeat of the Attorney General's argument lay in his failed attempt to securitize the African migrant issue, as envisaged by the Copenhagen School's concept of socially constructed securitization.[29] Put briefly, securitization is a conceptual–methodological approach which views security issues as socially constructed epistemological entities rather than ontologically independent givens existing separately from their socially ascribed interpretation. Fundamental features of securitization include the artificially constructed needs and meanings of what we come to know as "security." A security need is a construct of our perception, rather than being solely an ontologically independent issue.

Looking through the securitization "prism" so as to gauge Israeli policies towards the African migrants can be helpful in exposing the true thinking which underpinned government policies. Security is a consensus-generating mechanism – even more so in Israel, with its precarious and vulnerable security history. Tagging any single issue, person, object, or even train of thought as a security threat most often legitimizes excessive governmental policies against it.

The consensus about the need to guard Israeli society from imminent threats equates the existence of those threats with governmental license for excessive behavior, most often in breach of moral and legal principles. Any government success at convincing the Israeli public that a given issue is indeed a security threat almost certainly entails the licensing of excessive measures against that issue. With the human-rights NGO advocates understanding this mechanic full well, the battleground between governmental voices and those of the NGOs has shifted towards the contest over whether the African clandestine migration was to be considered a security threat *a priori* – or not.

The attempts by the Israeli Government to securitize the clandestine African migration had been rejected by the supreme court from the outset of this influx, back in 2005. These attempts had included the incarceration of migrants in 2006 on suspicion of being potentially utilized by terrorist organizations operating in the Sinai Peninsula. That attempt was rejected outright by the high court that same year.[30] In her 2013 ruling, Justice Arbel explicitly referred to the high court's rejection of the securitization of the African influx back in 2006, reaffirming the court's rejection of the usage of the 1954 Anti-infiltration Act by the government as it ordered the Israeli security forces to operate under the stipulations of the civilian-based 1952 Law of Entry into Israel.[31] In 2007, and following the judges' 2006 rejection of the security-based argument for the automatic detention of all African migrants, the Israeli State Comptroller launched an inquiry into security procedures and policies vis-à-vis the African clandestine migrants.[32]

As I have previously mentioned, upon apprehension by the Israeli Army, all tresspassers were to undergo a routine interrogation concerning their background, whereabouts, and reasons for illegally crossing into Israeli territory.[33] Once it had been determined that the detainee posed no security threat, they were to be dealt with under the legal stipulations enshrined in the 1952 Law of Entry into Israel, and not under the conditions laid down in the 1954 Anti-Infiltration Act.[34]

While the 1952 law contains measures to safeguard the rights of clandestine border crossers during their detention period and prior to their deportation, the 1954 Anti-Infiltration Act did not contain any such safeguards. This difference between the two laws first and foremost derived from the vital legal condition known as the "dangerousness threshold".[35] The determining factor in distinguishing whether illegal border crossers would be dealt with under the lenient 1952 Law of Entry into Israel or according to the harsh 1954 Anti-Infiltration Act was their potential for doing harm to Israelis. Though Rubenstein's orders were reiterated by his successor, Menahem Mazouz, in 2006, the security establishment did not follow suit with regard to these guidelines.

The State Comptroller's examination of 2007, concerning the handling of foreign migrants by the Israeli security establishment, yielded problematic findings which resulted in the Comptroller's recommendations for rectifying the situation:

> Amongst the different security bodies stood deep disagreement as to whether the dangerousness threshold ought to be administered over the entire population of Sudanese migrants. The position of the Secret Service [Shin Bet] was that the State must administer the dangerousness threshold toward all Sudanese migrants since Sudan is a State openly harboring terrorism. On the contrary, the Army [IDF] maintained that there is no justification for this position and that there is a need to interrogate every single Sudanese migrant in order to ascertain if he or she posed a threat to

> Israeli national security. Due to this disagreement, the Attorney General's guidelines were not executed.[36]

The Attorney General, knowing full well that his orders were not being implemented, turned the entire issue over to the acting prime minister at the time, Ehud Olmert, requesting the latter's intervention and an executive decision on the question of whether all Sudanese migrants passed the dangerousness threshold. Finally, in April 2007, Prime Minister Olmert ordered the security establishment not to implement the dangerousness threshold unless clear evidence was found suggesting a certain migrant was indeed a threat to Israeli national security.[37]

Interestingly, dangerousness threshold or not, the IDF took a general decision not to incarcerate any Sudanese women or children who arrived from across the Egyptian border. Tellingly, the army explained to the Attorney General that it was not equipped to deal with female and children migrants since these were the responsibility of the civil social services. The army bluntly admitted that it was releasing from custody all women and children, as a standard procedure, since they posed no threat whatsoever to Israeli national security.[38]

Though the State never repeated its open attempts to securitize the African influx, the government remained adamantly convinced of the alleged security threats posed by African migrants to Israeli society. In 2011, Prime Minister Netanyahu openly stated that the demographic implications of the coming influx of African migrants constituted a major threat to Israeli national security.[39] In 2012, *Haaretz* newspaper published a policy paper by the Israeli internal secret service (Shin Bet) concerning illicit money transfers by African migrants back to their home countries, and stressed that these funds would be used by terrorist organizations.[40]

The most important, and blatant, attempt by the State to securitize the African migrant issue was through its security-driven rationale forming the foundation of the 2012 Anti-Infiltration Act. The decision by the government to pursue the revitalization of the 1954 Anti-Infiltration Act, originally intended for use against the Fada'ayun militias, was an exercise in securitization *par excellence*. The government's decision to drop the 2008 anti-migrant legislation, after its defeat by the pro-migrant NGO lobby, in favor of the 1954 legislation had had a clear security-based logic. Recalling the objections of the Knesset's chief legal advisor, Eyal Yinon, to the use of the 1954 security-based legislation, Justice Uzi Vogelmann had written:[41]

> During the legislative proceeding in the Knesset Interior Committee, the parliamentary legal advisor cautioned the Committee to reconsider its position and legislate the proposed Act under the 1952 Law of Entry into Israel, however the representative of the Attorney General made it explicitly clear during the proceedings, that the government deliberately resolved to intentionally make usage of the of the 1954 Anti-Infiltration Act as the legal platform for this issue, so as to project "an extreme message of severity", and turn over the overall responsibility to the Minister of Defense. The rhetorical choices of the legislator are not subject to our judicial oversight. However, it is important that the rhetorical choice by the legislator does not hide the essence of the law. We are bound to remember, along every step of this debate, the complex character of our modern-day "infiltrators", who overwhelmingly are defined as asylum seekers.[42]

The above passage was preceded by a detailed explanation by Justice Vogelmann of the original grounds of the 1954 Anti-Infiltration Act as a legal platform for preventing terrorism. He explicitly referred to the 1954 "infiltrator," who was armed and who usually crossed the border deliberately to maim and kill Israelis. Justice Vogelmann continued here the general trend within the ruling as he deliberately differentiated between the evildoing border crossers of 1954 and the current stream of African migrants, who are all unarmed civilians:

> The legislator chose to regulate the issue at hand through an amendment of the 1954 Anti-Infiltration Act, and to consider the individual against whom this legislation is geared as an "infiltrator". On the top of it, this is merely a legal term designating "anyone who is not an Israeli citizen, who enters Israel not through a regulated and legal border crossing". However, one cannot disassociate between the new amendment and the original intention of this term in its original normative setting. The term "infiltrator" is very heavily burdened with the historical baggage laden on its shoulders.[43]

Referring to the fact that none of the over 70,000 migrants who had entered Israeli clandestinely had ever carried a firearm or posed a security threat to the State, Justice Arbel rejected the securitization of the African-migrants issue through their tagging with the historically laden definition of "infiltrators":

> We are driven towards complex confrontations with this issue of the migrants. We must remember that when faced with this issue, we are not confronted with people coming to harm the population of the State of Israel, but rather with a miserable population, who is arriving to our shores from a destitute humanitarianly stricken region, a population which conducts a miserable and poverty-stricken life in Israel too.[44]

At a deeper level, the high court's rejection of the security-based rationale which underpinned the adoption of the 2012 Anti-Infiltration Act was also a rejection of the Attorney General's argument for the exceptionalism of the Israeli case. As Justice Arbel explained in her main concurring opinion, Israel was *not* exceptional as she faced the challenge of incoming migratory influxes from the poor war-stricken and underdeveloped South. Europe, the US, Australia, Canada, and other countries were all experiencing similar migratory pressures:

> Israel is not the only country coping with clandestine migration phenomena, and with an influx of asylum seekers and refugees cramming and knocking on its gates. It might well be that Israel's unique geopolitical reality places her in a more complicated situation, and yet the basic coping is mutual for Israel together with many other countries in the world.[45]

In short, Israel had international legal obligations, based upon international universalist tools that it had originally helped shape in the form of the 1951 Refugee Convention.

Ironically, however, Israel's anachronistic use of historically laden terms ("infiltrators" in this case), relating to circumstances and perpetrators from bygone eras, was not specific to the country. Nor was the redeployment of harsh legislation from previous periods of extreme challenge to present-day national-security contexts a uniquely Israeli feature. In fact, this "legislative behavior" was becoming quite common in other nations that were experiencing migratory pressures. One such country, which experienced an acute crisis due to African migratory pressures almost at the same time as Israel did, was France.

On the night of October 27, 2005, two teenagers of African-immigrant origin were electrified to death in the northern Parisian suburb of Clichy-sous-Bois following a police pursuit whose grounds were later legally contested. The deaths of the teenagers in this poverty-stricken ghetto-like neighborhood, and the alleged police responsibility for them, prompted a wave of nationwide violence. These serious riots across the whole of France were seen as the worst instances of civil disobedience since the French–Algerian war of 1954–62. They resulted in the incarceration of over 5,000 suspects, over 10,000 vehicles torched, more than 900 state institutions (most notably schools, police stations, and governmental offices) burnt, and over 200 injured – 70 of whom suffered permanent life-changing injuries.[46]

At the height of these riots, President Jacques Chirac, upon the insistence of his then-interior minister, Nicolas Sarkozy, issued Decree 1386, which declared a state of emergency throughout metropolitan France.[47] Under the conditions of the state of emergency, the French security forces ordered night curfews, had the right to impose arbitrary detention without legal counsel to the detainees for a period of up to 14 days, and had the right to infringe upon the laws of informational privacy on telephones and the internet.

Of utmost importance was the legislative path chosen by the French Government as it opted to declare a national state of emergency. Decree 1386 was not newly introduced legislation; rather, it was a renewal of the infamous 1955 state of emergency declared by the French Government against Algerian rioters during the first year of the French–Algerian war, in April 1955.[48] Capturing faithfully the historical overtones of this newly re-enacted emergency legislation, the *New York Times* correspondent to Paris wrote:

> critics said the introduction of curfews carried a more distant, and troubling, historical echo. The government is dusting off a law last used to stamp out unrest during the war in Algeria. In an unfortunate bit of symbolism, the critics said, those most affected by the decree would be the descendants of North Africans who

> were caught up in that French colonial misadventure. "Exhuming a 1955 law sends to the youth of the suburbs a message of astonishing brutality," the Paris daily *Le Monde* declared, "that after 50 years France intends to treat them exactly as it did their grandparents."[49]

The implications of the reinstatement of the Algerian wartime state of emergency in 2005 metropolitan France were self-evident. From the perspective of African-French migrants, most of who had already become naturalized citizens, the reinstatement of military legal tools from a bygone war into the public sphere of civil disobedience triggered harsh memories of the past. Writing for a human-rights NGO network, the francophone intellectual Achille Mbembe explained:

> Through the byway of the fight against the right of asylum, illegal immigration and terrorism, the sphere of rights has been invaded by legal conceptions relating to war. These conceptions have in turn provoked a clear resurgence of State racism, which as we know was one of the corner stones of the colonial order. The law is now being used not as a tool for rendering justice and guaranteeing freedom but as a stratagem that, if it does not authorize extreme violence, at least exposes the most vulnerable and deprived populations to extraordinary methods of repression. The great advantage of these methods is that they can be used rapidly, arbitrarily, almost irresponsibly. To control immigration, a segmenting of the administration of justice has come about.[50]

Mbembe refers here most notably to the infamous use of the 1955 emergency legislation during the final stages of the French–Algerian war.[51] On October 17, 1961 – on the orders of Maurice Papon, the Paris police prefect – French armed security forces and police officers shot dead some 200 civilian Algerian protesters who were taking part in a peaceful demonstration along the Seine, throwing their bodies overboard into the river waters.[52] The pretext for the killings, some of them carried out in custody within police stations, was the breaking of the curfew regulations of the 1955 emergency laws – the very same laws which were resurrected overnight on November 8, 2005.

The words of Justice Vogelmann concerning the use of bygone terms were as pertinent to the French case as Achille Mbembe's were to Israel. As their legislation of preference concerning African migrants, both countries chose the use of legal tools articulated and designed for the most extreme external wars which had threatened them long ago. For both Israel and France, the "importing" of wartime legal tools, originally designed for external application, for use against civilian non-combatant migrants, provided a vital insight into the extent of the danger these migrants had come to embody in the eyes of government officials. If anything, the French case was even worse than the Israeli one, since the people being targeted by the French measure were naturalized citizens, while Israel at least enjoyed a remote benefit of the doubt as it was dealing with clandestine migrants who were also Sudanese enemy nationals.

Fall 2005 witnessed the coinage and frequent use of the term *L'Intifada des banlieues* by the French media with reference to the eruption of acute social violence in urban outskirts from Paris to Marseille.[53] This adoption of a linguistic term borrowed from the Israeli–Palestinian conflict to describe social unrest in France echoed several mutual aspects between French and Israeli political heritages. These include a shared, unfinished, decolonization process (France in West Africa and the *Department d'Outre-Mer*; Israel in the Occupied Palestinian Territories) and a shared history of acute violence during periods of political transition – for example, the repeated assassination attempts on President Charles de Gaulle during the evacuation of Algeria and the political murder of Israeli Prime Minister Yitzhak Rabin, which cut short the Israeli–Palestinian peace process in 1995.[54] Moreover, both France and Israel shared a strong affinity toward overarching ideologies which had epistemologically shaped their political psyche. In France, it was the deeply enshrined concept of republicanism; in Israel, it was the prevalence of a Jewish demographic majority within "The Jewish State," as originally framed by Theodor Herzl.

As with the French case, the Israeli legislation was not new but rather an amendment of a 1954 anti-border transgression law passed during Israel's border conflict with Egypt and its proxies, the Palestinian Fada'ayun militias. As with the case of Algeria for France, this border conflict resulted in Israel eventually embarking on a full-scale war when it occupied the entire Sinai Peninsula during the 1956 Suez Canal crisis. At the time, the conflict was seen as the highest existential threat to the nascent Israeli state, established only eight years earlier with the

Holocaust as its background. At the end of the day, "The Law of 1955," as it was laconically referred to in the France of November 2005, was just as laden with historical significance and emotional baggage as was the 1954 Anti-Infiltration Act when reinstated in the Israel of 2012.[55] Israel was exceptional neither in the African migratory challenge it faced nor in the harsh legislative measure that it opted for as a remedy.

The Migrant as an Instrument for Deterrence

At the heart of the ruling which invalidated the 2012 Anti-Infiltration Act stood the rejection by the high court of arbitrary detention as a means for deterrence against other migrants wishing to enter Israeli territory clandestinely. Fundamentally, the court could not accept the objectification of migrants as a tool used by the State for the prevention of actions undertaken by others, without any wrongdoing on behalf of the incarcerated individuals. The implications of turning the incarcerated individuals from subjects into objects, in the Kantian sense of these terms, effectively meant that the State of Israel was stripping them of their humanity so as to use them as instruments for its policy objectives. As Justice Arbel explained:

> The objective of this law as drafted by the State is to halt the migratory phenomenon [...] there can be no doubt that the halting of African migration to Israel is a worthy cause. However, the implication of this legal cause is deterrence. That is to say, the mere placing of migrants in incarceration creates deterrence for other potential migrants from coming into Israel, knowing full well that they too shall be incarcerated [...] the difficulty with the deterrence objective is clear. A human being is incarcerated not because he personally poses any danger to society, but in order to deter others. He is not treated as an individual, but rather as a means to an end. This treatment without doubt further dehumanizes him as a man. The dignity of man means seeing him as the objective, and not as a means towards achieving other ends. Human beings shall always maintain an objective standing of their own. One must not see them as means only, nor as a commodity to be traded, the ultimate goal being as noble as it is. I myself have hitherto referred to this point that one must never treat a man as a

> means to an end, so as to achieve other external ends, since this inherently means harming his dignity, as we have learned from the venerable doctrine of the philosopher Emmanuel Kant.[56]

Justice Arbel also referred to previous high court rulings concerning foreign aliens in Israel and their incarceration, pointing to the clear consistency of her interpretation with those of her predecessors:

> The placing of the migrants in incarceration is not according to the criminal legal process, but rather executed as an administrative measure, by an administrative authority. The fact that the objective of the incarceration is deterrence is extremely difficult, once the incarcerated migrant becomes a tool for the achievement of the State's objectives. The key to his jail is in the hands of others, not in his own hands.[57]

Justice Arbel framed the illegality of migrant incarceration as stemming from the irrevocable stature of human dignity, as referred to in the philosophy of Emmanuel Kant – a humanist interpretation of the stature of the migrant which draws upon deep ethical roots. This idea of the sanctity and dignity of man dates back at least to the Renaissance period, with Pico Della Mirandola's *Oration on the Dignity of Man*, and can be followed through in Kant's *Metaphysics of Morals* and in its modern-day application in Jean-Paul Sartre's *L'exitensialisme est un humanisme*. Justice Arbel's refusal to accept the State's instrumentalisation of existing African migrants as a tool in the service of the State's declared objective of deterrence, and her specific reference to Kantian ethical principles, projected the legal debate back into the spheres of natural-law theories and the centrality of man's inalienable rights.

Spanning the entire spectrum of Western philosophy, and therefore far beyond the scope of this study, one key element of natural-law theories since the Renaissance views man as the center of creation.[58] Put briefly, the history of the idea of man unequivocally maintains his *a priori* existence and subsequent rights and dignities, *prior* to any definition or category to which he belongs: social, political, racial, gender-based, or indeed migratory. In short, the African migrant is first a human being with certain rights stemming from his humanity *inter alia* – in this case, his rights to freedom and to protection from arbitrary detention.

This point is at the heart of Justice Arbel's reference to the concept of the dignity of man by Kant, who is explicitly quoted on this by Sartre. In relation to different definitions of migrants as refugees, asylum seekers, infiltrators, economic migrants, voluntary migrants, and so on, Arbel's reference to Kant inherently gave precedence to the humanity of migrants over their specific categorization. In Jean-Paul Sartre's *L'exitensialisme est un humanisme*, this idea is crystallized in the precedence given to human existence over essence:

> there is at least one being whose existence comes before his essence, a being which exists before it can be defined by any conception of it. That being is man [...] What do I mean by saying that existence precedes essence? We mean that man first of all exist, encounters himself, surges up in the world – and defines himself afterwards.[59]

In its recent ruling, from early 2012, the European Court of Human Rights reprimanded the Italian Government for illegally turning back refugees from its borders and territorial waters. The European Court emphasized that the obligations for refugee protections stemmed from the original humanitarian intentions of the drafters of the 1951 Refugee Convention, to which Italy is a signatory. The court also reiterated its belief in the precedence of the statue of man, prior to his categorization into a certain migrant category of, say, refugee or asylum seeker:

> A person does not become a refugee because of recognition, but is recognized because he or she is a refugee. As the determination of refugee status is merely declaratory, the principle of Non-Refoulement applies to those who have not yet had their status declared [asylum seekers] and even to those who have not expressed their wish to be protected.[60]

Non-Refoulement, Illegal Incarceration, and the Enhancement of Freedom

Perhaps the most important consequence, of the Israeli Supreme Court ruling which invalidated the 2012 Anti-Infiltration Act was the conjunction between the principle of non-refoulement and the illegality of arbitrary detention. The sequential combination of these two principles, in the case of migrants meriting protection, effectively turned the principle of non-refoulement into a freedom-securing legal mechanism. This evolutionary development in the implications of non-refoulement was definitely not envisaged by its original authors, Samuel Hoare and Jacob Robinson. Rather, it was due to the evolvement of international humanitarian law over the past five decades. The elevation of the principle of non-refoulement to the status of *jus cogens*, coupled with the progress in terms of the definitions and limitations of incarceration norms under international law, carry significant implications. This conjunction effectively meant that once Israel had applied the non-refoulement principle to Eritrean and Sudanese migrants, it had also implicitly necessitated their freedom so long as they posed no security threat and in so far as no third country of asylum would accept them.

The first reference to non-refoulement appeared at the very beginning of the high court's ruling, when Justice Arbel explained its importance to all migrants regardless of whether they had attained refugee status or not.[61]

In his concurring opinion to that of Justice Arbel, Justice Yoram Danziger further refuted the State's claim that all the asylum seekers were in fact economic migrants whose deportation was therefore allegedly merited:

> One cannot overlook the fact that the inconclusiveness as to the quality of these "infiltrators" and whether they are economic migrants or indeed refugees meriting political asylum – stems from the failed manner with which the State has treated them. For years, the State has refrained from examining their refugee status pleas tabled by these Eritrean and Sudanese nationals on a case by case basis, whilst on the other hand the State has accorded them temporary protection from Refoulement.[62]

The explicit interpretation of non-refoulement as freedom from detention lay at the heart of the Sudanese and Eritrean plaintiffs' plea against the State. The first and major legal argument by the plaintiffs was simple and straightforward: given that over 90 percent of the illegal African migrants originated from Sudan and Eritrea, they had come under the protection of the non-refoulement principle in any case. Once these migrants had obtained the right to reside in Israel by virtue of their non-refoulement protection, they were entitled to the right to freedom under Israel's Basic Law, a right denied them by the 2012 Anti-Infiltration Act.[63]

Justice Arbel proceeded to examine internal Israeli law and international law in tandem, both from the point of view of the explicit objective of the government legislation – namely, to deter further migrants from crossing into Israel. After an extensive review of UN High Commissioner for Human Rights' guidelines concerning non-refoulement and the justified detention of migrants, and the positions of the European Court of Human Rights, Justice Arbel concluded in the following words:

> The current situation is one where most migrants currently under imprisonment, are asylum seekers in any case, and this is not dependant on the question whether their requests for refugee status shall eventually be accepted or not. Thus, the overwhelming majority of these incarcerated migrants are subject to the principle of Non-Refoulement, which does not permit their return back to their countries of origin at this stage. International law is more stringent when concerned with asylum seekers and with the countries within whose territories they are present. In 2012 UNHCR published a set of updated detention guidelines concerning asylum seekers [...] briefly, I would conclude that even these guidelines stipulate that no detention can be arbitrary, and moreover, they specifically underscore the need for every detention to be based upon a particular weighing of the circumstances of each and every detainee.[64]

Thus, the conjunction between non-refoulement and freedom had been established. Once the State designated a group of migrants as asylum seekers worthy of non-refoulement protections, it had *inter alia* established their protection from arbitrary detention.

Justice Arbel's position, which maintained the inherent connection between non-refoulement and protection from arbitrary detention, was repeated by Justice Vogelmann. In his concurring opinion, Vogelmann refers to the Attorney General's official position (declared and highlighted in the State's reply to the plaintiffs) that Israel implemented a policy of "temporary Non-Refoulement" concerning the return of Eritrean nationals to Eritrea.[65] Justice Vogelmann rejected most of the Attorney General's legal arguments, and foremost amongst those was the distinction made by the State between "temporary Non-Refoulement," which the State claimed it was executing on its own humanitarian behalf, and the general principle of non-refoulement according to recognized international law:

> the State has claimed that its policy of temporary Non-Refoulement exercised towards Eritrean nationals, is a humanitarian step by the State of Israel, the result of an administrative authorities' decision according to internal Israeli legislation, and has no connection to any legal obligation by the state. On the contrary, the principle of Non-Refoulement, to which the state refers to in its arguments for defense, derives from Article 33 of the 1951 Refugee Convention, as well as from Article 3 of the 1984 Convention Against Torture, and is moreover not limited to these conventions alone. We are speaking of a *Jus Cogens* principle accepted throughout Customary International law, a universal principle also internalized into the Israeli legal system, whereby no man is expelled to a place where his life or liberty are endangered.[66]

The artificial distinction drawn by the State between its so-called "temporary Non-Refoulement" and a "permanent" protection from refoulement was conditioned upon the procedural mechanics inherent in the Refugee Status Determination (RSD) procedure Israel was supposed to undertake vis-à-vis every single migrant on a case-by-case basis. Though this was the explicit commitment which the state took upon itself – and which Advocate Sternberg vouched for during the legislative stages of the 2012 Anti-Infiltration Act – in reality, the State had never actually intended to execute the RSD procedure in the first place. Less than three months after the supreme court's ruling, the full extent of the State's intellectual dishonesty was unveiled.

Over a period of three years, between 2010 and 2013, 1,800 RSD requests had been officially tabled at the Israeli Interior Ministry. Of these requests (over a 3-year period!), a mere 250 had been examined by the Israeli authorities. Furthermore, of these, not one single RSD request was found worthy of refugee status. In comparison, during the same time period, the average European positive RSD request ratio in the cases of Sudanese and Eritrean nationals stood at 70 percent.[67]

As Vincent Chetail has convincingly explained, nowadays the practice of RSD has somewhat unofficially evolved into a two-staged procedure. Given UNHCR's explicit requirement that RSD be administered by states in a transparent and orderly fashion, and in order to exclude "preventive refoulement" (a situation whereby a State deliberately turns refugees away so as to avoid the "headache" of carrying out the RSD procedure) virtually all asylum seekers receive some sort of immediate "technical" protection from refoulement so as to provide the State with time to carry out the RSD procedure in full. Only once RSD has been concluded, and in the event that no sufficient grounds for granting refugee status have been established, can the migrant concerned be expelled.[68]

By administering its "temporary Non-Refoulement," the State opted for providing the first "unofficial" protection within Chetail's two-stage process, yet with the implicit intention never to reach the second "permament" stage of protection from refoulement, which could only be granted if and when an RSD procedure had been concluded. The State explicitly stated that its "temporary Non-Refoulement" did not consist of the granting of non-refoulement protection, but rather that it was doing so *ex gratia*.[69]

Ultimately, the high court revoked the State's inventive approach as it created a non-existent category within international refugee law: that of "temporary Non-Refoulement." As she quoted previous opinions from other verdicts by Justices Vogelmann and Esther Chayut regarding the problematic implications of the temporary nature of this State policy, Justice Arbel remarked:

> there is a problem in maintaining a policy of temporary protection permanently, and after a certain period of time the State must examine the entitlement for refugee status. The implications of Israel's policy vis-à-vis Eritrean nationals has never been sufficiently clarified by the State [...] as Justice Chayut has already established, this situation is "especially" undesirable. This normative fog creates a heavily burdening uncertainty for these

> people themselves [...] the Courts too are compelled to put up with the different and varied conditions and circumstances, which evidently, this living reality creates for these people.[70]

At the end of the day, the court's verdict effectively reiterated the permanence of non-refoulement, which the State deviously and deliberately wanted to avoid.

The Humanitarian Imperatives of Jewish Law and History

Some of the most important passages in the high court's ruling – which bestowed considerable measures of humanitarianism upon the African migrants, in contrast to the government's legislation and policies – were based on Jewish legal principles. Three of the nine presiding judges (Edna Arbel, Isaac Amit, and Neil Hendel) drew extensively from Jewish scriptures and legal commentaries as they substantiated their concurring legal opinions.

This recourse to Jewish legal scriptures has to be understood within its general context. In Israel, references to religious rulings and jurisprudence are often intuitively associated with right-wing settlement activities in the OPT, or with the curtailment of civic freedoms due to Israel's lack of separation between religion and state. That the main editorial in *Haaretz* on September 17, 2013 should begin with a direct quote from the verdict of the Israeli Supreme Court, based upon Jewish religious legal sources and written by a supreme court judge (Isaac Amit) with a religious background, was not self-evident. Nor were the ethical predicaments so bluntly expressed in Justice Amit's quoted words:

> With regard to those asylum seekers who have already reached our abode, after having crossed other countries and thousands of kilometers of wilderness by tortuous routes, and traversed hundreds of kilometers of the Sinai Desert, where some fell victim to evildoers who tortured them, abused them, raped their wives and daughters, and sometimes even killed some of them in various ways. Once they reached our borders, wounded in body and soul, we should have welcomed them [...] bound up their wounds of body and soul and treated them with generosity and compassion with respect to work, welfare, health and education.[71]

As with all selective quotes, the portions of the text omitted from the published quote were as interesting as the text included. Being a left-wing secular newspaper, *Haaretz* and its editors did not take the trouble to mention the fact that they had omitted Justice Amit's explicit reference to the Bible. In the missing quote towards the end of the paragraph, marked above by the ellipsis, Amit wrote what he, as a supreme court magistrate, expected to have been the message from the Israeli Government to the tortured asylum seekers from Sudan and Eritrea:

> We ought to have told them "Let a little water, I pray you, be fetched, and wash your feet, and rest yourselves under the tree".[72]

The educated reader would immediately recognize this famous passage from the Old Testament, where Abraham receives the three angels who bring forth the good news that his wife, Sarah, will bear their son, Isaac (Genesis 18:4). The well-known New Testament parallel to this passage unfolds as Jesus washes the feet of his disciples (John 13:5).[73] In both Jewish and Muslim traditions, Abraham's greeting of God's messengers bearing the news of Isaac's arrival is one of hospitality and protection, starkly contrasted with the evildoings of the people of Sodom and Gomorrah. Both the Old Testament (Genesis 18) and the Qur'an (Surat Al Hud 11:69–83) deliberately juxtapose Abraham's protection of the three strangers (God's angels, unbeknownst to him) in face of the evil, harmful intentions of the people of Sodom and Gomorrah against these seemingly defenseless strangers who had found refuge in his tent.[74] This human need for protection from evil, granted by Abraham in both Jewish and Muslim traditions, and its absence thereof towards African migrants in twenty-first-century Israel, was highlighted by Justice Amit as he referred to the world's indifference toward Jewish sufferings during World War II. Israel's vital involvement in the making of the 1951 Refugee Convention, as a direct consequence of the Jewish Holocaust, could not be overlooked:

> The State of Israel and the Jewish NGOs took an active part in the drafting of the 1951 Convention Relating to the Status of Refugees, in direct relation to the Second World War and the

> Jewish Shoa, and the State of Israel was also one of the first countries to sign and ratify this Convention. And not for nothing.
>
> The story of the passenger ship Saint Louis is still scarred within our flesh and consciousness as an open wound, as a historical lesson, and a byword to refugees and asylum seekers unwanted anywhere. The ship set sail from Germany in May 1939 after *Kristallnacht* with 1,000 Jewish passengers onboard whose entry was forbidden into the USA and Cuba. The ship finally returned to Europe, where a few countries agreed to receive some of its passengers, of whom many – with the exception of those who were taken in by the UK – were annihilated during the Jewish Holocaust.[75]

The most important references to Jewish law and jurisprudence (*Hamishpat Ha'ivri*) in the supreme court's revocation of the 2012 Anti-Infiltration Act were inserted towards the end of Justice Arbel's main concurring opinion. In her final remarks she wrote,

> I thought it appropriate to refer to our Hebrew Bible and the heritage of our Jewish forefathers, which serve as a primary guidance for us to this day. In the Book of Deuteronomy 23:15–17 it is written:
>
> "15: Thou shalt not deliver unto his master the slave which has escaped from his master unto thee. 16: He shall dwell with thee, even among you, in that place which he shall choose in one of thy gates, where it liketh him best: thou shalt not oppress him."
>
> Biblical interpreters have maintained that the above passage refers to a *non-Jewish* slave, fleeing his master in a foreign land and finding refuge in the land of Israel. One ought to cite here the teachings of nineteenth-century religious scholar and Jewish community leader Rabbi Samson Raphael Hirsch regarding these verses: Hirsch extends the responsibilities of the Israeli authorities of the time, compelling them to provide protection and care for this slave, to secure his release, and to grant him the full and equal rights of a citizen.
>
> The authorities of Israel are bound by law to provide this slave with protection and care, as per the decrees of Maimonides

> (Laws of Slaves 88), they must free this slave and for this purpose they must confront his master with the choice, either the master signs his writ of release receiving a debt certificate for his blood, and if the master refuses, the Jewish Court expropriates this slave from the master's hands and frees his blood. Once the slave is free, he becomes a permanent resident with full rights of any Jewish citizen and enjoys the protections of Jewish Public Law and the community.[76]

Justice Arbel's reference to the biblical commentary by Rabbi Hirsch carried special contextual significance. Hirsch had been born in Hamburg into a religious orthodox Jewish family that had produced a long lineage of rabbis dating back some 200 years. After receiving rabbinical ordination, Hirsch studied at the University of Bonn alongside Abraham Geiger, the main figure of nineteenth-century Reform Judaism in Germany. Hirsch rejected Geiger's drift away from orthodoxy, yet completely identified with the need to adapt his orthodoxy to modern-day European Jewish life. After a short and fruitful rabbinical tenure in the northern German city of Oldenburg, Hirsch came to lead the Jewish community in Frankfurt am Main, the main community heir to the medieval legacy of Rashi in Mainz and Worms, the epicenter of Ashkenazi Jewish thought. In Frankfurt, Hirsch established the neo-orthodox movement, with which he has been most prominently identified since his death in 1888.[77] At the heart of neo-orthodoxy stood the conjunction between Jewish law, as established in the Torah, and a universal morality which Hirsch identified as dating back to the venerable figure of Rabbi Gamliel in the Talmud. Justice Arbel's reference to Hirsch, in connection to the obligations vested upon the Jewish state, struck at the heart of the African migrant issue, since Hirsch was an unwavering advocate for universal moral values which, to his mind, were totally immersed in Jewish neo-orthodoxy. Some 20 years prior to Theodor Herzl, it was Hirsch who first began referring to "the Jewish State" in his biblical commentary on the Torah, which he wrote between 1867 and 1878.[78]

Hirsch's view of the obligations of the Jewish state are best observed in his commentary on the book of Exodus 22:20 and 23:9. Here, in the legal predicaments obligating the Jewish state vis-à-vis the most vulnerable members of society – the foreigner, the orphan, and the widow – Hirsch presented his views concerning foreign migrants coming into that state in terms almost identical to those of Justice Arbel's ruling.[79] Her quotations concerning foreign slaves in the book of Deuteronomy indeed rested upon previous definitions concerning the Jewish state's social and legal obligations toward the migrant foreigner, stated three books earlier in the book of Exodus:

> Thou shall neither vex a stranger nor oppress him: for ye were strangers in the land of Egypt (Exodus 22:20)

The pronouncement of the vulnerability of the stranger, and the Jewish need to identify with the suffering and hardships of foreign migrants, are again espoused in the next chapter of the book of Exodus:

> Also thou shalt not oppress a stranger: for ye know the heart of a stranger, seeing ye were strangers in the land of Egypt (Exodus 23:9)

The inconsistencies of the translation of The King James Version, switching between the terms "foreigner" and "stranger" are not to be found in the Hebrew original, which consistently uses the term – גר in Hebrew. Rashi's medieval commentary to Exodus 22:20 leaves no room for error as to whom the biblical text refers, by his use of the term גר:

> All references to גר: a person not born in that country, but who arrived from another country to reside there.[80]

With this clarification of the terms in mind, Hirsch explains:

> A person born as a non-Jew, once he has entered the custody of the Jews, while accepting he is under the fundamentals of Jewish life, he is therefore entitled to complete and utter equality (שיווין גמור), and to all rights amongst the Jews, according to the Jewish Law (Torah). The connection here between these different biblical verses reiterates a significant law which the Torah repeats in several places namely: Human dignity and citizenship, and human rights and residential rights are not conditioned in any way upon a person's country of birth [the German here is *Heimat*], his ancestry or his

> material assets, and are not conditioned by anything external or accidental, but are solely and only derived from the spiritual-moral value of the human inner personality. *Seeing ye were strangers in the land of Egypt* – comes to safeguard this principle from any qualification whatsoever. This is not the same as the reasoning "for ye know the heart of a stranger" since the scripture here speaks in the full affirmative "ye were strangers in the land of Egypt". Your entire calamity in Egypt was due to this fact that you were "strangers" there, and as such were devoid from any rights, thus according to the view of the other nations, rights to land, to a motherland, even to existence, and your masters could do with you as they pleased. As strangers – you had no rights in Egypt and this was the basis for your enslavement, and the torture vested upon you. Therefore beware – and this is the meaning of God's warning – beware of the establishment of human rights on anything else other than pure humanity (האנושיות הטהורה) which is vested in each and every single human being as a human. Any breach of human rights shall open the flood gates of social mal-intent and human abuse – the root causes of all the evil in Egypt [. . .] in most States foreigners are evilly discriminated against and their rights are revoked – by law, which is why the *Jewish State* has been warned of this practice.[81]

Hirsch's emphasis upon the State's obligation to uphold the human rights and civil liberties of the vulnerable portions of society (in this case, the foreign migrant, the widow, and the orphan) should be read within its nineteenth-century German context. While the language here, concerning the correct ordering of the State's affairs and the principles it ought to adhere to, was clearly Weberian, the emphasis on granting of civil rights by the State had specific Jewish connotations. As Shlomo Avineri has recently demonstrated in his seminal archival research on the family of Karl Marx in Trier, Jewish civil liberties (such as the right to practice as an attorney at law, in the case of Marx's father) were contingent and changed frequently – in the case of Marx, due to the European restoration of 1814 and the revocation of Napoleon's legal code.[82] The arbitrariness of Trier's return from French to German rule, and the demand from Marx's father to renounce his Judaism so as to continue practicing his legal profession as an attorney-at-law, served as the backdrop to Hirsch's thinking on how the envisaged Jewish state ought to treat the vulnerable.[83]

Hirsch's emphasis on the legal and specifically judicial implications of the religious protection provided by the Torah to foreign migrants was ultimately expounded upon in his commentary on Exodus 23:9. With the Pentateuch (the Torah) being a distinctly minimalistic text, any repetition in it usually commands an abundance of explanatory material from commentators. When coming to explain the repetition of the words "ye were strangers in the land of Egypt," which appeared in the earlier chapter, Hirsch provided a full conception of the basic legal precepts for the future Jewish state:

> In the previous reference the Torah opened and consecrated the two social principles of the Jewish State in Israel: the principle of *total equality in front of the law* and the *principle of love and charity towards all persons in society requiring social assistance*. All the correlating laws simply result from these two principles concerning the administration of *justice* according to the *principle of equality* and to the adherence of *society* to the charity principle. Our current verse repeats and reiterates the principles of equality and charity, and it is on these principles that the Jewish State shall administer its policies towards foreigners: these shall enjoy the full legal rights of a citizen, and shall benefit from an attitude of love and charity, and these shall always serve as the true benchmark [of] the State's humanity and rule of law [. . .] these laws serve to instill in the hearts and minds of the citizens the notion that they too will see themselves as nothing more than mere residents and foreigners in God's Country [. . .] while the granting of full human rights is a duty bestowed upon the entirety of society, the duty to charity is individual.[84]

The State Replies: Third-Country Forced Resettlement

As the legal challenge to the 2012 Anti-Infiltration Act mounted in the corridors of the Israeli Supreme Court, the State began to scramble for additional arguments to substantiate its claim for the justification of the inhumane, unlimited jailing of the African migrants. In June 2013, two months before the anticipated verdict by the enlarged nine-judge chamber of the supreme court, the Attorney General seemed to be "pulling rabbits out of hats." As a measure of last resorts, the state attorneys begged the supreme court to strike down the pro-migrant lobby's plea against the 2012 Anti-Infiltration Act, claiming that a settlement with a third-party country of voluntary asylum had been reached, rendering the plea non-relevant.[85] To the Court's astonishment, at the very same time that the Attorney General was arguing for the removal of the pro-migrant plea due to the finding of a designated country of asylum, another branch of government contradicted that very claim. As the court adjourned at the end of that day, the spokesperson for the Israeli Ministry of Foreign Affairs confirmed the official ministerial position: that Israel had not concluded any such agreement with any third country, let alone any country in Africa. The spokesperson confirmed that Israel had indeed proposed to 30 African countries the creation of agricultural farms with Israeli funding where foreign migrants were supposed to take up employment, yet no country had agreed to this trade-off.[86]

In mid-June 2013, the picture began to clear, as the State was compelled to make its final submissions to the supreme court concerning the NGO plea against the 2012 Anti-Infiltration Act. Countering the claims voiced by the Foreign Ministry, the Attorney General submitted an affidavit from Prime Minister Netanyahu's personal envoy charged with the African-migrant file, which further clarified the issues at stake. In his affidavit to the supreme court, Hagai Hadas clearly stated:

> Following the explicit request for complete secrecy tabled by the involved countries who have agreed to accept the discussed migrants, due to the high political sensitivity of the issue, we have committed ourselves and so have they, to refrain from exposing the identity of these countries, their willingness to engage and help on this issue and the details involved [. . .] the negotiations are at a very advanced stage, and during my last visit, this country has agreed to accept a part of these migrants. We still have to conclude the operative details and specific issues to conclude concerning this migrant group. We are speaking of an African country, to which these certain migrants shall arrive in civilian aircraft.[87]

Israeli cooperation with other countries, along with the attempted "outsourcing" of the African migrant issue, was being carried out in the utmost secrecy. This secrecy began with the biographical profile of the person chosen by Prime Minister Netanyahu as his personal envoy on the migrant issue. Hagai Hadas was neither a police official nor an immigration-service veteran, but rather a former senior spy who had served a decades-long career in Israel's foreign espionage organization, Mossad – a fact which also came to explain the Foreign Ministry's lack of any knowledge about his clandestine negotiations with other countries. The habitual features of the espionage world, of deniability and varying degrees of "truth management," began to make themselves apparent as the pressure from Israeli investigative journalists intensified. Hadas' alleged "agreement with certain African governments" was suddenly watered down into "a general understanding," finally becoming "a general objective" once an oath was required to be taken before the supreme court.[88]

A week after the hearing of June 9, 2013, further exposures of Hadas' half-truths, which he had declared before the supreme court, began to appear. In two separate reports by the two leading newspapers in Israel, *Haaretz* and *Yediot Aharonot*, journalists confirmed that at least 177 Sudanese and Eritrean nationals had been deported from Israel. According to both reports, the migrants had been coerced into signing "voluntary return requests" in a procedure which had received the legal endorsement of the Attorney General, Yehuda Weinstein.[89] In a combined journalistic investigative effort with news sources in Khartoum, and following the examination of the civilian flight records out of Israel, *Haaretz* confirmed that no aircraft had left Israeli airspace for Sudan, an enemy country, in July 2013. Rather, and in direct contradiction to the statements made by Hagai Hadas to the supreme court, the north-Sudanese migrants were secretly shipped over the border into Jordan. With the state of war between Israel and Sudan, and the lack of any consular facilities between the two countries, Israel had enlisted the help of the Jordanian secret-service authorities. These in turn had engaged with the consular section at the Sudanese embassy in Jordan's capital, Amman, ultimately issuing the international travel papers required by international law for the deportation of these migrants.[90]

With one month left before the verdict date of the supreme court regarding the legality of the 2012 Anti-Infiltration Act, the inconsistencies exposed in the government's line of argument began to extract a heavy political toll, especially with the pressure of the investigative media outlets.[91] By the end of August 2013, just two weeks before the verdict date, the Israeli system of military censorship which oversees all publications by media outlets in the country was forced by *Haaretz* newspaper to disclose information regarding the pending agreement with a third-party African country. Fearing the issuance of a freedom-of-information court order which would compel the State to disclose in full all the details concerned, a government spokesperson agreed to the release of details of the agreement, thus preempting the newspaper's plea to the court.[92]

As the investigative-journalism campaign intensified, the full extent of the government's actions began to come to light. As it turned out, Israel had forcefully returned over 2,000 north-Sudanese migrants, some of them victims of the Darfur Genocide, to Sudan via third countries, in most cases Egypt and Uganda, with some of the migrants being stranded between the two countries.[93] As the interior minister, Eli Yishai, began taking pride in his ability to supposedly solve the African migrant problem by instigating mass deportations, Israel gradually found itself in a diplomatic skirmish with in-country UNHCR representatives.[94] Attempting to halt the diplomatic and media tidal wave, the Israeli attorney general, Yehuda Weinstein, ordered the immediate halting of the deportation of the Eritrean migrants until further notice, or at least until he could find ample legal justification to explain the State's actions in court.[95]

As news emerged that agreement to deport the Eritrean and Sudanese migrants from Israel had supposedly been secured with Uganda, few eyebrows were raised – and definitely none among pro-migrant NGOs, given the special Israeli–Ugandan relationship. As *Haaretz* newspaper continued to badger government spokespeople for more information, its chief investigative correspondent, Anshel Pfeffer, managed to expose the secretive espionage trail which underpinned the alleged Israeli–Ugandan agreement:

> The secret agreement between the governments of Israel and Uganda over the deportation of African migrants to Uganda is not surprising considering the warm relations between the two countries in the seventeen years since Yoweri Museveni came to power. Museveni's government has maintained close ties with Israel and has signed numerous deals for weapons systems, agricultural

> technology and medical assistance. One of the key figures in the relationship has been Rafi Eitan, a former Mossad official, who was also the leader of the now-defunct Pensioners Party and a minister in the Olmert government. Eitan has business interests in Uganda and he is a confidante of Museveni. He accompanied the Ugandan president on his two visits to Israel [. . .] The Ugandan military, which has been involved in the fighting in Rwanda, in the Democratic Republic of Congo and in its own northern provinces against rebels, has received significant Israeli military aid. According to foreign media reports, Israeli weapons supplies have included self-propelled cannons and mortars, artillery shells, surveillance systems, modernization of its ageing MiG-21 fighter jets and the training of its pilots in Israel. There have also been reports of supplies of Israeli drones to Uganda.[96]

No sooner had Pfeffer's investigative article gone to press than the pro-migrant NGO lobby and the public radio and television talk shows began their all-out onslaught on the clandestine government agreement. The involvement of former senior Mossad agents such as Rafi Eytan and Hagai Hadas in the negotiations, and the clear trade-offs between firearms and military equipment and the "counter-currency" in the form of the deportation of the African migrants, all created high levels of hostility and disgust among the Israeli general public against the Israeli–Ugandan agreement. Even more alarming from the government's perspective was the fact that its distraction strategy vis-à-vis the upcoming supreme court verdict had now been exposed. In an additional submission of evidence to the supreme court, the advocates for the pro-migrant lobby who had tabled the plea against the 2012 Anti-Infiltration Act in the first place wrote:

> For years the Interior Ministry [has been] talking about a third country which would "purchase" Israel's African migrants, against hard currency and arms, and Uganda's name has already come up in the past. However, it has turned out that Uganda is not a safe country, and there is no way to guarantee the safety of those who shall be deported to it. The Ministry of Interior does not disclose when the agreement shall be taking place, how many people will be deported and who guarantees their safety.[97]

Referring to the government's failed legal strategy in attempting to circumvent the wrath of the supreme court, the pro-migrant attorneys clearly pointed to the deliciously savory "red herring" with which the government was trying to distract the court so as to avoid the ramifications of the latter's severe judicial criticism:

> The sole purpose of the publication of this theoretical and non-existent agreement with Uganda, is to reinvigorate and resuscitate the discussion concerning the deportation to a third country, so as to influence the decision of the justices of the Supreme Court via media outlet reports, so that they will not issue a harsh verdict on the plea against the Anti-Infiltration Act.[98]

The ink had hardly dried on the investigative reports by the *Haaretz* correspondents before swift and clear denials regarding the Israeli–Ugandan migrant-deportation agreement began coming through the wire from the highest government echelons and the spokesperson for the Ugandan Ministry of Foreign Affairs. Under pressure from the press, and confronted with the diplomatic embarrassment which resulted from the Ugandan swift and clear denials of any African migrant-deportation agreement with Israel, the Israeli Interior Ministry finally succumbed to pressure to provide public explanations. A ministry spokesperson confirmed that, indeed, no agreement had been either reached or signed with Uganda.[99] With over 60,000 migrants directly targeted by the Israeli Interior Ministry for incarceration or deportation, the discovery that Hagai Hadas' affidavit to the supreme court referred at best to a few hundred migrants further undermined government credibility. What had begun in June 2013 as an instantaneous government solution for the African migrant problem, presented to the high court by ex-security officials speaking on behalf of the Prime Minister, turned out to be nothing more than a series of inconclusive discussions used to throw sand in the eyes of the judges. This red herring, deliberately waved by the government, had begun to smell foul – if not to stink outright. On September 16, 2013, as the supreme court handed down its verdict, Justice Vogelmann eloquently put in writing how the members of the bench actually saw the whole third-country deportation farce:

In its reply to the plea, the argument has been made by the State that it is currently in negotiations with other countries, so as to facilitate the deportation from Israel of the Eritrean and Sudanese migrants not entitled to Political asylum in Israel. How does this argument bear upon our judicial criticism? if one would have spoken of a realistic option for the existence of deportation arrangements in the immediate future, arrangements which would have coincided with Israel's international obligations and its internal legislation, these might have brought the possibility of viewing this as a change in the evidence platform established before us. That is not the case here.

I do not see how these generalist comments brought before us on this issue change our ruling, even if we assume for the sake of the benefit of the State's argumentation, that it has any real truth in it.[100]

CHAPTER 8

INCARCERATION, FORCED RESETTLEMENT, AND THE ENSUING CONSTITUTIONAL CRISIS

The supreme court's revocation of the 2012 Anti-Infiltration Act caught the entire Israeli political establishment by surprise. It is safe to say that a significant portion of the country's political class did not believe that the high court would overturn government legislation in this case. Even the most stringent pundits, who did believe the high court would eventually intervene given the harsh inhumane measures stipulated by the new anti-migrant legislation, could not have anticipated the forcefulness and resolve shown by the court in its revocation. The flat-out concurrence of entire the bench against the government's position, and the unanimous voice of all nine judges without any dissenting opinion, was unequivocal; the government had failed colossally. Yet during the 18-odd months between the Knesset's adoption of the 2012 Anti-Infiltration Act and the high court's revocation thereof, a comprehensive government strategy designed to rid Israel of its existing African migrants had been enacted.

Durable solutions for refugees as stipulated by International law and UNHCR include three "classic" options: Repatriation (to the refugee's country of origin), local integration (in the refugee's current country of asylum), and resettlement (in third-party countries, which are neither the country of origin nor the country of asylum).[1] With repatriation excluded (due to the deteriorating humanitarian conditions in Eritrea and Sudan), and with the government's refusal to consider any local integration modalities, Israel's sole solution was one of resettlement. This, in essence, was what the government presented to the high court as its solution of choice, as per Israel's secret negotiations with African countries aimed at the resettlement of the migrants there in exchange for economic and military favors.[2]

"Venue Shopping" and Migrant Outsourcing by Western Countries

In recent years, several Western nations have resorted to agreements with under-developed countries so as to block illegal immigrant flows across their borders, using those countries as offshore detention centers for their clandestine migrants caught onshore. These migrants are then deported beyond the borders or territorial waters of those Western countries and are usually left, uncared for, to their own fate. Generic examples of this practice included Italy's secret agreements (during Silvio Berlusconi's premiership) with Libya under the dictatorship of Mu'ammer Gaddafi; Spain's arrangement with Morocco over the Gibraltar straits and the Melilla enclave; and Australia's deal for detention centers in Papua New Guinea, and its agreements with Indonesia.[3] In essence, all these bilateral interstate arrangements provided a remedy for the phenomenon of non-regulated migrant flows that overrode state controls as they entered these Western countries clandestinely. "Off-shoring" deprived these migrants from the ability to demand asylum as they stepped onto the host country's territory.

Refugee flows pose a perennial dilemma for states that are, on the one hand, committed to universal human-rights standards and, on the one hand, are determined to halt by all means the entry of people they do not desire into their territory. This conundrum is further exacerbated by the logical paradox of trying to maintain human-rights standards *within* one's territory while settling for, and sometimes actively instigating, major human-rights violations *beyond* one's borders so as to keep out the unwanted.

The actions of Western governments, working in close operational proximity to non-human-rights-abiding states from the developing world, can take different forms. These range from merely returning seafaring migrants back to the shores they came from to deep and continuous cooperation with local authorities, enticing the latter to take hard measures to prevent migrants from embarking on the outward maritime journey in the first place. The deep cooperation between the Libyan Coast Guard and Italian immigration authorities, later critically examined and criticized by the European Court of Human Rights, has already been mentioned.[4] The example set by Italy with its Libyan operation was also followed by Spain in its close cooperation with the immigration and security forces of Morocco, along with the latter's harsh onslaught on migrants and violent infringements of their human rights.[5] Much of the same could be said for Malta.[6]

The idea of "outsourcing" the responsibility for migrant asylum seekers, and their handing over to non-human-rights-abiding countries beyond the judicial sphere of Western democracies, is neither new, nor has it been tacitly disguised in any sort of way. As early as 2004, the European Union officially discussed the possibility of what it called the "off-shoring" and outsourcing of its migrant problems to other neighboring states. This proposal was fought long and hard by pro-human-rights advocates in Brussels, and was finally turned down thanks to the efforts of the British prime minister at the time, Tony Blair.[7] To a large extent, the American practice of using an offshore territory such as Guantanamo Bay for carrying out unconstitutional practices outside the limits of the US judicial system was not fundamentally different.

Silja Klepp has demonstrated the complex and covert mechanics underlying European diplomacy geared towards preventing African asylum seekers from entering "Fortress Europe." The African refugee and asylum-seeking tidal wave that engulfed southern Europe in 2009–11 prompted European border countries (Greece, Spain, Malta, and Italy) to enact proactive policies to halt the coming ashore of these migrants, along with their forceful return to the African continent.[8]

Klepp pointed to the troubling tendency whereby Western governments abused their diplomatic leverage in relations with economically weaker Third World countries bordering their Mediterranean territorial waters. These Third World countries then proceeded, on behalf of their "patrons," to prevent asylum seekers from leaving their African shores, thus curtailing their ability to apply for refugee status on European soil. In cases of undocumented asylum seekers, the Third World countries provided detention facilities for African detainees caught in Europe, whom the European countries often forcefully returned back to Africa. In most cases, the incarcerated detainees were not nationals of the African country that jailed them, and, without identity papers, lacked any prospects for humanitarian protection. In return for their cooperation, the Third World countries usually enjoyed development assistance in infrastructure, mostly for the construction of jailing facilities, aid in policing materials, and military aid which enhanced their armed naval and maritime policing capacities.[9]

On February 23, 2012, the European Court of Human Rights unanimously ruled that Italy had breached the non-refoulement principle by illegally turning back refugees from within and beyond its territorial waters, through its naval "push back operations" across Mediterranean waters, toward Libya.[10] This verdict effectively reversed ten years of European "venue shopping" policies, with EU states' navies now performing search-and-rescue operations so as to save African "boat people" and bring them to detention facilities on European shores.[11]

The European court's ruling set European policies distinctly apart from those of other Western countries that experienced incoming refugee flows, most notably Australia and the US. While Europe was compelled by its human-rights court to halt its venue-shopping policies, Australia and the US carried on unabated. In 2014, Australia reintroduced its policy of detaining all illegal migrants off its shores on the island territories of Nauru and Papua New Guinea, in privately administered jailing facilities with controversial human rights records.[12] In September 2014, the Australian Government further augmented its venue-shopping policy as it signed a refugee-transfer deal with Cambodia. Under its terms, Australia was to pay Cambodia for its services – to the dismay and open criticism of UNHCR officials.[13]

As for the US, it had already engaged in venue-shopping policies vis-à-vis Haiti since the early 1980s, with the Reagan Administration signing a dubious agreement with the then Haitian dictator Jean-Claude ("Baby Doc") Duvalier. This agreement instigated a "tow-back" policy of boats carrying asylum seekers, from US territorial waters toward Haiti.[14] In 1993, this policy was challenged before the US Supreme Court, which, in a verdict of eight against one, ruled that the non-refoulement principle could not be called upon to revoke the actions of the US Coast Guard as it returned asylum seekers to Haitian shores. The majority opinion held that the non-refoulement clause spoke of not returning a refugee to "frontiers and territories where their life would be in danger." The open high seas, so argued the majority opinion, was not a "territory" in the literal sense of the term, where the 1951 Refugee Convention allegedly intended that "the right of non refoulement be applied only to aliens physically present in the host country."[15] This majority opinion was forcefully contested by US Supreme Court Justice Harry Blackmun, who maintained that the issue of non-refoulement was unequivocally clear, and had to do with what the migrant was fleeing from (his tormentors) and *not* where this plight was taking place. In other words, the determining factor for the applicability of non-refoulement was humanity, not geography.

That this majority opinion of the US Supreme Court bordered on intellectual dishonesty, in the face of Justice Blackmun's powerful dissenting opinion, was further confirmed by the judicial decisions of the Inter-American Court for Human Rights as well as the British Court of Appeal, both of whom were highly critical of this verdict. The recent uncovering of the original archive materials of the 1951 Refugee Convention has confirmed that non-refoulement was *specifically* intended to apply to refugees on the high seas.[16]

Initial Israeli "Venue Shopping" Endeavors under Olmert

By mid-2007, as the half-baked measures of the Israeli security establishment failed to halt the African clandestine migration across the country's southern border, the Olmert Administration finally began to grasp the dire consequences of its inaction. Notwithstanding the strain on municipal social services due to the lack of planning and policy, the security concerns voiced by the Israeli Secret Service (Shin Bet) were beginning to trigger government action. The geographical proximity of the Gaza Strip, and the alleged utilization of ancient nomadic trails through the Sinai Desert by terrorist organizations (also used for smuggling and human trafficking of the African migrants) prompted calls for a secure barrier along the entire Egyptian–Israeli border.[17]

Sharon's cerebral incapacitation and Olmert's taking of office placed the latter more towards the center of the Israeli political spectrum as opposed to the right-wing Likud of his origins. The implications and electoral price Olmert would have to pay were he to opt for harsh government action against the African migrants were clear to him. With both public opinion and the supreme court on the side of the African migrants, Olmert anticipated that he would be viscerally attacked from the left of the political map, seriously jeopardizing his priceless achievement of political centeredness. Wishing to avoid a pointless confrontation with the left-wing NGOs regarding the African migrants, and given Israel's signed commitments according to the 1951 Refugee Convention, Olmert began exploring covert undercover options to halt the migrant influx. Sharing his concerns with Hosni Mubarak in the Egyptian resort of Sharm el-Sheikh, Olmert apparently managed to secure a commitment on the part of the Egyptian premier to prevent African migrants from approaching the Israeli–Egyptian border.[18]

The arbitrary killing of African migrants in front of the UNHCR offices in Cairo back in December 2005 rendered the agreements allegedly struck between Olmert and Mubarak in 2007 highly questionable vis-à-vis international humanitarian law. Given the well-documented harsh treatment of African asylum seekers in Egypt, Israel might well have breached its commitments to non-refoulement in a similar manner to the Italy–Libya agreements castigated in the European Court's 2012 verdict.

A deeper look into the diplomatic mechanics of the secretive 2007 Sharm el-Sheikh agreement between Olmert and Mubarak reveals some distinct resemblances and parallels with practices undertaken by other Western governments. The alleged agreement stipulated the immediate return of African asylum seekers to Egyptian territory, without recourse to Israeli judicial oversight or the examination of their pleas on a case-by-case basis, as mandated by UNHCR. The similarities between this Israeli pattern of behavior and the European *modus operandi* as explained by Klepp were clear.[19] The forceful denial of the alleged agreement espoused by the Israeli Ministry of Foreign Affairs in its July 1, 2007 communiqué inadvertently vindicated the suspicions of cooperation between Israel and its African rogue subcontractor, commissioned to execute policies which so-called "civilized" countries could not be seen to undertake.[20]

The State's Strategy Unfolds: Incarceration and Resettlement under Duress

Granted its unintentional, short spurt of "migrant outsourcing" under Olmert, it was not until 2013 under Netanyahu that the Israeli

Government began actively pursuing a harsh outsourcing policy for its African migrant population. Olmert's attempt to garner Egyptian support was tactical at best, and definitely did not stem from any "grand strategic" anti-migrant policy that he had in mind. If anything, Olmert was to be credited with a "dovish," soft, and humane approach to foreign migrants – as evident from the naturalization efforts of non-Jewish migrant children under his interior minister, Bar-On.[21]

With the benefit of hindsight, it seems that by early 2013 the Netanyahu Administration had elaborated a full-blown strategy to remove the entire African migrant community from Israel. It took human-rights groups almost a year to fully grasp its all-encompassing nature.[22] Netanyahu's strategy was built upon two pillars, both of which needed to exist simultaneously for the strategy to take full effect. The first pillar consisted of securing third-country locations for the migrants' resettlement, preferably in Africa. The second pillar saw the creation of a physical pressurizing mechanism, in the form of a jailing facility. The idea behind the conjunction of these two pillars was simple. Once all migrants were incarcerated, and once third-party resettlement countries became available, the State could entice and pressurize the migrants to agree to their resettlement outside of Israel, preempting problematic judicial scrutiny since the migrants would "voluntarily" agree to leave, allegedly of their own accord.

The first testimonies and evidence of application of this strategy came from the pro-migrant NGO community and UN agencies. In early February 2013, evidence began piling up, pointing to the fact that Israeli immigration officials were forcing Eritrean migrants to sign allegedly "voluntary" repatriation papers, committing them onto chartered flights from Tel Aviv to unknown African destinations via Cairo.[23] In August 2013, these migrants' final destination was revealed. Israel had decided to outsource its migrants in a venue-shopping mode to Rwanda and Uganda. As if prefiguring the supreme court revocation of the 2012 Anti-Infiltration Act some seven months later, the testimonies collected by *Haaretz* correspondents confirmed that state officials were threatening the migrants with unlimited incarceration so as to "blackmail" them into signing their own expulsion orders, of so-called voluntary return.[24] It is in light of this governmental two-pillar strategy that one can make sense of the ensuing chain of events over the subsequent 18 months, from the supreme court's revocation in September 2013 onwards.

In a blitz-like reaction to the supreme court's revocation, the government hastily re-legislated virtually the same amendment to the 1954 Anti-Infiltration Act, differentiated by two parameters. Rather than an indefinite incarceration, with an initial 3-year jailing period, the new legislation cut down the initial jailing term to a single year. The Saharonim penitentiary, which for all intents and purposes was tantamount to a full-blown jail, was exchanged for the Holot detention facility. The government claimed that the absence of impenetrable fences, and the fact that the migrants had to be present for only three daily roll calls, made it into a humane detention center rather than a harsh jail.[25]

The lightning speed with which the government legislated the new Anti-Infiltration Act (now officially known as the 4th amendment to the 1954 Anti-Infiltration Act) sounded alarm bells among the pro-migrant NGO lobby. Three days after parliament's rapid approval of the new legislation, the lobby tabled its renewed plea to the supreme court against the latest legislation.[26] Its ground was singular and simple: the government's sole purpose for locking up the migrants was deterrence – the very same ground previously struck down by the high court.[27] The impetus for speed in the passing of the new act stemmed from the State's desire not to have to release the migrants it already had in custody. The longer any migrant remained jailed, the higher the chances that they would eventually succumb to the prospect of being released (provided they boarded an airplane to Uganda or Rwanda).

The danger inherent in the supreme court's revocation of the 2012 Anti-Infiltration Act was that it entirely undermined the government's two-pillared strategy of incarceration and resettlement. As long as there would be no incarceration, there would be no impetus for the migrants to consider resettlement. Once it had managed to jail a certain migrant, the State's explicit objective was to psychologically push them toward signing their own deportation orders:

> State officials do not hesitate to harass incarcerated inmates brought before them to return to their countries of origin. Thus, for example, in the testimony of "H", who was incarcerated in the Saharonim jail for two years. During this time she was repeatedly summoned before a State official named Mart Dorfmann: "The only thing the official told me was that I had to return to Chad, if I do not wish to

> die in jail. He said the same thing each and every time [...] he repeated that I needed to return or that I would die in jail". "I don't understand this official", said "M" currently jailed at the Saharonim prison for the past year. "Its already one full year that this official Dvir Peleg asks me the same two questions: how do I feel, and if I am prepared to return. I told him: "do you think that if I would have wanted to return I would not have done so a year ago?"[28]

January 2014 saw the most significant demonstrations yet by the African migrant community against the State's polices of mass incarceration, as over 10,000 migrants peacefully gathered in central Tel Aviv demanding that the State recognize their refugee status.[29] During the same month, UNHCR officially warned that Israel could be in breach of international law due to its policy of indefinite detention for asylum seekers. As UNHCR's Adrian Edwards explained,

> Since Holot is housing people who cannot be returned to their countries of origin for reasons to do with non-forced returns, we're concerned that this facility will in effect result in indefinite detention with no release grounds [...] People in Holot are going to be in circumstances where their only means of being released is to volunteer to return to their country of origin. And clearly that's of concern to us since it is tantamount to being returned under duress.[30]

In February 2014, the Ministry of the Interior published its monthly report regarding the departures of African migrants from Israel. Whereas 325 migrants signed their deportation requests in December 2013 and 765 migrants in January 2014 following the re-enactment of incarceration under the newly re-legislated Anti-Infiltration Act, February 2014 saw the departure of 1,705 migrants in total. Boasting the merits of his government's strategy, the extreme right-wing interior minister, Gideon Sa'ar, could not disguise his satisfaction:

> This data concerning the previous month is positively surprising. If the tendency we are witnessing now continues, and I have been informed that in March 2014 it looks to continue, we will have massive departures out of the country this year. This is very important.[31]

The administration's strategy was thus unmasked, thanks to its representative's boastfulness. As the government pounded the asylum seekers with indefinite incarceration, the State's attorneys played judicial "cat and mouse" with the NGO lobby on the supreme court's marble floors.[32] Neither the State Comptroller's report on Israel's breach of its commitments towards the African migrants nor the supreme court's reprimand of the government as it stressed that there can be no separate administrative law for migrants, divorced from the common administrative law of the land, deterred the government from its chosen path.[33] The migrants had to be deported. Judicial universalism had no business interfering with sacred attempts to preserve racial purity. The somber reality that Eritrean asylum seekers previously incarcerated in Israel, who left the country under duress, were later caught and beheaded on camera by ISIS vigilantes in Libya was merely a sad reminder of the savage surroundings encompassing "civilized" Israelis.[34]

An Israeli Constitutional Crisis

On September 22, 2014, the Israeli Supreme Court revoked for the second time the governmentally legislated Anti-Infiltration Act.[35] Never in the history of Israel had the supreme court revoked the same legislation, enacted by the Knesset, twice in a row. In contrast to the supreme court's first revocation, which took many by surprise, this time round several experts correctly anticipated the resulted verdict.

As with the initial revocation, the Knesset's parliamentary legal advisor, Eyal Yinon, was first in line to warn the legislators *not* to go forward with their "softened" version of the Anti-Infiltration Act.[36] As Yinon correctly anticipated early on, the newly mandated incarceration period of one year stood no chance of passing the high court's judicial-worthiness benchmark.[37] Moreover, said Yinon, the government attorneys' claims that the Holot incarceration facility was fundamentally different from a jail would not stand the test of judicial oversight.[38] Even within the State's Attorney General's office, officials at the highest level decided to sound alarm bells as they feared a second debacle before the high court. Orit Koren, the deputy attorney general for legislation, warned that the proposed new law was unconstitutional. Attorney General Weinstein, nevertheless, decided to support it.[39]

As Eyal Yinon correctly assumed it would, the supreme court revoked the 2013 Anti-Infiltration Act on the very same grounds that it had revoked its predecessor, reinstating the migrants' right to freedom and their protection from arbitrary jailing. In a verdict spanning over 200 pages, seven high court judges supported Justice Vogelmann's majority opinion against the court's President Gronis and Justice Neil Hendel, who opted for the government-supporting minority opinion. Adopting a strong universalist voice, Justice Vogelmann wrote:

> The incarceration of cross border infiltrators whose deportation is not immediately foreseeable, for a period of one full year – not as a punishment to any act on their behalf, and without any ability of their own to promote their release – harms their rights severely [. . .] Incarceration exerts a high toll from the person being jailed. One hardly has any right which is not harmed by incarceration. Incarceration takes away one's freedom, and harms one's right [to] dignity; it violates one's right to privacy, obliterates one's ability to maintain a family life, and hinders the individual's autonomy in its most basic sense. The deprivation of physical freedom, therefore, leads to infringements of other constitutional rights, and influences all spheres of the individual's life. Jailing a person for one full year derails that individual's life from its course. It "freezes" for a considerable period of time – his ability to run his life and exercise his autonomy. It is no accident that many Western countries in the world have therefore instilled stringent limitations upon the maximal time periods for holding in detention, which are no longer than a few weeks or months.[40]

While Justice Amit did not share Justice Vogelmann's view of the need to completely do away with the new law's stipulation of a one-year incarceration period, he too could not accept the implications of prolonged incarceration. The Holot detention facility resembled a jail for all intents and purposes. The State's legitimate desire for control and oversight over the migrants could not negate their humanity. Referring to the individual humanity of each and every single migrant, Justice Amit wrote:

> Even if our opinion is not at ease with the situation which has evolved, we are bound to raise the curtain beyond that "block" of infiltrators and level our eyes toward each and every one of them. That is the concentrated essence of humanity – the acknowledgment that what is seen from afar as a blurred human grouping, is construed of human beings, and each and every man has a name, and every name his own face, and his own language, and his own way to execute his human dignity. Towards this facial profile of each and every infiltrator one can add a pinch of compassion, towards those thousands who have undergone a horrifying abuse in the Sinai desert and who have come to us when they are deeply wounded in their body and soul.[41]

Experts aside, however, most Israelis were surprised by the high court's repeated revocation of the Anti-Infiltration Act – if only because the spectacle of a twofold legislative revocation by the high court was unprecedented in Israeli history. As the surprise dwindled, things became clearer. The government, for its own part, was not going to change its chosen strategy. It was not prepared to lose its only means to exert the required pressure needed so as to coerce the migrants to sign their own suicide warrents in the form of their so-called voluntary deportation orders. If the supreme court continued its stubborn approach and blocked the government-sanctioned incarceration, parliament would resort to its constitutional "doomsday weapon." It would change Israel's constitutional Basic Law of Human Dignity and Liberty so as to exclude from its purview the issue of clandestine migrants.

Any change to the Basic Law of Human Dignity and Liberty would amount to an amendment of Israel's material constitution. As one senior Justice Ministry official put it, this would be tantamount to the use of a "non-conventional weapon" in the escalating confrontation between supreme court and parliament:

> The altering of a Basic Law is a catastrophe to the democratic State. In doing so, the State admittedly confirms that it cannot persuade its own judiciary that its actions are indeed legal. The amendment of a Basic Law would mean admitting that although we have a Constitution – it does not apply to certain people.[42]

One day after the supreme court's renewed revocation, Interior Minister Sa'ar confirmed his wish to change Israel's Basic Law.[43] On the very same day, the extreme right-wing MK Ayelet Shaked from the Habait Hayehudi party revived a motion she had already tabled to the Knesset some nine months earlier in anticipation of the high court's decision. In it, Shaked proposed to enact a special clause which would override the supreme court's decision through legislation to be passed with a special absolute majority of 61 members of parliament.[44] One month later, the government discussed the proposed law and, despite the vehement objections of the Attorney General and several coalition members, the proposal was endorsed in the ministerial legislation committee.[45] Ultimately, it was thanks to the government that this motion was dropped. Netanyahu, it seemed, was not ready to go down in history as the person who turned Israel into a declared legal ethnocracy.[46]

On December 9, 2014, the Knesset legislated for the third time the amendment to the 1954 Anti-Infiltration Act. Appropriately this time, the title of the endorsed act mirrored its true content. The new Anti-Infiltration Act finally included in its title the government's overall objective: "The Law for the Prevention of Infiltration and for the Promotion of Departure of Infiltrators from Israel – 2014."[47]

CONCLUSION

In January 1950, Foreign Minister Moshe Sharett instructed Jacob Robinson to represent the nascent State of Israel in ECOSOC's first session of the Ad Hoc Committee on Statelessness. In preparation, Robinson drafted what would become Israel's diplomatic strategy paper for the 1951 Refugee Convention. In it, Robinson prophetically foresaw how the plight of persecuted non-Jews would push refugees into Israel in search for protection from torment:

> I wish now to state our line and the factors capable to influence our attitude vis-à-vis the problem of protection of refugees and stateless persons. In the first place, we have to think in general categories of all states, which for well known reasons do not like to commit themselves to any far-reaching obligations. At the moment, a problem of non-Jewish refugees hardly exists in Israel. But the Convention on Refugees (if and when signed and ratified) is supposed to be concluded for an indefinite period. We have to have in mind that Israel is the only stable country in the region. If and when normal relations will be established, between us and our Arab neighbors, we may find ourselves in the position of a country of refuge for various types of political, racial, and religious refugees coming from this troubled region. *Caution qualified by humanitarianism is therefore imperative.*[1]

Over the next four years, Robinson fought, haggled, and arm-twisted as he and others worked to secure the endorsement of the 1951 Refugee

Convention and the 1954 Convention on Statelessness. Through these documents, the "Robinson network" breathed life into the non-refoulement principle and the non-discrimination clause. These measures underpin the international refugee regime as we know it today. Robinson himself invented the generic term which underpinned this new global refugee regime back in 1950: he named it the "Universalist" approach.[2]

Israel's approach toward asylum-seeking migrants and non-Jewish refugees was definitely universalist, in the Robinsonian sense, at its outset. Six decades later, this universalist ethos was pitted against the rise of "Exceptionalist" tendencies which came to the fore as African asylum-seeking migrants began flowing into Israel in ever-growing numbers. While Israeli exceptionalism manifested itself through the rise of the country's extreme-right parties, along with their politically driven xenophobia, these were by no means the only actors on the field. In the opposing corner stood a strong and determined coalition of pro-migrant NGOs, who cherished the humanitarian precepts fundamental to the universalist refugee regime. Nonetheless, the dissenting trend toward exceptionalism eventually prevailed as Israel opted for an open-ended incarceration of its African asylum seekers under the terms of the 2012 Anti-Infiltration Act, passed by Netanyahu's government.

This descent into exceptionalism was then temporarily halted with the unanimous revocation of the anti-migrant legislation by the Israeli Supreme Court in 2013, and its unprecedented repeated revocation by the high court in 2014. These revocations were grounded upon both Jewish and international legal principles. Ultimately, though, the government's inhumane strategy of indefinite incarceration and deportation under duress partially bore fruit, as the number of African asylum seekers dropped from around 60,000 to approximately 47,000.[3] As Galia Sabar and Elizabeth Tsurkov have recently observed:

> Israeli governments faced obstacles in implementing the most draconian components of this policy, in the form of repeated High Court rulings that forced the state to allow asylum-seekers to work and struck down laws mandating prolonged detention without trial for asylum-seekers. Over and over again, the Israeli government managed to circumvent the rulings and successfully pushed through measures that helped to achieve its goal of ridding Israel of asylum-seekers.[4]

To be sure, Israel's behavior towards asylum seekers was not fundamentally different from that of other developed countries confronted with clandestine migratory flows. Australia's refusal to aid stranded Rohingya refugees off its coast, as it undertook tow-back operations of boat people to Indonesia, was in no way better than Israel's behavior towards asylum seekers.[5] The rising levels of xenophobia in Hungary and Greece against asylum seekers, and those governments' complacency over the public onslaught against them, mirrored the behavior in Israel.[6] As the number of the world's refugees crossed the 50 million threshold for the first time since the end of World War II, Israel's challenges in dealing with 47,000 African migrants seemed to be dwarfed by the death of almost half that number in Mediterranean waters alone.[7] Israel had become an affluent, developed country, and as such a target for asylum-seeking migrants. Robinson's prophecy had materialized. The plight of African asylum seekers coming across Israel's southern frontier was, if anything, a token of the country's normality. The ensuing constitutional crisis, between its high court and its parliament, over the treatment of asylum seekers was no more than the dichotomist clash between universalism and exceptionalism – each side represented by these now-opposing state organs. The high court saw itself as the guardian of universal, humanitarian norms. The parliamentary legislator had become the promoter of ethnocentric exceptionalism.

This book opened with two intuitive hypothetical equations, and their respective normative corollaries, concerning universalism and exceptionalism. Universalism was equated with international law and norms. The resulting normative extrapolation identified universalism with tolerance, humanitarianism, and Western liberal values. Exceptionalism, on the other hand, invoked the traits of ethnocentric Jewish purity. It implied that Judaism in its stark, ethnocentric form was the source of the harsh racial governmental treatment accorded to African migrants.

The findings of this study, however, bitterly refute both of these abstruse paradigms, if only because the picture which has emerged regarding asylum in Israel has proved infinitely more complex. The universalism of Western international law and norms also included the dangerous concepts of "national security" and "exceptional measures." From the outset, in the drafting of the 1951 Refugee Convention, these terms were regularly being abused by Western states, who declared their support for humanitarian principles, but de facto legalized inhumane anti-migrant administrative measures. These measures were habitually cloaked in pseudo-legal "national security" jargon, fundamentally intended to free governments from any legal constraints in their battering of persecuted asylum seekers. In 1951, it was Jacob Robinson, the Israeli representative, who fought hardest against these measures – advocated at that time by Australia. In the case of Israel, the refusal to resort to "national security" arguments came from the least expected protagonist: the Israeli Army.

The second key hypothesis, which equated exceptionalism with an ethnocentric ethos of Jewish racial purity as the source of migrant hate-mongering, has been forcefully refuted as well. Surprisingly, it was greatly to the credit of religious Jewish jurists, and their reliance on ancient Jewish law, that non-refoulement could be called upon to protect asylum seekers the world over. This Jewish humanitarian spirit continued unabatedly in 2011, as the ultra-orthodox Knesset Interior Committee chairman, Amnon Cohen, refused to continue legislating the 2012 Anti-Infiltration Act, because "as a Jewish state, we have morals which must be applied."[8]

Any reader conversant with contemporary Middle Eastern history will immediately question the very possibility of any claim to humanitarianism on the part of Israel vis-à-vis refugees, given the never-ending plight and ongoing suffering of the Palestinian refugees. As their fate in the Syrian Yarmouk refugee camp unfolded along with the writing of this book, avoiding this question seemed like deliberately turning one's face away from "the elephant in the room".[9] To add any new findings to the already exhausted body of literature on the Palestinian refugee tragedy seemed impossible. Yet to speak about Israeli universalism vis-à-vis African refugees, and to argue for humanitarianism – the very essence of what Palestinian refugees have been consistently deprived of for almost seven decades – felt like *mauvaise foi*. To my surprise, the answer to this conundrum came from none other than Jacob Robinson himself.

Of all the primary sources examined in the course of this study, none has been more striking and indicative of Israel's humanitarianism during its early years than Robinson's attitudes towards the tragedy of Palestinian refugees after Israeli independence and their *Nakba* of 1948.

Upon the explicit request of the Israeli foreign minister, Moshe Sharett, Robinson drew up a lengthy legal opinion detailing a prospective compensation-and-resettlement plan for Palestinian refugees in their countries of residence after the 1949 Arab–Israeli armistice agreements were signed in Rhodes.[10] Robinson's plan for this compensation fund and evaluative mechanism for Palestinian assets was strikingly similar to the model he later established as the chief negotiator in the German–Jewish reparations agreements of 1952.[11] For Robinson, the prospect of refugees returning to their homes was moot, be they Jewish refugees wishing to return to post-Holocaust Europe or Palestinian refugees seeking to travel back across the already-sealed Israeli borders of 1949. Universalist and humanitarian values translated in this case into the amelioration of conditions for refugees, by providing them with compensation for their lost assets and renewed means of livelihood, so as to rebuild their lives in their respective host countries.

Drawn up probably during the last months of 1950, marked "Top Secret," and handed directly to Sharett, the plan was dated January 9, 1951 – between Robinson's participation in the UN Ad Hoc Committee's second session of August 1950 and the Refugee Convention's Plenipotentiaries' Conference in July 1951. In this compensation plan, Robinson unequivocally stressed the need for justice and full compensation for all the Palestinian refugees. As he envisaged it, this compensation process had to be administered by a non-partisan international body, preferably a UN agency, so as not to fall under the purview of any one member state.[12] In his top-secret reply regarding this compensation plan, Foreign Minister Sharett demanded clarification as to how this proposed fund would actually operate. In a rare and hitherto unheard of statement by any Israeli foreign minister, Sharett, for the first time, morally acknowledged Israel's responsibility towards the Palestinian refugees – a responsibility that Israel has never officially acknowledged to this day:

> A warm heartfelt thank you for your eye-opening and illuminating report from the 9th of this month. When we concluded our telephone conference as I left New York [. . .] I posed to you a question which has remained unanswered and it is: assuming each payment we deposit into this compensation fund shall be credited to our favor, how are we guaranteed that we will not be required to

> make more payments beyond these compensations, by the need to comply and settle claims of individuals who will not be able to, or will refuse to enjoy the benefits of this compensation claims fund?
>
> From the bottom of my heart I fear we cannot safeguard this. If all Palestinian refugees demand their compensation from this fund it could be that this fund will not be sufficient for them all. And thus there shall remain a certain number of refugees, who have done no harm nor crime or bad deed, who will not reach their peaceful tranquility and resting. As to these people one is bound to ask: and these sheep how have they sinned? And we shall not be able to renege upon our responsibilities unto them.[13]

Both Robinson and Sharett received a religious Jewish upbringing, which resulted in their excellent command of biblical Hebrew.[14] The meaning of Sharett's reply, using the famous biblical proverb from the second book of Samuel (24:17) must have been very clear to Robinson. When the Lord kills 70,000 Israelites in punishment for the sins of David, the Jewish king requests the Lord's wrath be inflicted upon himself using this proverb, sparing the innocent people who have done no wrong. Thus its usage leaves very little room for misinterpretation. The Palestinian civilian population, according to the passage above, became refugees not because of their wrongdoings but because of the realities of a war, of which they were mere victims.

This was most certainly not the official position advocated publically by the Israeli Government at the time, yet the Foreign Minister states here his own humanitarian view in unequivocal terms. Sharett shared Robinson's approach, as stated in his compensation report, that Israel had a profound moral and legal responsibility to aid all Palestinian refugees and eventually correct the injustice suffered by them. However, Sharett did not state this opinion so forcefully anywhere, at any other time, and definitely not in writing. It is safe to assume that he did so only with Robinson, precisely because he was so well acquainted with the humanitarian convictions of his interlocutor.

It is against this backdrop of humanitarianism shown towards its bitterest enemies that one must pose the question as to why Israel had descended so swiftly down the moral ladder towards institutionalized xenophobia against the African migrants some six decades later. After all, by the end of the Sharon–Olmert Administration in 2008, the majority of illegal migrant children were being voluntarily naturalized by Israel's Interior Minister Bar-On.

How did it come about that a mere three years later, MKs Ben-Ari and Eldad from the extreme right and MKs Regev and Danon from the ruling Likud party all came to participate in an orchestrated xenophobic campaign against the African migrants? Moreover, how does one explain the fact that the conductor of this anti-migrant orchestra was no less than the State's second-highest-ranking official: the deputy prime minister and interior minister, Eli Yishai? The shift from the humane policies of the Sharon–Olmert Administration towards the vile hand of racism in MK Regev's "cancer in our body" speech, and the subsequent anti-migrant arson attacks, demand an explanation.

One could claim that these MKs were merely voicing their genuine xenophobic views, without paying heed to the fact that they were alienating themselves from the general Israeli electorate. This was certainly true for the extreme right-wing MKs Eldad and Ben Ari, who suffered acute electoral punishment as they were swiftly voted out of parliament by the Israeli public in the 2013 elections.[15] Much of the same holds true for Interior Minister Yishai, whose voicing of similar views eventually resulted in his own political suicide.

These voices were at the fringe of the Israeli political spectrum. Nevertheless, they managed to consistently mobilize strong anti-migrant parliamentary majorities which recurrently legislated the 2012 and 2013 Anti-Infiltration Acts – unconstitutional as these were. It was these consistent anti-migrant parliamentary majorities, not the extreme-right fringe, that were resaponsible for the Knesset's exceptionalism. The entire Israeli political class participated in the hounding of the African migrants: Likud, the liberal center (Yesh Atid and Kadima), and in some cases even the left-wing Labor party.[16] To provide a proof-based answer as to why the majority of Israeli parliamentarians behaved in this way is beyond the scope of this book, whose objective has been limited to establishing that this is indeed what took place. The evidence gathered here does, however, point strongly towards one plausible explanation.

The African migrants were the "softest" of all possible social targets in Israel at the time. Pounding them, harassing them, and demonstrating one's "hardline-ness" on the backs of this group seemed to carry no political risk. They were expedient, and as such became easy prey for parliamentarians who wished to demonstrate they were tough on something – anything. Israeli society was running out of "social targets" (Arabs, homosexuals, women) which could be struck without paying an electoral price. Being hard on people with a different skin color, beyond the pale of one's own religious kin, came "free of charge." The number of parliamentarians who actually spoke out against this trend was staggeringly low, and those who did so were the ones with strong ethical and moral backbones – either from socialist (Dov Hanin) or Jewish-religious (Amnon Cohen) backgrounds.

The Likud administrations on Netanyahu's watch held the record for the highest levels of foreign labor importation, when this measure was advocated by strong financial lobby groups such as those of the construction sector.[17] These imported migrants were no more Jewish than the African asylum seekers, nor did they leave the country after their migration visas expired. The African migrants were a political opportunity in waiting for Machiavellian pundits who, just a few years earlier, had condoned the exact opposite in migrationary policies.[18]

Therein lies a strong lesson: once the racial genie had been released from its bottle, the legislator followed its exceptionalist precepts far beyond reasonable, normative limits. The African migrants' individual faces were now lost; their voices, which uttered the tormented stories they had experienced in the Sinai Desert, silenced. They metamorphosed into a menacing black "block," in the words of Supreme Court Justice Amit. Their Sartreian essence as "infiltrators" came to preclude their existence as human beings.

As the Israeli legislator descended into his exceptionalist moral abyss, he was unexpectedly confronted by two formidably mobilized and powerful adversaries: the pro-migrant NGOs and the Israeli Supreme Court. In its firm stance and unwavering commitment to international humanitarian norms and Jewish values, the high court partially saved Israel from the exceptionalist moral debacle that its parliamentarians pursued.

Over the years, much criticism has been leveled against the Israeli Supreme Court, from all sides of the political spectrum. To right-wing religious Israelis, it is a bastion of left-wing secularism. To left-wing people, the high court is seen as complacent over Israel's atrocious occupation of the Palestinian people's land. The "context heavy" conditions of the Israeli–Palestinian conflict serve as the prism through which, inevitably, most people view the court and its decisions.

Yet the question posed at the beginning of this book was precisely and deliberately divorced from this prism. The whole point of examining Israel's reaction towards the coming of the African migrants was to try and obtain a sense of its behavioral character around an issue free of Israel's habitually existential security concerns.

And it is here that the Israeli Supreme Court's gleaming-white moral light has shone through. In the growing global schism between supreme courts that stand idle at the plight of refugees on their shores and those which still adhere to universalist values, the Israeli court, like its European peer, emphatically belonged to the latter group. As the court reverted to the original, humane ethos of Jacob Robinson and his peers, it exhumed their sprits, breathing life into their Jewish and universalist moral values – especially after the appalling events at Kadesh Barnea in late 2013. The command of the Robinsonian ethos over the Israeli judicial heritage proved to be more profound than the recent exceptionalist tendencies of Israeli society, despite the 62 years that had elapsed since the the signing of the 1951 Refugee Convention.

The fact that the Israeli Court maintained this position by drawing from both its Western and Jewish legal traditions confirms the intimate symbiosis between the two pillars upon which it stands. Any attempt to simply equate ethnocentric exceptionalism with Judaism collapsed in the face of Justice Arbel's revocation of the 2012 Anti-Infiltration Act, based upon the teachings of Rabbi Samson Raphael Hirsch. No fewer than 36 biblical reiterations of the need to protect and safeguard the rights of the migrant-stranger were more than sufficient to prove the deep humanitarian dictums of Judaism. No other group of people received so many protective references in the Jewish legal code (the Torah) as the migrant did.[19] Three millennia ago, the most vulnerable people in society were the migrant, the orphan, and the widow. Society would be judged according to the way it treated its most vulnerable members. George Mosse recalibrated these categories of social vulnerability into modernity, as he stressed women, minorities, and homosexuals as the groups meriting protection. He might have added a biblical fourth category: asylum seekers.

In 1950, Jacob Robinson was nominated as deputy president of the UN General Assembly's Sixth (legal) Committee, a unique feat in the notoriously troubled context of UN–Israel relations. The only abstention to Robinson's candidature was proclaimed by the Egyptian delegate. He explained his abstention, rather than outright objection, to Israel's nomination on the grounds of the discrepancy between the personal attributes of the Israeli delegate and the member state he represented. Egypt could not accept this nomination since Israel was its primordial enemy, yet he could not find it in himself to turn down such a worthy candidate as Dr Robinson.[20] An admirable voice from a bygone diplomatic era. One can only imagine how the Palestinian refugee problem might have been ameliorated had more of Robinson's universalist–humanitarian convictions prevailed in Israeli and international policy-making circles. As with so much of his universalism, here, too, the precepts of ancient Jewish law shone through. In his eyes, international law and Jewish law were totally compatible and complementary, since both advocated a universal humanitarianism. Exceptionalism – as in the naked hand of a racial, nationalistic ethos – was a danger to civilized societies. As he told the delegates of the 1951 Conference of Plenipotentiaries:

> Countries should accept refugees as human beings, with all the infirmities and weaknesses inherent in the human condition.[21]

One can only hope this approach will finally be accorded to the African migrants, who long for asylum in the Promised Land, far away from their tormentors in Darfur, Sinai, and Eritrea. Jacob Robinson would surely have wished it.

NOTES

Introduction

1. Ruud Koopmans and Paul Statham, "Migration and Ethnic Relations as a Field of Political Contention: An Opportunity Structure Approach," in Ruud Koopmans and Paul Statham (eds), *Challenging Immigration and Ethnic Relations Politics* (New York: Oxford University Press, 2000), p. 20 n.3.
2. Ilan Lior and Revital Levy-Stein, "Tens of Thousands of African Migrants Protest in Central Tel Aviv", *Haaretz*, January 5, 2014; "Tausende Flüchtlinge demonstrieren gegen israelische Lagerhaft", *Die Zeit*, January 6, 2014; Oded Shalom, "The Bearers of the Black Flag", *Yediot Aharonot*, Weekend supplement, January 10, 2014; Isabel Kershner, "Africans Continue to Protest in Israel" *New York Times*, January 6, 2014; "En Israël, manifestation monstre de migrants africains clandestins", *Le Monde et Agence France Presse*, January 5, 2014.
3. Isaiah 42:6 and Numbers 23:9. All biblical quotations in English in this study are taken from the King James version unless stated otherwise. A full exposition of the historical–theological sources for this particular dichotomy lies well beyond the scope of this study; however, a few words of clarification seem appropriate here. The contradiction between "a light unto the nations" (אור לגויים) and its nemesis, "a people who shall dwell alone" (עם לבדד ישכון), can already be found in the Talmud, with the perplexing issue of how to reconcile the legalistic traditions and moral decrees of Judaism with those of the pagan nations around it. Talmudic figures in the second and third centuries AD came to reconcile the dilemma by stipulating that the Seven Laws of Noah were universal decrees for all mankind, and universally applicable (Talmud-Sanhedrin 56 a:61). Rabbi Yehuda Halevi (Spain, twelfth century), who wrote one of the most famous medieval Spanish-Jewish texts – the Kuzari – settled this dilemma by providing Judaism a leading role in regulating the affairs of nations, yet definitely within them and not ostracized from them (Kuzari 2:36). The Kuzari

is set as a dialogue between a Jewish Rabbi and a pagan sage, so that the question as to the inclusion or exclusion of the Jews from the world's nations – be their exclusion of their own making or as a result of actions of others – is at the epicenter of this classical theological text. This discussion has followed through the ages with Renaissance Jewish thinkers such as Don Yithak Abarbanel (Spain, fifteenth century); the enlightenment thinkers of the eighteenth century, Shlomo Maimon and Moses Mendelssohn; and up the twentieth-century roots of Zionism, in the famous debate between Martin Buber and his close friend the Marburg philosopher Hermann Cohen. As Buber emigrated from Germany and established the Hebrew University in Jerusalem, he tried to persuade Cohen to follow in his Zionistic footsteps. Cohen vehemently rejected the Zionist vision, since he saw it as a Jewish drift towards particularism, shifting away from the universalist approach that he adhered to, stressing to Buber, "Are the Jews really asking just to be content like all other nations?" With bitter sarcasm, Cohen asked, "Was it in order to create yet another small and nationalistic Albania that we have so insurmountably endured the great suffering of Jewish History? Shall we take the great duty that the Jewish people have taken upon themselves to be a moral and spiritual light unto the nations, and exchange it for circus amusements such as flags and parades?" Quoted in an article by the well-known Israeli author Abraham B. Jehoshua, "Is there any Practical Meaning to the term Light unto the Nations?" in *Homeland Grasp: Twenty Articles and One Story* (Tel Aviv: Hakibbutz Hameuchad, 2008), pp. 68–73 [translation from the Hebrew by the author].

4. Uri Bialer, "Between a Light unto the Nations, a Nation who Shall Dwell Alone and Political Realism: Israeli Foreign Policy and its Coping with the Zionist Vision in 1948," lecture delivered at the research seminar "Following 1948: Coping with the Realization of the Dream of Israel," Ben-Gurion University in Sede Boker, April 24, 2012. Many of Bialer's points in this lecture are also based on his seminal book capturing these dichotomies in Israeli foreign policy. See: Uri Bialer, *Between East and West: Israel's Foreign Policy Orientation 1948–1956* (Cambridge: Cambridge University Press, 1990).
5. See: United Nations General Assembly Resolution 3379, adopted November 10, 1975. For revocation of this 16 years later, see: United Nations General Assembly Resolution 46/86 December 16, 1991. For the full texts of both resolutions, see the internet site of the Israeli Ministry of Foreign Affairs, available at: www.mfa.gov.il/mfa/foreignpolicy/mfadocuments/yearbook8/pages/260%20general%20assembly%20resolution%2046-86-%20revocation.aspx (accessed April 2016).
6. Avi Beker, *The United Nations and Israel: From Recognition to Reprehension* (Tel Aviv: Bar Ilan University Press, 1985) [in Hebrew].
7. See the obituary of Israeli prime minister Yitzahk Shamir: Juian Ozanne, "Unflinching Supporter of Greater Israel", *Financial Times*, June 30, 2012. See also: Kati Marton, *A Death in Jerusalem* (New York: Pantheon Books, 1994), especially the introductory notes by Richard Holbrooke – US special envoy to the former Yugoslavia and the architect of the Dayton Accords.

See also the positive book review on Marton's book by the *New York Times* correspondent to Jerusalem during the Oslo peace process, Clyde Haberman: "Books of the Times: Terrorism Can be Just Another Point of View," *New York Times*, February 22, 1995.

8. The metaphor of "throwing the Jews into the sea" was coined by Ahmad Shuqayri (The first PLO chairman) on June 3, three days before the begning of the Six Day War, and alongside Egyptian President Gamal Abdel Nasser's closing of the Tiran maritime straits. See: Moshe Shemesh, "Did Shuqayri Call for 'Throwing the Jews into the Sea'?" *Israel Studies 8* (2) 2003, pp. 70–81 at 72. The traumatic metaphor of "the destruction of the third Temple" was used on the second day of the Yom Kippur War (October 8–9, 1973) by Moshe Dayan, who served as Israel's defense minister and who displayed a keen sense of despair that eventually prompted Prime Minister Golda Meir to replace him as spokeperson in a press conference of October 9, instead placing the more moderate and calm General Aharon Yariv in front of the microphones. It is disputed whether Dayan actually did utter the words during the famous meeting with the head publishers of the Israeli press on October 9. What is unequivocally clear is that he did use these words to the then acting head of the Israeli Air Force, General Benni Peled, as he requested air support in the Golan Heights during the hard armored-corps battles aginst the Syrian Army there. Regarding Mahmoud Ahmadinejad's explicit call for the destruction of Israel, see: Yair Sheleg, "Hasanegor Hagadol ['The Great Apologist' – translated G. B.N.]" in the weekend supplement of *Makor Rishon*, December 26, 2014. In 2012, the Iranian President repeated his calls to "eliminate" the State of Israel, which he initially voiced in 2006. See: Louis Charbonneau, "In New York, defiant Ahmadinejad says Israel will be 'eliminated'", as reported by Reuters, September 24, 2012. Available at: www.reuters.com/article/us-un-assembly-ahmadinejad-idUSBRE88N0HF20120924#QSDbhi7DCWtz66Fw.99 (accessed April 2016).
9. Illouz' considerable intellectual influence and clout is worth mentioning here, especially given her active participation in the Israeli public sphere of debate. Born in Fez and educated in France and then in the US, Illouz lectured at Princeton in 2004, the same year in which she won the best book award from the American Sociological Association. She delivered the Adorno Lecture, and in 2009 was marked as one of the 12 most important future forward thinkers in the world by the influential German newspaper *Die Zeit*. See: Elisabeth Von Thadden, "Am Seelenmarkt: Was macht die moderne Ökonomie mit unseren Gefühlen?" *Die Zeit*, April 16, 2009.
10. Eva Illouz, "Words That Must Never be Uttered," *Haaretz*, June 25, 2012.
11. See Part 3, below.
12. Judith Shuval and Elazar Leshem (eds), *Immigration to Israel: Sociological Perspectives* (New Brunswick, NJ: Transaction Publishers, 1998).
13. Naama Carmi, *Immigration and The Law of Return: Immigration Rights and their Limits* (Tel Aviv: Tel Aviv University Press, 2003) [in Hebrew].

14. Samir El-Youssef, *The Illusion of Return* (London: Halban Publishers, 2008).
15. For the full text of the law in Hebrew see: www.nevo.co.il/law_html/law01/189_003.htm (accessed April 2016).
16. Ilana Salama Ortar, *Uprooting, Refugeeism and Immigration* (Herzliya Museum of Contemporary Art, Herzliya: Hakibbutz Hameuchad, 2005).
17. Paul Weis, *The 1951 Refugee Convention: The Travaux Préparatoires Analyzed, with a Commentary* (Cambridge: Cambridge University Press 1995), pp. 144–8.
18. Benny Morris, *Israel's Border Wars 1949–1956*, (Oxford: Oxford University Press 1997).
19. Ibid., pp. 99–100.
20. Ibid., pp. 110–17.
21. Anti Infiltration Act 1954. See the text of the law at: www.nevo.co.il/Law_word/law01/247_001.doc (accessed April 2016).
22. Knesset Protocol of December 16, 1953, p. 126.
23. Morris, *Border Wars*, p. 432.
24. Sarah Willen (ed.), *Transnational Migration to Israel in a Global Comparative Context* (Lanham, MD: Lexington Books, 2007).
25. Adriana Kemp and Rebeca Raijman, *Migrants and Workers: The Political Economy of Labor Migrants in Israel* (Jerusalem: Van Leer Institute and Hakibbutz Hameuchad Publishers, 2009) [in Hebrew], pp. 80–94; Roby Nathanson and Lea Achdut (eds), *The New Workers: Wage Earners from Foreign Countries in Israel*, (Tel Aviv: Friedrich Ebert Stiftung and Hakibbutz Hameuchad 1999).
26. Zeev Rosenhek, "Challenging Exclusionary Migration Regimes," in Willen (ed.), *Transnational Migration*, pp. 217–32.
27. Zvi Eckstein, "Report of the Israeli Governmental Inter-Ministerial Committee for the Establishment of Governmental Policy regarding Non-Israeli Workers," published upon the Israeli Government's request by *Israel Democracy Institute – Caesarea Form,* June 2010. See: www.idi.org.il/media/575451/Foreign_Workers.pdf (accessed April 2016).
28. Willen (ed.), *Transnational Migration*, pp. 1–27, at 15.
29. Michael Alexander, "Tel Aviv: The Limits of Liberalism in a Guest Worker Regime," in Michael Alexander, *Cities and Labour Responses: Comparing Policy Responses in Amsterdam, Paris, Rome and Tel-Aviv* (Hampshire: Ashgate, 2007), p. 91.
30. Ibid., pp. 89–93. See also: Galia Sabar, "The Rise and Fall of African Migrant Churches: Transformations in African Religious Discourse and Practice in Tel Aviv," in Willen (ed.), *Transnational Migration*, pp. 185–202, at p. 189 n. 9. On the cross-continental exchanges between the West African migrant workers in Israel and their diasporic impacts in their countries of origin, see: Galia Sabar, *"We're Not Here to Stay": African Migrant Workers in Israel and Back in Africa* (Tel Aviv: Tel Aviv University Press, 2008) [in Hebrew].
31. Shlomo Avineri, Liav Orgad, and Amnon Rubinstein, *Managing Global Migration: A Strategy for Immigration Policy in Israel* (Jerusalem: Metzilah Center

for Jewish Zionist Liberal and Humanist Thought, 2009), p. 47 [in Hebrew]. Regarding the deterioration of the conditions of East African refugees and asylum seekers in Egypt, which triggered their flight towards the Israeli border, see: Amnesty International, *Egypt/Sudan: Refugees and Asylum seekers face Brutal Treatment, Kidnapping for Ransom, and Human Trafficking* (London, 2013). Available at: https://www.amnesty.org/en/documents/afr04/001/2013/en/ (accessed April 2016).

32. Lisa Anteby-Yemini, "Les 'réfigiés soudanais' en Israël: discours, representations, mobilizations," *Maghreb-Machrek* 199 (Spring 2009), pp. 71–84, at 81.
33. Moshe Arens, "African Migrants Could Destroy Israel," *Haaretz*, January 14, 2014.
34. Amnesty International, *Egypt/Sudan*, p. 5.
35. Médecins Sans Frontières, *Violence, Vulnerability and Migration: Trapped at the Gates of Europe*, a report on the situation of sub-Saharan migrants in an irregular situation in Morocco, March 2013. Available at: http://www.msf.ie/document/violence-vulnerability-and-migration-trapped-gates-europe (accessed April 2016).
36. Silja Klepp, "Negotiating the Principle of Non-Refoulement in the Mediterranean Sea: Mission, Visions, and Policies at the Southern Borders of the European Union," Working Paper Series No. 1 (Leipzig: Global and European Studies Institute – University of Leipzig, 2008).
37. Haim Yacobi, "Let Me Go to the City: African Asylum Seekers and the Politics of Space in Israel," *Journal of Refugee Studies* Vol. 24 (1) (2011), pp. 48–68, at 52.
38. Moti Basok, "By Year's End 2012 Israel had 256,000 Foreign Migrants, of whom only 40 Percent were Legal," *Haaretz*, July 30, 2013.

Chapter 1 The Origins of the 1951 Refugee Convention and Non-Discrimination

1. Anshel Pfeffer, "Reserve Soldiers Actively Opposed the Forceful Refoulement of Infiltrators to Egypt – and the Order has been Suspended," *Haaretz*, April 22, 2011.
2. J. McAdam, "The Interpretation of the 1951 Convention," in A. Zimmermann, J. Dörschner, and F. Machts, *The 1951 Convention Relating to the Status of Refugees and its 1967 Protocol: A Commentary* (Oxford: Oxford University Press, 2011), pp. 75–116, at p. 101.
3. T. Einarsen, "The Drafting History of the 1951 Convention and the 1967 Protocol," in Zimmermann, Dörschner, and Machts, *1951 Convention*, pp. 37–74, at p. 49. See also: McAdam, "Interpretation," p. 102.
4. The United Nations Year Book (1946–7) quoted in: Seymor M. Finger, "Beyond the conflict – the United Nations," in D. S. Wyman and C. H. Rosenzweig (eds),

The World Reacts to the Holocaust (Baltimore, MD: Johns Hopkins University Press, 1996), p. 811.

5. Israeli State Archives (ISA), Foreign Ministry Files container 2416, December 1950: statement by Arthur Lourie, Israeli consul general in New York, dated December 13, 1950, to the UN General Assembly Negotiating Committee on contributions to programs of relief and rehabilitation, p. 6. Cross-checked and confirmed – *United Nations Archive – New York (UNA) restricted document A/AC.41/SR.5*. It should be noted here that in both the UN archive and the Israeli foreign affairs ministry an abundance of documents confirms the fact that from a volume and "management attention" perspective the Korean war refugees, together with the Palestinian refugee issue, had occupied the priority slots in terms of policy attention of world governments, overriding refugees in other parts of the world, also from the IRO perspective.
6. Mark Mazower, *No Enchanted Palace: The End of Empire and the Ideological Origins of the United Nations* (Princeton, NJ: Princeton University Press, 2009), pp. 104–48.
7. Avi Beker, *The United Nations and Israel: From Recognition to Reprehension* (Tel Aviv: Bar Ilan University Press, 1985), pp. 38–42 [in Hebrew].
8. Gabi Sheffer, *Moshe Sharett: Biography of a Political Moderate* (Oxford: Oxford University Press, 1996), pp. 337–712.
9. A glance through the biographies of Sharett's immediate staff reads more like a "diplomatic dream team" than the usual image of a foreign service. His ambassador to the UN (and for a time to the US) was Abba Eben, his subordinate director general of the ministry was Walter Eytan, and his legal advisor was Shabtai Rosenne. All three were British nationals and British officers during World War II (Eytan had been part of the Enigma code-breaking team; Eban, a senior intelligence officer to Field Marshal Montgomery; and Rosenne, an intelligence officer in the Royal Air Force). Eytan was nominated the youngest German-history reader of his Oxford class, while Eban graduated in Semitic linguistics from Cambridge with high marks, speaking fluent Arabic, Turkish, Farsi, and Hebrew – not to mention his capacity for European languages. Rosenne studied law at the University of London, and by the age of 30 was a senior lecturer in international law at the Royal Naval College in Greenwich. See: Walter Eytan, *The First Ten Years: Diplomatic History of Israel* (New York: Weidenfeld & Nicholson, 1958).
10. ISA Foreign Ministry Files container 2406, October 28, 1949: Agreement between the Government of Israel and the International Refugee Organization concerning permanent provision for institutional care. Ibid., October 27, 1950 and October 30, 1950, exchange of letters from Donald Kingsley, director general IRO to S. Adler-Rudel, representative of the Government of Israel.
11. Itamar Rabinovich, *The Road Not Taken: Early Arab-Israeli Negotiations 1949–1952* (Jerusalem: Maxwell-Macmillan-Keter, 1991), p. 27 [in Hebrew].
12. ISA Foreign Ministry Files container 1829/8 – the legal advisor, September 18, 1950: top-secret cable from Shabtai Rosenne, chief legal advisor to

Dr Jacob Robinson in New York. Rosenne informs Robinson, based upon secret service information at his disposal, that the UN Conciliation Commision mandated to see the execution of the return and compensation of Palestinian refugees according to GA Resolution 194 is considering a property exchange of Jewish refugees from Iraq and Yemen against Palestinian property belonging to Palestinian refugees within Israeli borders.

13. ISA Foreign Ministry Files container 93.38.1.29, 19/8צח, February 26, 1952: letter from Dr Paul Weis, Chief legal advisor for the UNHCR, to Dr Menachem Kahany, the Israeli representative to the UN European office in Geneva, concerning travel documents and the applicability of the law of return removing refugee status from Jewish refugees who have obtained citizenship in Israel.
14. Irial Glynn, "The Genesis and Development of Article 1 of the 1951 Refugee Convention," *Journal of Refugee Studies* 25 (1) (2011) pp. 134–48, at 3.
15. Ibid., p. 4.
16. Ad Hoc Committee on Statelessness and Related Problems, UN Doc. E/1618, E/AC.32/5, February 17, 1950 (hereinafter: Ad Hoc Committee, "Draft").
17. ISA Foreign Ministry File number 2416, Doc. 775, Robinson to Director General, July 8, 1951: "The Convention regarding refugees and stateless people 1st report" (hereinafter: Robinson Report 1), point 1.
18. H. Pundik, *Die Flucht der dänischen Juden 1943 nach Schweden* (Husum: Husum Verlag, 1995), p. 42.
19. ISA Foreign Ministry File number 1976/7, April 1, 1952: letter from Robinson to Sharett and to Kidron, director of international organizations at the Israeli Foreign Ministry. Letter M/32400, dated March 14, 1952.
20. J. Robinson, "Book Review – Knud Larsen 'Nationality Laws'", *American Journal of International Law* Vol. 45 (July 1951), pp. 617–18.
21. See Abba Eban's biography at the online Jewish Virtual Library website. Available at www.jewishvirtuallibrary.org/jsource/biography/Eban.html (accessed April 2016).
22. For Dr Jacob Robinson's biography, see: Omry Kaplan-Feuereisen, "Im Dienste der jüdischen Nation: Jacob Robinson und das Völkerrecht," *Osteurope* 58th Year/Issue 8–10 (August–October 2008), pp. 279–94; Omry Kaplan-Feuereisen, "Robinson, Jacob," in Gershon David Hundert (ed.), *The YIVO Encyclopedia of Jews in Eastern Europe* (New Haven, CT: Yale University Press, 2008), pp. 1, 567–8, also available at www.yivoencyclopedia.org/article.aspx/Robinson_Jacob (accessed April 2016); "Robinson, Jacob," in *Encyclopedia Judaica,* vol. 14, col. 207 (Jerusalem and New York: Macmillan publishers, 1971).
23. M. Marrus, "A Jewish Lobby at Nuremberg: Jacob Robinson and the Institute of Jewish Affairs 1945–1946," paper prepared for The Cardozo Law Review Conference: "The Nuremberg Trials: A Reappraisal and Their Legacy," Benjamin N. Cardozo School of Law, New York, March 27–29, 2011.

24. Eglė Bendikaitė and Dirk Roland Haupt (eds), *The Life, Times, and Work of Jokūbas Robinzonas – Jacob Robinson*, (Sankt Augustin: Academia Verlag, 2015), p. 12.
25. For his biography, see: "Nehemiah Robinson," in *Encyclopedia Judaica*, vol. 14, col. 208; also, "Dr Nehemiah Robinson, Director of WJC Institute, Dead; Funeral Today," *Jewish Telegraphic Agency*, January 13, 1964.
26. W. Grimes, "Louis Henkin, Leader in Field of Human Rights Law, Dies at 92," *New York Times*, October 16, 2010.
27. S. Power, *A Problem from Hell: America and the Age of Genocide* (New York: Harper Perennial, 2002), pp. 48–50.
28. ISA Foreign Ministry File number 1976/7: letter from Robinson to legal advisor Shabtai Rosenne, July 1, 1954.
29. ISA Ministry of Justice File number 4524/: Jacob Robinson to Israeli Attorney General Chaim Cohn, August 18, 1954, handwritten Doc. 18638: "Dearest Chaim, please allow me to thank you deeply for sending me a copy of your ratification letter and I am hopeful that the original ratification document will reach New York soon, so as to permit us to help and take action for thousands of Jews in the Diaspora, time is short whereas the convention relating to stateless people opens on the 13th September, and I hereby sign in the blessing of peace. Yours, Jacob." The wording in Hebrew of the signature is reminiscent of the priestly blessing (Numbers 6: 24–26), in Hebrew of the Cohanim, the priests to whom Chaim Cohn was related as shown by his family name – and which both Cohn and Robinson implicitly understood given their religious upbringing.
30. Jacob Robinson, *Das Minoritäten-Problem und seine Literatur; kritische Einführung in die Quellen und die Literatur der europäischen Nationalitätenfrage der Nachkriegszeit, unter besonderer Berücksichtigung des Völkerrechtlichen Minderheitenschutzes* (Berlin and Leipzig: Institut für ausländisches öffentliches Recht und Völkerrecht in Berlin – Walter de Gruyter & Co, 1928). And see: Jacob Robinson, *Minorities and the League of Nations* (Washington, DC: American Council on Public Affairs, 1941); Jacob Robinson et al., *Were the Minorities Treaties a Failure?* (New York: Institute of Jewish Affairs, 1943).
31. Jacob Robinson, *The Metamorphosis of the United Nations: Extract of the Recueil des Cours*, (Leiden: The Hague Academy of International Law A.W. Sijthoff publishers, 1958), pp. 495–592.
32. For a biography of Paul Weis, see: Paul Weis Archive document PW/PR, Intro 1; also "Nansen Ring awarded to Dr Paul Weis," *Association of Jewish Refugees Bulletin*, June 1974.
33. Paul Weis, *Nationality and Statelessness in International Law* (London: Stevenson and Sons, 1956).
34. Paul Weis Archive PW/WR/WMSC/2 Doc. 11.
35. Glynn, "Genesis," p. 7.
36. Paul Weis Archive PW/PR/IRO-6 Doc. p. 32, at 3.
37. S. Hoare, *Nine Troubled Years* (London: Collins, 1954), p. 239.

38. Ibid., p. 240.
39. Paul Weis Archive PW/WR/WMSC/2. Weis held in his papers several copies of Hoare's speeches and legal motions in the House of Commons in favor of British intervention in the Jewish cause and on behalf of Jewish refugees from continental Europe.
40. Les Archives Diplomatiques – Royaume de Belgique, Dossier Numéro PERS: 2159 – Albert Herment, declassified and opened for public reading April 2014.
41. Ibid., letter from Herment to the Secretary General of the Foreign Ministry, December 31, 1939; letter from Herment to Billen, December 13, 1944.
42. Les Archives Diplomatiques – Royaume de Belgique, Dossier Numéro 13717 / I – Apatrides et Definition de Réfugiés. All translations from the French by the current author.
43. Herment 2159 – Personal Confidential Files; the reverse side of the file lists Herment's pension-fund remunerations.
44. Kaplan-Feuereisen, "Im Dienste," p. 164 n. 26.
45. Robinson Report 1, p. 2 point 9.
46. Einarsen, "Drafting," p. 54.
47. G. Goodwin-Gill and J. McAdam, *The Refugee in International Law*, 3rd edn. (Oxford: Oxford University Press, 2007), p. 9.
48. Robinson Report 1, p. 2 point 10; exclamation mark is in the original.
49. UN Doc A/CONF.2/6/Add. 2; see also: A. Takkenberg and C. C. Tahbaz, *The Collected Travaux Préparatoires of the 1951 Geneva Convention Relating to the Status of Refugees*, Vols I–III (Amsterdam: Dutch Refugee Council / European Legal Network on Asylum, 1990), p. 247.
50. ISA Foreign Ministry Files, container 2416, Doc. 788: Robinson to Director General, July 22, 1951 – "The Convention regarding Refugees and Stateless People 3rd Report" (hereinafter: Robinson Report 3), p. 1.
51. Glynn, "Genesis," p. 7.
52. Glynn, "Genesis," p. 6.
53. Robinson Report 1, at 2.
54. Ibid., p. 2 point 9.
55. Ibid., p. 2 point 10.
56. Ibid., p. 2 point 9.
57. I. Friedman, *The Question of Palestine 1914–1918* (London: Routledge & Kegan Paul, 1973); J. Robinson, *Kommentar der Konvention über das Memelgebiet* (Kaunas: Spaudos Fondas Verlag, 1934); S. Yerasimos, "Le sandjak d'Alexandrette: formation et integration d'un territoire," *Revue de l'Occident musulman et de la Mèditerranée* No. 48–49 (1988), pp. 198–212. M. Khadduri, 'The Alexandretta Dispute' in *The American Journal of International Law* 39 (3), 1945, 406–25.
58. Michael Marrus, *The Unwanted: European Refugees from the First World War Through the Cold War* (Philadelphia: Temple University Press, 2002) pp. 70, 160.
59. Robinson et al., *Minorities Treaties*, p. 8.

60. Ibid., pp. 109–24.
61. Marrus, *The Unwanted*, pp. 158–9.
62. Gilad Ben-Nun, "The Israeli Roots of Article 3 and Article 6 of the 1951 Refugee Convention," *Journal of Refugee Studies* Vol. 27 (1) (2014), pp. 101–25, at 103–6.
63. Statement by Rochefort (France), UN Conference of Plenipotentiaries on the Status of Refugees and Stateless Persons, Summary Record of the Nineteenth Meeting, July 13, 1951, A/CONF.2/SR.19.
64. Ibid.
65. ISA/Foreign Ministry Files 19/10/ RG 93.38/1-31: Jacob Robinson to Moshe Sharet and Walter Eytan – "Geneva – Forth and final report on the Conference of Plenipotentiaries on the status of Refugees and Stateless Persons," August 1, 1951 (hereinafter: Robinson Final Plenipotentiary Report), p. 4.
66. ISA/Foreign Ministry Files 19/10/ RG 93.38/1-31: Jacob Robinson to Moshe Sharett and Walter Eytan – "Geneva – First Interim report - Conference of Plenipotentiaries on the status of Refugees and Stateless Persons," July 8, 1951, Doc. 775, p. 2 point 6. [Originally in Hebrew].
67. See the text of the convention issued by UNHCR marking its 60th anniversary, available at: www.unhcr.org/3b66c2aa10.html, p. 3 (accessed April 2016).
68. Robinson Report 1, p. 2 point 10.
69. UN Doc. A/CONF.2/72, July 11, 1951.
70. Ad Hoc Committee, "Draft," p. 13.
71. UNHCR, *The 1951 Convention and Protocol Relating to the Status of Refugees* (ed. 2010), available at: http://www.unhcr.org/pages/49da0e466.html (accessed April 2016) (hereinafter: UNHCR, 1951 Refugee Convention).
72. Robinson Report 3, p. 1 point 2.
73. R. Marx and W. Staff, "Article 3 of the 1951 Refugee Convention," in Zimmermann, Dörschner, and Machts, *1951 Convention*, pp. 643–56, at 645. See also: Weis, *Commentary*, p. 39.
74. ISA Foreign Ministry File number 2416, Doc. 782: Robinson to Director General, July 11, 1951 – "The Convention regarding Refugees and Stateless People 2nd Report" (hereinafter: Robinson Report 2), p. 1 point 4.
75. Marx and Staff, "Article 3," p. 655. See also: Weis, *Commentary*, p. 39.
76. Marx and Staff, "Article 3," p. 654.
77. Ibid., p. 655.
78. A. Grahl-Madsen, *Commentary on the Refugee Convention 1951: Articles 2–11* (Geneva: UNHCR, 1963) p. 8 n. 4. Available at: www.unhcr.org/3d4ab5fb9.html (accessed April 2016). See also: Weis, *Commentary*, p. 36 n. 83; Marx and Staff, "Article 3," p. 647 n. 21.
79. Marx and Staff, "Article 3," pp. 643–56, at 647.
80. UN Document A/CONF.2/72, Articles 4, 5, 6, and 7.
81. Takkenberg and Tahbaz, *Collected Travaux Préparatoires,* Vol. II p. 369.
82. Robinson Report 1, p. 1 point 6.

83. Rules of Procedure for the Conference of Plenipotentiaries, July 2, 1951, *Traveaux preparatoires*. Available at: www.unhcr.org/3ae68cd9c.html (accessed April 2016).
84. Takkenberg and Tahabaz, *Collected Travaux Préparatoires*, p. 231.
85. Ibid., p. 242.
86. R. Marx and F. Machts, "Article 6 of the 1951 Refugee Convention," in Zimmermann, Dörschner, and Machts, *1951 Convention*, pp. 707–14, at 709.
87. The 1951 Refugee Convention drafts never had an Article 6 (b). The confusions of Article 3(b) with Article 6(b) in the text of Marx and Machts' "Article 6" are to be found on pp. 709 § 7 and pp. 710 § 8.
88. Takkenberg and Tahabaz, *Collected Travaux Préparatoires*, pp. 238–9.
89. Ibid., p. 243. The Australian amendment was filed under the reference UN Doc. A/CONF.2/14.
90. Weis, *Commentary*, p. 39.
91. UN Doc. A/Conf.2/SR.84, p. 5.
92. Takkenberg and Tahabaz, *Collected Travaux Préparatoires*, p. 244.
93. Robinson Report 2, point 5.
94. Weis, *Commentary*, p. 223.
95. A. Perry, "Solving Israel's African Refugee Crisis," *Virginia Journal of International Law*, Vol. 51 (1) (2010), pp. 157–84, at 170.
96. Gamal Nakrumah, "Here Today Gone Tomorrow: Why are Increasing Numbers of Sudanese Refugees Fleeing Egypt for Israel?" *Al Ahram Weekly*, issue No. 856, August 2–8, 2007.
97. Lisa Anteby-Yemini, "Migrations africaines et nouveaux enjeux de la frontière israélo-égyptienne," *Cultures & Conflits: Frontières et logiques de passage*, 72 (Winter 2008), pp. 77–99, at 81.
98. Ruti Sinai, "The High Court of Justice Forbids Keeping the Sudanese Refugees in Administrative Detention without Recourse to Judicial due Process," *Haaretz*, May 9, 2006.
99. Sarah S. Willen, "Darfur through the Shoa Lens: Sudanese Asylum Seekers, Unruly Biopolitical Dramas, and the Politics of Humanitarian Compassion in Israel," in Byron J. Good et al. (eds), *A Reader in Medical Anthropology: Theoretical Trajectories – Emergent Realities* (New York: Wiley-Blackwell, 2010), pp. 505–18, at 506.
100. Sinai, "High Court Forbids."
101. Willen, "Darfur," p. 509.
102. Weis, *Commentary*, p. 50.
103. During last 15 years of his life, Jacob Robinson embarked upon an extensive enterprise of compiling edited bibliographical volumes and historical bibliographic guides of the written sources concerning the Jewish Holocaust. To this end, Robinson fundraised and created the Memorial Foundation for Jewish Culture in New York, under the auspices of the WJC, under the same institutional housing of the IJA, which he had created a quarter of a century earlier. The first bibliographical volumes were conducted jointly between the

Yad Vashem memorial in Jerusalem and the YIVO institute for Research of Judaism in New York. The printing and editing was undertaken exclusively in Jerusalem, first under the biggest Israeli publishing house at the time – Keter – and, from the 1970s onward, by the Hebrew University Press. In 1970, Robinson relocated the work and housed it under the Institute for Contemporary Jewry of the Hebrew University on Mount Scopes. Here, he engaged his young protégé, Yehuda Bauer, in continuing these publications, of which two volumes in English were produced and supervised by himself and Bauer – both of whom wrote separate prefaces to these volumes. All in all, Bauer and Robinson worked closely for over 10 years, from the time of Bauer's early assignments at Yad Vashem until the last edited volumes' publication in 1974, three years prior to Robinson's death in 1977. See: Jacob Robinson and Yehuda Bauer, *Guide to Unpublished Materials of the Holocaust Period* (Jerusalem: Hebrew University Press, 1970). See also: Jacob Robinson, *The Holocaust and After: Sources and Literature in English*, (Jerusalem Yad Vashem Memorial Authority & YIVO Institute for Jewish research: Israel University Press, 1973).

Chapter 2 The Origins of the Non-Refoulement Principle

1. European Court of Human Rights, *Hirsi Jamaa v. Italy*, Application No. 27765/09, 23 February 2012. Available at: www.hudoc.echr.coe.int/sites/eng/pages/search.aspx?i=001-109231#{"itemid":["001-109231"]}(accessed April 2016).
2. Justice P. P. de Albuquerque, "Concurring Opinion to the Ruling of the European Court of Human Rights," *Hirsi Jamaa v. Italy*, Application No. 27765/09 (Eur. Ct. H. R. Feb. 23, 2012), pp. 62–82 notes 2–62.
3. Ben-Nun, "British-Jewish Roots", pp. 8–10.
4. Albuquerque, "Concurring Opinion," pp. 68–72.
5. Gilad Ben-Nun, "The British–Jewish Roots of Non-Refoulement and its True Meaning for the Drafters of the 1951 Refugee Convention," *Journal of Refugee Studies* 28 (1) (Oxford: Oxford University Press, 2015), pp. 93–117.
6. W. Kälin, M. Caroni, and L. Heim, "Article 33, para 1 (prohibition of Expulsion or Return ['Refoulement']),” in Zimmermann, Dörschner, and Machts, *1951 Convention*, pp. 1,327–96, at 1,341.
7. Takkenberg and Tahbaz, *Collected Travaux Préparatoires*, Vol. 1, p. 163.
8. Ibid., p. 162.
9. Ad Hoc Committee on Statelessness and Related Problems, UN Doc. E/AC.32/L.25 (1950).
10. Ibid.
11. Ben-Nun, "Israeli Roots," p. 20.
12. UK National Archives, File #HO/ 274/9: Evans to Hoare, 16 October 1951, following Hoare's request for consultations with Robinson in New York so as to postpone the submission of the protocol relating to stateless persons, pending the ratification of the Refugee Convention.

13. Ben-Nun, "Israeli Roots, " pp. 9–12.
14. ISA/Foreign Ministry Files RG 130.2.1.1008 Box # 2416/ 10 Jacob Robinson to Walter Eytan {Dirctor General Israeli MFA} 'Ad Hoc Committee on Statelessness and Related Problems: Final Report, 21 February 1950. p. 2
15. Ibid., p. 2; all underlining in the original.
16. UK National Archives, File BT 271/349: I.O.C. (51) 125, "Steering Committee on International Organizations, Conference of Plenipotentiaries on the Status of Refugees held at Geneva from 3rd to 25th July, 1951: Previous reference I.O.C. (51) 68 and Addendum," 16 August 1951, p. 17.
17. Ibid., p. 3.
18. Robinson Final Plenipotentiary Report, p. 3 point 3.
19. K. Neumann, *Refuge Australia: Australia's Humanitarian Record* (Sydney: University of New South Wales Press, 2004), pp. 15–42.
20. Takkenberg and Tahbaz, *Collected Travaux Préparatoires*, Vol. 2, p. 242.
21. Robinson Report 1, p, 2 point 2; quotation marks in the original.
22. European Court of Human Rights, *Hirsi Jamaa v. Italy*, pp. 75–6 n. 44.
23. U. Davy, "Article 32 of the 1951 Refugee Convention," in Zimmermann, Dörschner and Machts, *1951 Convention*, pp. 1,277–1,325, at 1,285–286. Grahl-Madsen, *Commentary*, pp. 110–12. See also: J. Hathaway, *The Rights of Refugees under International Law* (Cambridge: Cambridge University Press, 2005), pp. 663–6; N. Robinson, *The Convention Relating to the Status of Refugees. Its History, Contents and Interpretation: A Commentary* (New York: Institute for Jewish Affairs and World Jewish Congress, 1953), pp. 65–74.
24. Weis, *Commentary*, p. 203.
25. I. Lewin, *In Defense of Human Rights* (New York: Research Institute of Religious Jewry, 1992), p. 13.
26. I. Lewin, *Religious Jewry and the United Nations: Addresses before the United Nations* (New York: Research institute for Post-War Problems of Religious Jewry, 1953), p. 1.
27. Ibid., p. 7.
28. Ibid., pp. 11–41.
29. Ibid., p. 320.
30. *New York Times*, Obituary: Isaac Lewin, 25 August 1995.
31. Lewin, *In Defense*, pp. 44–122.
32. Ben-Nun, "Israeli Roots," pp. 2–8.
33. Lewin, *In Defense*, pp. 94–5.
34. Ibid., pp. 121–2.
35. S. Troebst, "Speichermedium der Konflikterinnerung zur Ost (Mittel) Europäischen Prägung des Modernen Völkerrechts, " in Martina Keilbach (ed.), *IPP Kolloquium Papers (Winter)* (Leipzig: Graduate Institute for Global and European Studies, University of Leipzig, 2012).
36. Power, *A Problem from Hell*, pp. 48–50.
37. S. Troebst, "Lemkin and Lauterpacht in Lemberg and Later: Pre- and Post-Holocaust Careers of Two East European International Lawyers," paper given

at the Annual Conference of the Imre Kertész College at Friedrich Schiller University, Jena on "Catastrophe and Utopia: Central and Eastern European Intellectual Horizons 1933 to 1958," Budapest, 13–15 June 2013. Available at: www.iwm.at/read-listen-watch/transit-online/lemkin-and-lauterpacht-in-lemberg-and-later-pre-and-post-holocaust-careers-of-two-east-european-international-lawyers (accessed 1 April 2016).

38. Power, *A Problem from Hell*, pp. 48–50.
39. ISA/RG 93.3/1-254, archive address: 02-110-01-03-05 – Israeli Foreign Ministry files concerning the UN Genocide Convention. Letter dated 9 November 1949, from Foreign Ministry legal advisor Shabtai Rosenne to Abba Eban, Israeli ambassador to the UN, demanding Israel's ratification of the Genocide Convention and quoting Raphael Lemkin's meeting with Israeli attorney general at the time, Jacob Shapira, along with a former colleague of Dr. Jacob Robinson from the WJC: Leon Kubowitzki. See also in this file: Foreign Minister Sharett's demand that Israel ratify the Genocide Convention instantly (cable dated 29 November 1949). See also in this file: letter from the ministry's director general, Walter Eytan, demanding that all parties first consult with Jacob Robinson on the legal and diplomatic implications of an Israeli ratification of the Genocide Convention *prior* to action. Eytan letter to Israeli consul general in New York, Arthur Lourie, dated 4 April 1950.
40. Ben-Nun, "Israeli Roots," p. 6.
41. I. Lewin, *Ten Years of Hope: Addresses before the United Nations* (New York: Shengold Publishers, 1971), p. 1.
42. Lewin, *In Defense*, p. 318.
43. Lewin, *Religious Jewry*, pp. 9–57.
44. ISA Foreign Ministry Files (MFA): ISA reference ISA/RG 130.2.1.1008 Box # 2416/10 – Jacob Robinson to Walter Eytan, director general of the Israeli Foreign Ministry, "Ad Hoc Committee on Statelessness and related Problems - Final Report," 21 February 1950, p. 5 point 5.
45. Ad Hoc Committee on Statelessness and Related Problems, UN Doc. E/C.2/242 reprinted in E/AC.32/SR.19 (1950).
46. Davy, "Article 32," pp. 1,285–92; Weis, *Commentary*, pp. 220–30.
47. Ad Hoc Committee on Statelessness and Related Problems, UN Doc. E/C.2/242 reprinted in E/AC.32/L.25 (1950).
48. Davy, "Article 32," p. 1,286.
49. Ibid., pp. 1,284–5.
50. Weis, *Commentary*, p. 225.
51. ISA/RG 130.2.1.1008 Box # 2416/10: Jacob Robinson to Walter Eytan, director general of the Israeli Foreign Ministry – Secret, "Third interim Report - Ad Hoc Committee on Statelessness and related Problems," 6 February 1950, pp. 1–2 point 4; quotation marks on the word "success" in the original.
52. Ben-Nun, "Israeli Roots," p. 8 n. 13.
53. Ibid., pp. 5–6.

54. Eytan, *First Ten Years*, pp. 108–37.
55. Ad Hoc Committee on Statelessness and Related Problems, UN Doc. E/AC.32/SR.19 (1950), pp. 9–11.
56. Ad Hoc Committee on Statelessness and Related Problems, UN Doc. E/AC.32/SR.20 (1950).
57. Lewin, *In Defense*, p. 161.
58. Ibid., pp. 161–2. Lewin's reading of Amos, and his view of it as the first precedent for some sort of international law guaranteeing the protection of refugees, stems from the words "whole captivity" and "brotherly covenant." Lewin refers in his address to Amos 1:9: Thus saith the LORD; For three transgressions of Tyrus, and for four, I will not turn away the punishment thereof; because they delivered up the whole captivity to Edom, and remembered not the brotherly covenant. Lewin's reference to expulsion of refugees stems from the Hebrew words. This translates correctly into "entire exiled people." The English of the Bible's King James Version mistakenly translates גלות שלמה as "whole captivity." The correct translation, which ought to have been "entire exile," appears only in very modern translations of the Bible such as the Holman Christian Standard (2004). This mistranslation originates in the earliest Greek Septuagint translation of the Old Testament, where גלות was translated into the Greek word αιχμαλωσία, later carried forward into St. Jerome's Vulgate translation into Latin as *Captivitatem*. Lewin's reference to some early form of international law, regarding the abrogation of a "brotherly covenant" and God's reprimanding thereof as proof of it, stems from medieval Jewish thought. Rashi (died 1105 in France), foremost among biblical commentators, explicitly refers to the "brotherly covenant" ברית אחים as the regional political pact between the pagan King Hiram of Tyre and the Jewish King Solomon in Jerusalem. See 2 Samuel 5:11 and 1 Kings 5:14–25, and also 1 Kings 9:10–16. The conjunction between the expulsion of exiles back to their tormentors (Edom) and the breaking of existing, regional diplomatic agreements was the basis for Lewin's seemingly anachronistic claim in favor of biblical international law.
59. Glynn, "Genesis," pp. 3–6.
60. ISA/RG 130.2.1.1008 Box # 2416/10: Jacob Robinson to Walter Eytan, director general of the Israeli Foreign Ministry – Secret, "Second interim Report - Ad Hoc Committee on Statelessness and Related Problems," 30 January 1950, p. 3 point 6b.
61. Ad Hoc Committee on Statelessness and Related Problems, UN Doc. E/AC.32/L.25 (1950).
62. UNHCR, 1951 Refugee Convention, Art. 33 para. 1.
63. Weis, *Commentary*, p. 226.
64. Ibid., p. 59.
65. Conference of Plenipotentiaries on the Status of Refugees and Stateless Persons, UN Doc A/CONF.2/9 (submitted 2 July 1951). This amendment by the Swedish Government was meant to – and, indeed, did – change the

definition of a refugee, inserting the words "membership of a particular social group or political opinion" into Article 1, A paragraph 2. From there, the words were copied and inserted into Article 33 concerning non-refoulement as well.

66. Einarsen, "Drafting," pp. 62–5. See also: A. Zimmermann and P. Wennholz, "Article 33, para 2 (prohibition of Expulsion or Return ('Refoulement'), in Zimmermann, Dörschner, and Machts, *1951 Convention*, pp. 1,397–423, at 1403.
67. UN Conference of Plenipotentiaries on the Status of Refugees and Stateless Persons, *Draft Convention Relating to the Status of Refugees. Agudas Israel World Organization: Amendment to Article* 27, received 4 July 1951 (submitted 29 June 1951), considered by the conference 6 July 1951; UN Doc, A/CONF.2/NGO/6.
68. Lewin, *In Defense*, p. 168; italics and inverted comas in the original.
69. IOC (50) 193, "Steering Committee on International Organizations General Assembly Fifth Session – Draft Brief on Supplementary Agenda Item No. 4," 25 September 1950, UK National Archives File BT 271/349, signed H. N. Edwards, 18/SEP/1950. Handwritten remarks by H. N. Edwards, legal advisor to Undersecretary of Trade P. J. Mantle.
70. "On the Mass Deportations in Hungary," statement by the President of the United States of America, Public Papers of the Presidents, Harry S. Truman, Document # 173, 27 July 1951. Available at: www.trumanlibrary.org/publicpapers/index.php?pid=387 (accessed April 2016).
71. See press release of the Jewish Telegraphic Agency, 2 August 1951, from Geneva. Available from JTA Online archives at: www.jta.org/1951/08/03/archive/america-and-britain-may-complain-to-u-n-against-hungarys-mass-deportations (accessed April 2016).
72. Robinson Final Plenipotentiary Report, p. 5 point 5.
73. Ibid.
74. Zimmermann and Wennholz, "Article 33, para 2," p. 1,403.
75. Ibid.
76. The 1951 Refugee convention text is on the UNHCR website. Available at: www.unhcr.org/3b66c2aa10.html (accessed April 2016).
77. Conference of Plenipotentiaries on the Status of Refugees and Stateless Persons, amendment proposed by Belgium, UN Doc A/CONF.2/10; and amendment proposed by France, A/CONF.2/18.
78. Conference of Plenipotentiaries on the Status of Refugees and Stateless Persons, UN Doc A/CONF.2/SR.6, pp. 6–7. Also in Takkenberg and Tahbaz, *Collected Travaux Préparatoires*, Vol. 2, pp. 246–7.
79. Ben-Nun, "Israeli Roots," p. 11.
80. Ibid., pp. 11–12.
81. Ibid., pp. 3–9.
82. Ibid., p. 2.
83. Robinson Final Plenipotentiary Report, p. 6 point 5, underlined phrases and insinuation points in the original.

84. UN Conference of Plenipotentiaries on the Status of Refugees and Stateless Persons, *Draft Convention Relating to the Status of Refugees. France - United Kingdom: Amendment to Article 28*, 11 July 1951, A/CONF.2/69. Available at: www.refworld.org/docid/3ae68ce08c.html (accessed April 2016).
85. Zimmermann and Wennholz, "Article 33, para 2," p. 1,403; Weis, *Commentary*, p. 235.
86. Robinson Report 1, point 10D.
87. Robinson Final Plenipotentiary Report, p. 9 point 7.
88. ISA Foreign Ministry Files (MFA), ISA reference ISA/RG93.38/1-31/MFA – Memorandum # 111, from the Director General, Ministry of Foreign Affairs, to Dr. Menachem Kahany, the Israeli delegate to the UN Headquarter offices Geneva, instructing Dr. Kahany to Sign the 4th Geneva Convention on behalf of the State of Israel, and providing him with signing powers, 9 December 1949. In the same file – letter from Ezekiel Gordon in Jerusalem to Kahany, providing four signed copies of the powers of attorney to sign the convention on Israel's behalf. Gordon's letter to Kahany, dated 18 November 1949, carrying the original filling code of: FO/M/3201/6049 [letter in French].
89. ISA Foreign Ministry Files (MFA), ISA reference ISA/RG93.38/1-31/MFA – Internal - confidential letter from Kahany to the Director General, dated 8 December 1954, confirming Kahany's role as the chair of the UNHCR advisory council on behalf of Israel – Hebrew reference.2289 /מכ/יד Received by the Foreign Minister's chamber on 12 December 1954.
90. Ben-Nun, "Israeli Roots," p. 5.
91. UN Conference of Plenipotentiaries on the Status of Refugees and Stateless Persons, Draft Convention Relating to the Status of Refugees. France: Amendment to Article 2, 3 July 1951, A/CONF.2/18. Available at: www.refworld.org/docid/3ae68ce04.html (accessed April 2016).
92. Ibid.
93. Ben-Nun, "Israeli Roots," p. 13 n. 25.
94. Weis, *Commentary*, p. 239.
95. Ibid., p. 239 n. 656.
96. For the Swedish amendment, which enlarged refugee protections for people of a certain social group or political opinion, see the French version of the amendment text: A/CONF2.9: UN Conference of Plenipotentiaries on the Status of Refugees and Stateless Persons, *Projet de Convention Relative au Statut des Réfugiés. Suède: Amendement à l'article premier*, 2 July 1951, A/CONF.2/9; available at: www.refworld.org/docid/3ae68ce848.html (accessed April 2016). For the French amendment limiting the scope of refugee protections, introducing a mechanisim for the revocation of refugee status, see: text I French: UN Conference of Plenipotentiaries on the Status of Refugees and Stateless Persons, *Projet de Convention Relative au Statut des Réfugiés. France: Amendement à l'article 2*, 3 July 1951, A/CONF.2/18; available at: www.refworld.org/docid/3ae68ce830.html (accessed April 2016). For the Belgian amendment of Article 2, see: UN Conference of Plenipotentiaries on the Status

of Refugees and Stateless Persons, *Projet de Convention Relative au Statut des Réfugiés. Belgique: Amendement à l'article 2*, 2 July 1951, A/CONF.2/10; available at: www.refworld.org/docid/3ae68ce020.html (accessed April 2016).

97. Ben-Nun, "Israeli Roots," pp. 11–18.
98. Ibid., p. 13.
99. Ibid., pp. 13–16.
100. Ibid., p. 7.
101. UK National Archives, file BT 271/349.
102. IOC (50) 193, "Steering Committee on International Organizations General Assembly Fifth Session – Draft Brief on Supplementary Agenda Item No. 4," 25 September 1950, UK National Archives File BT 271/349.
103. Ibid., p. 27.
104. Ibid., p. 28.
105. Ibid., p. 29.
106. IOC (50) 193 Corr. 1, Steering Committee on International Organizations General Assembly Fifth Session – "Draft Brief on Supplementary Agenda Item No. 4," 4 November 1950, UK National Archives File BT 271/349, pp. 27–8; current-author italics.
107. IOC (51) 68, "Steering Committee on International Organizations, Conference of Plenipotentiaries on the Status of Refugees and Stateless Persons," draft brief for the United Kingdom representatives, prepared by the Home Office, 26 June 1951, UK National Archives File BT 271/349 (hereinafter: Hoare Final Report), p. 10.
108. Ibid., p. 17.
109. Ibid., pp. 1–2.
110. Robinson final Plenipotentiary Report, p. 5 point 5.
111. Glynn, "Genesis," p. 6.
112. Robinson final Plenipotentiary Report, p. 2 point 2.
113. Hoare Final Report, p. 6, "Israeli did not sign because it was Saturday, the Jewish Sabbath, but was to sign the following week."
114. This term was coined by UNHCR, as it hastily published the insufficiently proof-read text of the Refugee Convention (with its French spelling error: "Refaulement" rather than "Refoulement"), two weeks after its signing in August 1951. UK National Archives File LCO 2/4317.
115. Gili Cohen, "African migrants trapped in the no-man's land zone between Israel and Egypt," *Haaretz, 4 September 2012.*
116. See, among others, the in-depth research undertaken by Michael Obert and Moises Saman, "Im Reich des Todes," *Suddeutsche Zeitung* magazine, 29 March 2013. Available at: sz-magazin.sueddeutsche.de/texte/anzeigen/40203/Im-Reich-des-Todes (accessed April 2016). And see also: Mirjam van Reisen, Meron Estefanos, and Conny Rijken, *The Human Trafficking Cycle: Sinai and Beyond* (Oisterwijk: Wolf Legal Publishers, 2013). This report was discussed in a special session of the European Parliament dedicated to the humanitarian problem of human trafficking in Sinai, on 3 December 2013.

117. "I Wanted to Lie Down and Die: Trafficking and Torture of Eritreans in Sudan and Egypt," Human Rights Watch report, February 2014. Available at: www.hrw.org/reports/2014/02/11/i-wanted-lie-down-and-die-0 (accessed April 2016).
118. Israeli Supreme Court Ruling 7146/ 12 from 16 September 2013, p. 81.
119. Gili Cohen and Talila Nesher, "A High Court plea against Defense Minister Barak and Interior Minister Yishai: Explain the blocking of entry of the trapped migrants at the border," *Haaretz*, 5 September 2012. On the courageous action undertaken by Physicians for Human Rights, see: Roy Chiki-Arad, "The Soldiers and the Doctors Looking at each other suspiciously," *Haaretz*, 7 September 2012.
120. "Let the refugees in," *Haaretz* editorial, 6 September 2012. Also see: Yossi Sarid, "Open them a gate while locking gates," *Haaretz*, 6 September 2012.
121. Moshe Zimmermann, "Between the fences 1938, 2012," *Haaretz*, 9 September 2013.
122. Talila Nesher and Gili Cohen, "UNHCR: Israel must grant immediate entry to the stranded migrants on the border fence," *Haaretz*, 6 September 2012.
123. Talila Nesher, "First testimony by the African female migrants stranded at the border: the Army refouled and actively pushed the male migrants back into Egyptian territory," *Haaretz*, 11 September 2012.
124. One methodological – or, rather, meta-logical – feature of the historical narrative presented here concerns its embedded assumption, overtly and openly made, that the delegates and protagonists of the "Robinsonian network" were indeed paramount in mustering the diplomatic power required for the 1951 Refugee Convention to come to life in its overtly humanitarian form. Nevertheless, one is bound to ask in this regard: Where were the governments? Could it really be that these delegates had such a free hand as to legislate and bind their own governments to a document so far-reaching in its consequences without strong controls by those govenments over their delegates? The answer to this question is of course far beyond the scope of this study, and it is questionable whether one can speak of a general attitude of governments, as opposed to a general group of cross-country committed diplomats, which is what the notion of the 'Robinsonian network' would *ipso facto* imply. A more cautious approach (and probably one which would make more methodological sense) would be to examine the attitudes of each and every government and its respective inter-ministerial connection between ambassadors and superiors in capitals, and then to try and draw some answers to question as to the role of the 'States'. In the case of Israel, and specifically of Jacob Robinson, the sources are rather clear in that the Israeli officials from Foreign Minister Moshe Sharett down, did not actually care much for what Robinson was really doing in his endeavors to secure refuge rights, both in the drafting of the 1951 Refugee Convention, and in his drafting of the 1954 Convention on Statelessness. For a strong confirmation of this view regarding Robinson and Israel see: Rotem Giladi, 'A 'Historical Commitment'? Identity

and Ideology in Israel's Attitude to the Refugee Convention 1951–4' in *The International History Review 37* (4) 2015, pp: 745-767. For the attitudes of the French, Belgian and British governments see: Gilad Ben-Nun, 'From Ad-Hoc to Universal: The international refugee regime from fragmentation to unity' in *Refugee Survey Quarterly 34* (2) 2015, pp. 23-44 at 43-44. The analysis of the archival evidence in these studies do somewhat point to the fact that in the case of the 1951 Refugee Convention, the people (that is the humanitarianly committed delegates) did indeed 'make the history' much more than their individual governments. That said, at least in the case of the British government, the evidence seems absolutely clear that a keen and deep humanitarian motivation for the amelioration of the conditions for refugees, existed in Whitehall all along. In this regard, Samuel Hoare was indeed probably directly executing the policies of His Majesty's government, which in this case – were deeply humanitarian.

Chapter 3 The Moderateness of the Sharon–Olmert Administrations, 2005–8

1. For the best analysis of the conflation between "left" and "right" in Israeli politics, and of how Ariel Sharon – the archetypal "hawk" – shifted from the fringes of right-wing thinking to the center of consensus of Israeli politics, see chapter 5 of one of the most balanced and erudite accounts of the making and collapse of the Oslo peace process, written by the former president of Tel Aviv University, and former Israeli ambassador to Washington under the late Yitzhak Rabin: Itamar Rabinovich, *Waging Peace: Israel and the Arabs 1948–2003* (Princeton, NJ: Princeton University Press, 2004), pp. 181–219.
2. Michael Feige, *One Space Two Places: Gush Emunim, Peace Now and the Construction of Israeli Space* (Jerusalem: Hebrew University Magnes Press, 2002).
3. Rabinovich, *Waging Peace*, p. 184.
4. Robert Fisk, *Pity the Nation: Lebanon at War* (Oxford: Oxford University Press, 1990). See also Ehud Ya'ari and Ze'ev Schiff, *Israel's Lebanon War* (New York: Touchstone Books, 1985). For the report of the Israeli Supreme Court, see the website of the Israeli Ministry of Foreign affairs: www.mfa.gov.il/MFA/Foreign%20Relations/Israels%20Foreign%20Relations%20since%201947/1982-1984/104%20Report%20of%20the%20Commission%20of%20Inquiry%20into%20the%20e (accessed April 2016).
5. Sarah S. Willen, "L'hyperpolitique du 'Plus jamais ça!': demandeurs d'asile soudanais, turbulence gouvernementale et politiques de contrôle des réfugiés en Israël," *Cultures & Conflits* no. 71 (Fall 2008), pp. 93–112, at 95.
6. Sabar, "Rise and Fall," p. 188.
7. See the memoir by the former US Secretary of State under the Bush Administration and during Sharon's disengagement from the Gaza Strip and

parts of the West Bank: Condoleezza Rice, *No Higher Honor: A Memoir of My Years in Washington* (New York: Random House, 2011), pp. 280–4.

8. Vered Leibowitch, "23 casualties in a suicide bombing in Tel Aviv," *YNET*, January 6, 2003.
9. Sarah Willen, "Flesh of our Flesh," in Willen (ed.), *Transnational Migration*, pp. 159–84.
10. Gary Sussman, "The Challenge to the Two-State Solution," *Middle East Report* (34) (2004). Available at: www.merip.org/mer/mer231/challenge-two-state-s olution (accessed April 2016).
11. Unfortunately, no full and in-depth account of the Sharon–Olmert administrations and their impacts upon Israeli society has been published in English. For one of the best accounts to date concerning Sharon's disengagement from Gaza, and Olmert's war in Lebanon in the aftermath of the disengagement in 2005, see the account by the well-respected Israeli journalist and commentator Dan Margalit: *Awakening* (Tel Aviv: Kineret-Zmora Bitan Publishers, 2009) [in Hebrew].
12. Dennis B. Ross, "Stop Giving Palestinians a Pass," *New York Times*, January 4, 2015.
13. Rice, *No Higher Honor*, pp. 613–21.
14. Rabinovich, *Waging Peace*, p. 310.
15. Itamar Rabinovich, *The Lingering Conflict: Israel, The Arabs, and the Middle East 1948–2012* (Washington, DC: Brookings Institute Press, 2012) pp. 163–82.
16. Shahar Ilan, "The Naturalization Process has been Concluded," *Haaretz*, June 19, 2007.
17. Ibid., p. 1.
18. Ibid.
19. Channel 2 evening news, June 20, 2007. See also: Ilan, "Naturalization process," pp. 1–2.
20. Ilan, Naturalization process," p. 2.
21. See the official website of the Israeli Government for the Winograd Commission: www.vaadatwino.gov.il (accessed April 2016).
22. This subject is well beyond the scope of the current volume, yet is nonetheless important for an understanding of the mindset of Olmert Administration legislators, framing their decision to bring forward their new anti-infiltration legislation and enshrining it within a security-driven discourse. Over the years, several vital issues have torn Israeli society apart at the juncture between the need for security and the safeguarding of civil liberties. The right for journalistic free speech versus military censorship of the media when concerned with material deemed harmful to national security, and the usage of torture against "ticking bomb" suicide terrorists are just two examples of the complex dilemmas confronting an Israel torn between security needs and its democratic liberties. On this, see (in Hebrew): M. Hofnung, *Israel – Security Needs vs. The Rule of Law* (Jerusalem: Nevo Publishers, 1991).
23. Ibid., p. 28.

24. See: ibid., p. 341. See also: A. Dowty, "The Use of Emergency Powers in Israel," *Middle East Review* Vol. 30 (1) (1988), pp. 34–46.
25. For the full text of the 2008 proposed Anti Infiltration Act, see the official website of the Israeli Knesset: www.knesset.gov.il/Laws/Data/BillGoverment/381/381.pdf (accessed April 2016) translated from the Hebrew, and italics added, by current author (hereinafter: Anti Infiltration Act 2008).
26. See Chapters 2 and 3.
27. Anti Infiltration Act 2008, Article 2, p. 550.
28. Ibid., Article 3, p. 550.
29. Ibid., Article 20, p. 560.
30. Ibid., Article 11, p. 555; italics added.
31. See official full text of the 1951 convention at the UNHCR website: www.unhcr.org/3b66c2aa10.html (accessed April 2016). For Article 33 of the convention, see p. 30.
32. For all the NGOs mentioned above, see their websites: "The Hotline" – www.hotline.org.il; ASSAF – www.assaf.org.il; ARDC – ardc-israel.org/en (all accessed April 2016).
33. For P4HR, see: www.phr.org.il; for Worker's Hotline, see: www.kavlaoved.org.il/default_eng.html (both accessed April 2016).
34. Shahar Ilan, "First Draft Approved: up to Five Years Incarceration for any Border Trespasser; Seven Years for a Trespasser from Darfur," *Haaretz*, May 20, 2008.
35. Vered Lee, "What have I Voted?: How Do the Members of Parliament Explain their Endorsement for the New Anti Infiltration Act," *Haaretz*, July 30, 2009.
36. See the official response of MK Dr Dov Hanin to the decision to refrain from continuing governmental efforts to legislate the 2008 Anti Infiltration Act, on his official web-based blog page. Available at: www.dovblog.org/dov/2088.htm l (accessed April 2016) [in Hebrew; current author's translation from Hebrew].
37. Interview, in Jerusalem, by current author with "G.L.", a pro-migrant activist with the coalition for the protection of the Darfur refugees in Israel. Interview number 5, dated July 16, 2012.
38. For the full work of the ACRI, its history and activities, see its website: www.acri.org.il/en (accessed April 2016).
39. Hofnung, *Security Needs*, pp. 107–224.
40. See the annual report by the Israeli national state comptroller for 2006, Justice Micha Lindenstraus, reports of the year 2007, and fiscal reports for the monetary year 2007. ISSN: 0334-9713, catalogue number: 958/1-2008, pp. 97–120, at p. 98, published on May 20, 2008 (hereinafter: Lindenstraus Report 2007). PDF version available at: old.mevaker.gov.il/serve/contentTree.asp?bookid=514&id=190&contentid=9582&parentcid=9581&bctype=1&sw=1366&hw=698 (accessed April 2016).
41. Anti-Infiltration Act 2008, Article 1 – General Terms, p. 548.
42. See the special blog created under the website of the ACRI for mobilization against the 2008 biometric database act at: acri-antibiometric.blogspot.de/2009/05/blog-post_30.html (accessed April 2016).

43. Liat Schlezinger, "The UN: 90 Percent of Asylum Seekers in Israel are Considered Under Refugee Status," *Maariv*, February 2, 2010.
44. See: ACRI, Amnesty International etal., "The draft Anti Infiltration Act – Lies and reality," position paper published by the pro-migrant coalition, Tel Aviv, 2010. Available for download from the website of the daily newspaper *Maariv* at: www.nrg.co.il/images/news1/report.doc (accessed April 2016).
45. Lindenstraus Report 2007, p. 110.
46. Shai Niv, "Objection in the Knesset Rising towards Endorsement of the 'Infiltration Law'", *Globes*, February 3, 2010. Also see: Lee, "What have I Voted?": "How do the Knesset members explain their endorsement for such dubious legislation? Here are their explanations for eternal disgrace: Nizan Horowitz [far-left gay Meretz MK, and senior gay rights advocate – G.B.N.] 'the government filled in a long list of laws for contiguity between parliaments, and I just walked in and voted affirmatively by mistake, even though I'm against the law [. . .] MK Daniel Ben Simon [Labor – advocate of socialist legislation, women's rights, and Arab minority rights – G.B.N.] 'There is a huge burden of legislation, we cannot learn all the laws being passed and I say this honestly, I voted affirmatively for this law out of ignorance. Really I did not know this concerned the Darfur refugees and would have never voted for it had I known so [. . .]'."
47. Dana Weiler-Polak, "The Government has Decided to Withdraw the Anti Infiltration Act," *Haaretz*, July 29, 2010.

Chapter 4 The Rise of the Israeli Extreme Right, 2009–12

1. I owe here a debt of gratitude to Professor Michael Daxner, former president of Oldenburg University and former chief civilian administrator of UNMIK (United Nations Interim Administration Mission in Kosovo) for delving into the development of my ideas concerning societal extremization.
2. On this distinction in Plato's theory of knowledge, and the difference between "True Belief" and "Knowledge," see: "The Meno," in W. K. C. Guthrie, *A History of Greek Philosophy* (Cambridge: Cambridge University Press, 1975) Vol. 4, pp. 236–65, at 256, and also see p. 265. For an earlier and somewhat simplified distinction between "true belief" and "knowledge," see what is nowadays considered a "canonical" study of Plato's theory of knowledge and education: R. L. Nettleship, *The Theory of Education in Plato's Republic* (Oxford: Oxford University Press, 1935), pp. 106–7. Nettleship's essay was originally published in 1880 (so just under 100 years before Guthrie's study), and uses the term "knowledge" as distinct from "opinion" as per Plato's own theoretical evolvement from the *Meno* to *The Republic*. Nevertheless, the meanings are basically the same.
3. George L. Mosse, *Nationalism and Sexuality: Middle-Class Morality and Sexual Norms in Modern Europe* (Madison, WI: Wisconsin University Press, 1988).

Mosse's point about the vulnerability of women, homosexuals, and ethnic minorities was amply presented and discussed by Mosse's student, and current history professor at the Hebrew University in Jerusalem, Steven Ascheim in his seminar, "The Modern Culture of the *Fin de Siecle*," concerning the anti-Semitic sentiments rampant in Theodor Herzl's and Sigmund Freud's Vienna in the late nineteenth century. Oddly enough, Mosse's observation is vindicated in cultural settings far removed from his own Western European societal spheres of research. One need only consider the recent anti-gay legislation by Uganda's ethics and integrity minister, Simon Lokodo, decreeing a possible death sentence for people charged with homosexual practices. Lokodo's recently proposed legislation demanding that women dress in long-sleeved clothes, against the cultural traditions and even climate of sub-Saharan Africa, merely validate Mosse's observation, albeit in societies that Mosse most probably never even considered. See: David Smith, "Uganda Proposes Ban on Miniskirts in Move Against Women's Rights," *Guardian*, April 5, 2013.

4. Leon Wieseltier, "Fevers," *New Republic*, January 25, 2012.
5. "MK Zeev: 'Homosexuals are Sick People Who have a Serious Defect'", report, Walla News Agency, March 19, 2001.
6. I. Marciano, "MK Zeev against the 'Disgusting Homosexual'", *YNET*, July 23, 2003.
7. A. Shumfalvi, "Eli Yishai: Homosexuals and Lesbians are People with an Illness," *YNET*, February 22, 2006.
8. S. Mizrachi, "MK Zeev: 'One should Treat Homosexuals like Bird Flu'", *Maariv* internet portal, "NRG," January 29, 2008.
9. A. Bender, "MK Zeev is Inciting and Calling for the Murder of Homosexuals," *Maariv* internet portal, "NRG," February 5, 2008.
10. Y. Goren, "Two Teenagers Murdered in a Youth Event of the Gay and Lesbian Community in Tel Aviv," *Haaretz*, August 2, 2009.
11. Amnon Meranda, "SHAS Condemns Attack on Gay Center," *YNET*, August 2, 2009.
12. Yusuf Jabarrin, "A New Politics? Between Conditional Citizenship and Full Equal Citizenship," *Van Leer Institute Bulletin* (1) (April 10, 2013) [in Hebrew].
13. ACRI, Amnesty International et al., "Lies and reality," p. 2.
14. "300 Rabbis Oppose Selling or Renting Apartments to Arabs," Israeli Channel 2 Television Report, December 9, 2010, broadcast at 07:28 hours.
15. "Betar Fans Demonstrated against the signing-on of Muslim Players," Israel Broadcasting Association – Channel Beth, February 1, 2013, 12:43 hours. See also: Yuri Yalon, "Betar Shall Remain Clean of Arabs," *Israel Today*, February 1, 2013.
16. Daniel Blatman, "If I were an American Jew, I'd worry about Israel's Racist Cancer," *Haaretz*, March 7, 2014.
17. Including the party leader and now Israeli foreign minister, Avigdor Lieberman, a settler from Tequoa near the Palestinian city of Bethlehem.

18. The KIC held four sessions where it considered, and finally adopted, the new draft legislation against migrants. These discussions were recorded by the Knesset clerks, and unofficial version of these protocols and transcripts were obtained by the author. The four sessions were held on the following dates: August 10, 2011, November 14, 2011, and December 13 and 19, 2011 – the last-mentioned being the final session where the draft legislation was voted on and adopted by the committee, and passed on to the Knesset plenary floor for the last call of voting.

Chapter 5 The Legislative Process and Modern Adaptation of the 1954 Anti-Infiltration Act

1. Knesset public record of legislative proposals, *Governmental legislation proposal number* 577, dated March 28, 2011, כ"ב באדר ב' התשע"א in the Hebrew calendar.
2. See the official call for public participation on the Israeli Government's official website for legislative participation. Available at: http://www.kr8.co.il/BRPortal/br/P102.jsp?arc=111317 (accessed April 2016)
3. Knesset Interior Committee (KIC) protocol meeting, Protocol Number 436, August 10, 2011, 11:30 hours. Available upon request from the Knesset (unrevised version obtained by the author).
4. Statement of the chairman, MK Amnon Cohen, ibid., p. 1.
5. Statement of Advocate Tomer Rosner, legal advisor to the KIC, ibid.
6. Statement of Advocate Avital Sternberg, director of the Department of Legislation, the Israeli Ministry of Justice, ibid., p. 3.
7. Statement of Advocate Avital Sternberg, ibid., p. 5.
8. Statement of Advocate Avital Sternberg, ibid., p. 6.
9. Statements of MK Michael Ben Ari for the extreme-right party Haichud Haleumi, ibid., pp. 8, 11, 13, 17.
10. Opening statement of Chairman Cohen, KIC Protocol 448, November 14, 2011, 09:30 hours, p. 2.
11. Ibid.
12. Opening statement of the chairman, Cohen, and following statement by Advocate Eyal Yinon, Knesset Chief legal Counsel, KIC protocol 465, December 13, 2011, 09:00 hours, pp. 3–4; italics added (hereinafter: KIC Protocol 465).
13. Omry Efraim, "The Knesset Chief Legal Counsel: The proposed anti infiltration act is exceptionally irregular," *YNET*, December 13, 2011; see also: "Israel's Anti Infiltration Law is a Disgrace," *Haaretz* main editorial, January 11, 2012: "Even the courageous objections of Knesset legal advisor Eyal Yinon were to no avail, and the law was passed."
14. Talila Nesher, "The High Court Suspends the Application of the Anti Infiltration Act," *Haaretz*, March 12, 2013.

15. Shuki Sadeh, "A Fence, but not a Solution on the Israel-Egypt Border," *Haaretz*, November 25, 2011.
16. KIC Protocol 465, p. 9, italics added.
17. Ibid., p. 10.
18. Ibid., p. 14.
19. Ibid., p. 46.
20. Ibid., pp. 34–47. The whole last hour, and corresponding 14 pages of KIC protocol 465, consist of a direct confrontation between the Chairman and both governmental legal advisors: Advocate Avital Sterberg and Advocate Achaz Ben Ari, chief legal counsel for the Ministry of Defense. The discussion was one where the chairman demands to read point by point, word for word from the new act, and the legal advisors repeatedly provide excuses of why the articles are formulated this way, stressing that they will correct the text before bringing it to the final vote at the Knesset plenary. Noteworthy, and characteristic of the thorough legal culture of Chairman Cohen, he refuses to accept these excuses and finally dismisses the KIC session until further notice, refusing to set either a deadline or a timetable for the following sessions until a fully fledged, coherent legal draft is provided for the KIC members to discuss. The final stretch of legislation took place a week later at the last session of the KIC, with a fully comprehensive draft which already incorporated the non-penalization of NGO workers and a reaffirmation of Israel's obligations according to the UNHCR 1951 Refuge Convention.

    See: KIC protocol # 467, December 19, 2011, 09:30 hours, pp: 22–5: statement of Advocate Yochi Gennesin, director of the newly created legal department for African migrants at the Israeli Ministry of Justice.
21. Azri Amram, "Police suspects Molotov Cocktail – a Vengeance Act Against the Rape," Channel 2 news report, April 30, 2012.
22. Globes News Service report, May 17, 2012.
23. Shoham Smith, "A Day Between Locals and Foreigners at the Helm of the Conflict in the Shapira Neighborhood," *Haaretz*, May 18, 2012.
24. Yaniv Kobovich and Ilan Lior, "Molotov Bottles Thrown Last Night at Migrants' Dwellings in South Tel Aviv: A Rise in the Degree of the Onslaught," *Haaretz*, April 27, 2012.
25. Yaniv Kobovich, "A Gang of South Tel-Aviv Residents had been Attacking Migrants," *Haaretz*, May 23, 2012.
26. Dana Weiler-Polak and Ilan lior, "Tension in the South Tel Aviv Neighborhoods: After the Molotov Cocktails Thrown at Migrant Dwellings – Threats to Humanitarian Aid Workers," *Haaretz*, May 7, 2012.
27. "Eli Yishai: We Need to Incarcerate all Migrant Workers and Refugees in Penal Facilities," *Haaretz* Daily News Service report, May 16, 2012.
28. Ibid., p. 1.

Chapter 6 The Israeli Extreme Right's Anti-Migrant Onslaught

1. Ibid., p. 2.
2. Yaniv Kobovich and Talila Nesher, "Netanyahu Threatens: we Might Easily Reach 600,000 Foreigners – the PM and the Interior Minister Warn that the Influx of Foreign Migrants Threatens the 'Zionist Dream'", *Haaretz*, May 20, 2012.
3. Yanir Yagne, "Yishai: A State which does not Want Infiltrators Shall not Allow Them Employment," *Haaretz*, May 22, 2013.
4. Yehonatan Lis, "A Stormy Knesset Debate – Police Representative at the Knesset Confirms: A Rise in Migrant Crime Rates – the State Must Allow them Employment," *Haaretz*, May 21, 2013.
5. *Haaretz* Daily News Service report, May 23, 2012 at 23:57 hours. See also: Atila Shumfalvi and Gilad Morag, "A Counter Demonstration in Jerusalem Following Yesterday's Anti Migrant Riots: Racism in the Knesset and the Country is Collapsing," *YNET* News Agency report, May 24, 2012.
6. Ibid., *Haaretz*, May 23.
7. Yaniv Kobovich, "Suspicion: A Gang of Tel Aviv Residents has been Attacking Migrants," *Haaretz*, May 23, 2012. See also: Eli Senior and Gilad Morag, "A ninth suspect apprehended regarding the attack on migrants in Tel Aviv," *YNET*, May 25, 2012; "Indictment in Court: Beating and Robbing of African Migrants with Clubs," *Haaretz*, May 31, 2012.
8. Anat Shalev and Mor Shimoni, "Molotov Cocktails Thrown at Migrant Dwellings and an African Kindergarten in South Tel Aviv," Walla News Agency, April 27, 2012.
9. Yaniv Kobovich, "Aharonovich to Members of the Knesset: your Words can Incite More Violence Like what we had Yesterday in Jerusalem," *Haaretz*, June 4, 2012.
10. Ibid.
11. Tamar Rotem, "Lessons in Incitement: Migrant Children Speak of their Life in Fear," *Haaretz*, June 3, 2012. See also: Dana Weiler-Polak, "Growing Concern in the Migrant Community: we're Afraid Leave Our Homes," *Haaretz*, June 11, 2012.
12. Sarah Willen, "Blood Rhetoric and Danger: Foreign Workers, Suicide Bombings and the Politics of Non-Visibility in the Realms of Mourning," in E. Lomsky-Feder and Tamar Rapoport (eds), *Visibility in Immigration: Body, Gaze, Representation* (Jerusalem: Van Leer Jerusalem Institute and Hakibbutz Hameuchad Publishing House, 2006), pp. 329–53 [in Hebrew].
13. Dana Weiler-Polak, "From Today: New African Migrants shall be Immediately Incarcerated for up to 3 Years," *Haaretz*, June 3, 2012.
14. Gili Cohen, "District Court Authorizes the Deportation of South Sudanese Back to their Homeland," *Haaretz*, June 7, 2012.
15. Yaniv Kobovich, "Yet Another Attack Against Migrants: Fire Bombs Thrown at an Eritrean Pub in Tel Aviv," *Haaretz*, June 17, 2012.

16. Aviad Glickman, "Attorney General: South Sudanese can be Deported," *YNET*, May 23, 2012.
17. Menachem Rahat, *SHAS the Spirit and the Power* (Tel Aviv: Alfa Communications Publications, 1998) [in Hebrew].
18. On the moderate views of SHAS concerning the Arab minority in Israel, and the party's sporadic cooperation with Arab – and even Islamist – factions in supporting initiatives promoting religious freedoms, see the 2004 International Crisis Group report regarding the Arab Minority in Israel: *Middle East Report No. 25* (Amman/Brussels: International Crisis Group, March 4, 2004), available at: www.crisisgroup.org/~/media/Files/Middle%20East%20North%20Africa/Israel%20Palestine/Identity%20Crisis%20Israel%20and%20its%20Arab%20Citizens.ashx (accessed April 2016). In this report, see especially the parallel drawn by SHAS members of the Knesset between their own educational autonomy of the Jewish ultra-religious educational system and possible correlative prospects for a moderate religious-Islamite educational system, p. 18 of the report (footnote 114).
19. Arye Dayan, *As the Spring Overflows: The Story of SHAS* (Jerusalem: Keter Publishers, 1999) [in Hebrew]. On Deri's resignation, see: Yoel Nir, *Arye Deri: The Rise, The Crisis and the Pain* (Tel Aviv: Yediot Aharonot, 1999) [in Hebrew].
20. Arnon Sofer (ed.), *Refugees or Migrant Workers from African States?* (Tel Aviv: Research Center of the Academy for National Security, 2009) [in Hebrew]. For a counterview of how the government was manipulating the African asylum-seeking influx, see: Haim Yacobi, "From Non-Policy to Politics of Fear," in Haim Yacobi, *African Refugee's Influx in Israel from a Socio-Political Perspective* (Florence: European University Institute, Robert Schuman Center for Advanced Studies, 2009). Available at: ardc-israel.org/sites/default/files/carim_rr_2009_04.pdf (accessed April 2016).
21. Interview with Eli Yishai to Israeli television, Channel 2, October 10, 2009, quoted in: Dana Weiler-Polak, "Yishai: Many Women who have been Raped by Migrants are Afraid to Come Forward and Report their Abuse for Fear of Being Tagged as AIDS Carriers," *Haaretz*, May 31, 2012.
22. "Eli Yishai: We Must Immediately Lock up all Migrant Workers and Refugees in Jail Houses or Detention Facilities," *Haaretz*, May 16, 2012.
23. Uri Misgav, "I am Pacifist," *Haaretz*, May 21, 2012.
24. Jonatan Lis, "Stormy Knesset Debate regarding the African Migrants: Police Chief in the Knesset – a Rise in Migrant Crime Rates, We must Allow Them Employment," *Haaretz*, May 21, 2012.
25. Shalom Yerushalmi, "Eli Yishai in a Special Interview: Its Either Us or Them," *Maariv*, June 1, 2012.
26. Ibid.
27. Dana Weiler-Polak, "From Today Onwards: Newcomer Migrants from Africa will be Immediately Jailed for an Initial Period of up to Three Years," *Haaretz*, June 3, 2012.

28. Gideon Levy, "A Larger Danger than the Migrants," *Haaretz*, May 31, 2012. See also: Yossi Sarid, "Nice to Meet you, Israel the Deporter," *Haaretz*, June 12, 2012; "Mass Jailing," *Haaretz*, editorial, June 5, 2012.
29. Levy, "Larger danger." Levy is reffering here to MK Miri Regev's speech at the anty-migrant demonstration on the May 23, 2012 where she refered to migrants as "a cancer in our body."
30. On the mass Israeli anti-capitalist and anti-government demonstrations, see: Asher Schechter, *Rothschild Boulevard: The Anatomy of Protest* (Tel Aviv: Hakibbutz Hameuchad Publishing House, 2012) [in Hebrew]. Also see: Orly Vilnai and Guy Meroz, *Suddenly a People Arises* (Tel Aviv: Modan Publishers, 2011) [in Hebrew].
31. Sivan Rahav Meir, "After the Jewish Festivals: Tens of Thousands of Migrant Trespassers will be Jailed," Channel 2 News report, August 29, 2012.
32. Talila Nesher, "State Attorney: Yishai's Declarations Concerning the Mass Incarceration of the Sudanese Migrants, were Misguided," *Haaretz*, October 25, 2012.
33. Ibid.
34. Ibid.
35. Ibid.
36. Barak Ravid, "Israel's Pillar of Defense Achieved its Goals," *Haaretz*, November 22, 2012.
37. Jeremy Bowen, "Israel-Hamas Ceasefire comes into Effect in Gaza," BBC News report, November 21, 2012.
38. "The Minister for Incitement Affairs," *Haaretz*, editorial, November 20, 2013.
39. Ariana Melamed, "The African Migrants have not Infiltrated Anybody's Political Campaign," *YNET*, December 20, 2012.
40. Yaniv Kobovich, "Media Ban Lifted: An 83 Year Old Woman was Raped Near her Apartment in South Tel Aviv," *Haaretz*, December 31, 2012.
41. Ibid.
42. For a cumulative account of African-migrant sexual violence and the explicit prior knowledge and cooperation of the media outlets with the media bans, see: Azri Amram, "Suspected: Rape of an Elderly Woman on her Premises," Channel 2 News report, December 31, 2013 at 09:02 hours. Also see: "Rape of Elderly Woman Concludes an Excessively Violent Year in South Tel Aviv," Walla News Agency, December 31, 2012 at 10:40 hours.
43. "Following the Rape of an Elderly Woman: SHAS Launches an Anti-migrant Campaign," *Maariv* internet portal, "NRG," December 31, 2012 at 17:15 hours.
44. 'Yishai: Determined to Deport All the Infiltrators' on *National Army Radio – Galei Zahal*, January 1, 2013, at 11:41 hours.
45. Akiva Novik, "Yishai's 'Doomsday Electoral Weapon': Watch SHAS' Secret Campaign Pitch," *YNET* News Agency report, December 31, 2012,
46. "SHAs Launches Anti-migrant Campaign."
47. Shabtai Bendet, "How did the Rape of an Elderly Woman Make its way into the Electoral Campaign?" Walla News Agency report, December 31, 2012 at 22:05 hours.

48. Novik, "Doomsday Weapon."
49. Jonatan Lis and Talila Nesher, "After a Negative Right Wing Campaign: A Researcher in the Knesset's Research Authority has been Removed from Office Due to his Left-Leaning Opinions," *Haaretz*, January 6, 2013.
50. "Liberalism with Limited Liability – the Removal of Dr Nathan," *Haaretz*, editorial, January 10, 2013.
51. Or Kashti, "The Campaign to Purge State Bureaucracy of Left-leaning People," *Haaretz*, January 12, 2013.
52. "The Removal of Dr Nathan."
53. Dana Weiler-Polak, "Knesset Member Katz Deliberately Withheld a Report Contradicting Prime Minister Netanyahu's Claims for a Refugee Tidal Wave," *Haaretz*, February 19, 2010.
54. For chart data, see: Talila Nesher, "Amid Drop in Entry of African Migrants: 80,000 Working Permits for Aliens were Issued this Year by the Interior Ministry," *Haaretz*, December 31, 2012. See also: Arik Bender, "Knesset Research Unit Report: Over a Quarter of a Million Aliens in Israel," *Maariv*, January 8, 2012. Also see: "Eli Yishai has Issued an Unprecedented Mumber of Working Permits for Aliens," Globes Economic News Agency, November 9, 2009; Dana Weiler-Polak, "Interior Minister Eli Yishai has issued a record number of working permits for aliens this year," *Haaretz*, November 9, 2011; Gilad Nathan, "Aliens in Israel," special report commissioned by Knesset Member Nitzan Horowitz for the special session of the Knesset Interior Committee concerning alien migrants into Israel, December 13, 2011.
55. A note of caution on the statistics for foreign migrants into Israel: during the 3-month research and data-collection period undertaken for this chart, strong discrepancies and contradictions arose between two government agencies: the Interior Ministry's population and immigration authority on the one hand, and the Israeli national Central Bureau of Statistics on the other. While the immigration authority's number of foreign workers stood at 90,000 and 88,000 for the years 2010 and 2011 respectively, The Central Bureau of Statistics' numbers were over 20 percentage points higher than those of the Interior Ministry. Given that the population and immigration authority had, in fact, been created in 2011 specifically to deal with the African migrant challenge, it was tainted in the sense that it wished as early as possible to exhibit a drop in foreigners resident in Israel, attributing this anti-migrant success to its own actions. The author of these lines has chosen to side with the objective and notably independent numbers emanating from the well-researched papers of the Israeli Central Bureau of Statistics. This choice stems primarily from the strong political implications attached to these statistics – especially given that the 2011 numbers were published in July 2012, just after the mass anti-migrant riots and as parliamentary elections were being announced.
56. Interview number 3, conducted by the author with SHAS officials in Jerusalem, July 2012.

57. Ibid. See also: Yacobi, "Let Me Go to the City," p. 60.
58. Interview number 5, conducted by the author with SHAS officials in Jerusalem, July 2012.
59. For this extreme view of Yishai as a racist, see the eloquent, if somewhat unfair, extrapolation of Yishai's legacy in: Ariana Melamed, "My Home and SHAS Racism," *YNET* News Agency, January 16, 2013.
60. For a fascinating discussion on the concept of "otherness" and how this acts as a differentiator within different societies, see the comparison of ideas of "otherness" in Germany, France, and the US by Riva Kastoryano: "Codes of Otherness," *Sociological Review*, Vol. 77 (1) (Spring 2010), pp. 79–100.
61. See Chapter 2, above.

Chapter 7 The Revocation of the 2012 and 2013 Anti-Infiltration Acts

1. See: Supreme Court President Aharon Barak, "The Place of Jewish Law in the Law of State," in Chaim Cohn & Yitzhak Zamir (eds), *Aharon Barak: A Collection of Writings* (Jerusalem: Nevo publishers, 2000), Vol. 1, pp. 97–105 [in Hebrew; title translated by author].
2. On the supreme court's history, image, and tendencies, see the book by current Supreme Court Justice Elyakim Rubenstein: *Judges of the Land* (Tel Aviv: Schoken, 1980) [in Hebrew].
3. Fania Oz Salzberger and Eli Salzberger, "The Secret German Roots of the Israeli Supreme Court," *Israel Studies* Vol. 3, No. 2 (Fall 1998), pp. 159–92.
4. Roger Cohen, quoted in: Lars Trägårdh and Michael Delli Carpini, "The Juridification of Politics in the United States and Europe: Historical Roots, Contemporary Debates and Future Prospects," in Lars Trägårdh (ed.), *After National Democracy: Rights, Law and Power in America and the New Europe* (Oxford: Oñati International Institute for the Sociology of Law and Oxford University Press, 2004), Ch. 3, pp. 41–78.
5. Salzberger and Salzberger, "Secret German Roots," p. 164.
6. Ibid., p. 180. See also: Pnina Lahav, "American Influence on Israel's Jurisprudence of Free Speech," *Hastings Constitutional Law Quarterly*, 9 (1981), pp. 21–40.
7. Pnina Lahav, *Judgment in Jerusalem: Chief Justice Simon Agranat and the Zionist Century* (Berkeley, CA: University of California Press 1991), p. 144.
8. Avigdor Feldman, "My Ideal Supreme Court," *Haaretz*, January 2, 2010 [translated from Hebrew by G.B.N.].
9. On the seizure of private Land in the OPT and the security establishment's approach, which was struck down in 1979 by the Israeli Supreme Court, see the very authoritative website of B'Tselem, the Israeli Information Center for Human Rights in the Occupied Territories, available at: www.btselem.org/settlements/seizure_of_land_for_military_purposes (accessed April 2016).

10. The second Netanyahu Administration (2009–14) indeed attempted to restrict the rights of NGOs to appeal to the supreme court, mainly on technical grounds. In 2011, the right-wing justice minister, Yaacov Neeman, attempted to change the Basic Law of the Judiciary to prevent NGOs from tabling public pleas to the supreme court. One of his main concerns was the pleas made on behalf of the African migrant community by pro-migrant NGOs. This initiative ultimately failed, due to informal consultations with legal dignitaries who reiterated the unconstitutionality of such an act. See: Hagai Amit, "Not Faithful: The Knesset is Waging War on the Judicial System and the Justice Minister Remains Silent," *Haaretz*, November 25, 2011.
11. KIC Protocol 465, p. 9, see also Chapter 4, above.
12. "High Court Exhibits New Commitment to Defending Human Rights," *Haaretz* main editorial, September 18, 2013.
13. Israeli Supreme Court Ruling 7146/2012, delivered September 16, 2013, revoking the 2012 Anti Infiltration Act. Available at: elyon2.court.gov.il/files/12/460/071/B24/12071460.B24.htm (accessed April 2016 [in Hebrew]) (hereinafter: High Court Ruling 7146/2012). For a concise 10-page summary of the over 100-page verdict, see the website of the Association for Civil Rights in Israel (ACRI), at: www.acri.org.il/he/wp-content/uploads/2013/09/hit7146psd-takzir.pdf (accessed April 2016) [in Hebrew].
14. See Chapter 2, above.
15. High Court Ruling 7146/2012, pp. 3–20.
16. Ibid., p. 4.
17. Ibid., p. 6.
18. Ibid., pp. 6–8.
19. Ibid., p. 6 para. 7.
20. Ibid., p. 7 Para. 8. Italics added.
21. Ibid, pp. 9–19.
22. For the court's analysis of the construction of the Israeli–Egyptian border fence and efforts with African governments for resettlement, see: ibid., p. 16. For the court's analysis of the legislative process leading up to the final endorsement of the Anti Infiltration Act (2012), see: ibid., pp. 16–20.
23. Ibid., p. 20 para. 37.
24. Ibid., p. 24. para. 48.
25. Ibid., p. 30 para. 67.
26. Ibid., p. 38 para. 82.
27. Ibid., pp. 39–44 paras 84–94.
28. Ibid., p. 58 para. 119.
29. Broadly speaking, the concept of "securitization" refers to conditions where political, economic, or societal issues are framed as threats or needs of national or community security – thus moving the debate from a social or political one, and turning it instead into a threat-based security-needs one. The concept was developed at the Copenhagen Peace Research Institute in the late 1990s through the work of Barry Buzan and Ole Wæver. See: Barry Buzan, Ole

Wæver and Jaap de Wilde, *Security: A New Framework for Analysis* (Boulder, CO: Lynne Reinner Publishers, 1998).

30. See Chapter 1, above.
31. High Court Ruling 7146/2012, p. 15 para. 24. See also Chapter 2, above.
32. "The treatment of political asylum seekers in Israel," *Annual report of the Israeli State Comptroller for 2007*, Vol. 58 b, pp. 97–120. Hard copy of this report obtained by the author from the Israeli National Archives, July 2012.
33. See Chapter 3, above.
34. Ibid., p. 99.
35. Ibid., p. 98.
36. Ibid., p. 99.
37. Ibid.
38. Ibid.
39. Arik Bender, Yael Friedson, and Yoval Goren, "The evacuation of the infiltrators has begun. Netanyahu: They must either be locked up or in their countries," *Maariv*, December 17, 2013.
40. Tamir Cohen, "Terrorist Organizations are operating a money laundering scheme using African migrants," *Haaretz*, July 24, 2012.
41. On the legal disagreement between the legal advisor of the Knesset and the Attorney General regarding the appropriate legal platform for the proposed anti-migrant legislation, see Chapter 4.
42. High Court Ruling 7146/2012, p. 66 para. 13.
43. Ibid., p. 65, para. 10.
44. Ibid., p. 59 para. 120.
45. High Court Ruling 7146/2012, p. 50 para. 105.
46. C. Tshimanga, C. D. Godola, and P. J. Bloom (eds), *Frenchness and the African Diaspora: Identity and Uprising in Contemporary France* (Bloomington, IN: Indiana University Press, 2009), p. vii.
47. For the full text of Decree 1386, see the webpage of the French Justice Ministry, available at: www.legifrance.gouv.fr/affichTexte.do?cidTexte=JORFTEXT000000263710 (accessed April 2016).
48. Ibid. The literal title name of this legislation reads: Decree No. 2005–1386 of 8th November 2005 concerning the application of Law No. 55–385 of 3rd April 1955 (translated from French by the author).
49. Mark Landler, "France Declares State of Emergency to Curb Crisis," *New York Times*, November 8, 2005.
50. Achille Mbembe, "The Republic and its Beast," in Tshimanga, Godola, and Bloom (eds), *Frenchness and the African Diaspora*, p. 52.
51. Ibid, p. 5, n. 11 and n. 12.
52. The issue of the trial of Maurice Papon is worthy of its own exploration in terms of parallels of state use of force and violence. Some two decades prior to his ordering of the Paris massacre of October 17, 1961, Papon had been responsible for the deportation and extermination of the 1,690 Jews of Bordeaux under the Vichy Government in its collaboration with the Nazi

occupation of France. In 1954, Papon took part in the repression of Moroccan nationalists who rejected the French protectorate there, and in 1956 he took active part in the use of torture and harsh military tactics as prefect of the district of Constantine in Algeria during the French–Algerian war. See: Jean-Luc Einaudi, *La Bataille de Paris. 17 octobre 1961* (Paris: Seuil, 1991).

53. Michel Feher, "Le Proche-Orient hors les murs. Usage francais du conflit israelo-palestinien," in D. Fassin and E. Fassin, *De la question Sociale a la question Racial* (Paris: La Decouverte, 2009), pp. 99–113.
54. See the sub-chapter on "Palestinization" by Achille Mbembe in "Republic and its Beast," pp. 51–4.
55. For the use of "The Law of 1955" – quotation marks in the original – see: Philippe Bernard, "Banlieues: la provocation colonial," *Le Monde*, November 18, 2005.
56. High Court Ruling 7146/2012, p. 40 para. 86.
57. Ibid., p. 41 para. 90.
58. Giovanni Pico Della Mirandola (1490–1534) was a Florentine humanist, who in 1520 published his *Oration on the Dignity of Man*. A contemporary of the luminary Marsilio Ficino of the Florentine academy, and the painters Michelangelo Buonarroti and Leonardo da Vinci, Pico Della Mirandola worked under the patronage of the Medici rulers of Florence. This text came to epitomize the renewed belief in the qualities of man, and the changing focus of attention from God to man. See: Pico Della Mirandola, *Oration on the Dignity of Man*, paras 1–7. Available at: www.fordham.edu/halsall/med/oration.asp (accessed April 2016).
59. Jean-Paul Sartre, *Existentialism & Humanism*, translated by Philip Mairet (London: Methuen Press, 2007), pp. 29–30.
60. See: Albuquerque, "Concurring Opinion," p. 65.
61. See Chapter 7, above, n. 20.
62. High Court Ruling 7146/2012, p. 104 para. 1.
63. Ibid., p. 20 para. 37.
64. Ibid., p. 43 para. 100, with an explicit referencing in the high court verdict text of the UNHCR detention guidelines for asylum seekers as published by UNHCR. See: UNHCR, *Guidelines on the Applicable Criteria and Standards relating to the Detention of Asylum-Seekers and Alternatives to Detention* (Geneva: UNHCR, 2012). Available at: www.refworld.org/docid/503489533b8.html (accessed April 2016).
65. High Court Ruling 7146/2012, p. 64 para. 8; quotation marks in the original.
66. Ibid., p. 64 paras 8–9. Interestingly, the principle of non-refoulement, translated into Hebrew as עקרון אי ההחזרה, is refered to in the text while explicitly adding in brackets the English legal term ("Non-Refoulement"). The reiteration of both languages in the text, as well as the quotation marks around the Attorney General's new legal invention of "temporary Non-Refoulement," serves Justice Vogelmann when making his deliberate point

of *a lack of distinction* between this particular Israeli application of non-refoulement and the general legal principle, long accepted in international law, of non-refoulement as an ultimate *jus cogens*.

67. Ilan Lior, "Israel examined 250 Asylum requests out of a total of 1800: not one has been approved," *Haaretz*, January 1, 2014.
68. Vincent Chetail, "Le Principe de Non-Refoulement et le Statut de Réfugié en Droit International," in V. Chetail and J. F. Flauss (eds), *La Convention de Genève du 28 Juillet Relative au Statut des Réfugiés – 50 Ans Après: Bilan et Perspectives* (Brusells: Bruylant, 2001), pp. 3–61, at 22.
69. High Court Ruling 7146/2012, p. 7 para. 9.
70. Ibid.
71. "The High Court has Prevented Shame," *Haaretz*, editorial, September 18, 2013. See also: High Court Ruling 7146/2012, p. 82 para. 2.
72. High Court Ruling 7146/2012, p. 82 para. 2.
73. See also: Gospel of St Luke 7:33.
74. I owe here a debt of gratitude to Professor Dr Amr Abdallah for explaining to me the similarities and mutuality between the Jewish Bible and the Qur'an concerning the protection assigned by Abraham to the strangers at his tent, from the wrath and sexual assault of the people Sodom and Gomorrah. Author's interview with Prof. Abdallah in Addis Ababa, November 6, 2013.
75. High Court Ruling 7146/2012, p. 83 para. 3.
76. Ibid., p. 58 para. 119. This final passage by Supreme Court Justice Arbel is significant in several regards from a Jewish point of view, irrespective of the self-evident legal significance of grounding the high court's verdict in the Jewish legal tradition. Paragraph 119 of the verdict is a masterful compilation and interweaving of Jewish legal traditions with the psychological, intuitive correlations of religious Judaic values, coupled into the general theme of the protection of helpless and vulnerable foreigners – in this case, the African migrants. The title of the paragraph, "Before Closure," using the Hebrew words לפני נעילה, refers directly to the name of one of the most holy of all prayers in the Hebrew calendar: the last prayer at the end of the Day of Atonement – Yom Kippur. The Day of Atonement begins with a prayer to desolve all vows (*Kol Nidrei* כל נדרי), and ends 24 hours later with the concluding prayer, *Neila* (נעילה). According to the Jewish faith and custom, the gates of the over-worlds are open during these 24 hours. *Neila* (נעילה) is considered to be man's last opportunity to repent and receive the clemency of God, in the final moments prior to the closure of the gates of the sky. It is this notion of a "help of last resort," pleaded for by the incarcerated African migrants and graciously provided by the high court, to which the psychological implications of *Neila* point to. Perhaps the most famous words in the Neila prayer concern the plea before God to "open us a gate – as the gate closes" (פתח לנו שער בעת סגירת שער). When one considers the time proximity of the Kadesh Barnea events to the court's ruling, these words

become charged with some acutely relevant meanings concerning Israel's conduct during this dark episode.

77. On Rabbi Hirsch, see his web-page biography published by the University of Calgary in Canada: people.ucalgary.ca/~elsegal/363_Transp/Orthodoxy/Hirsch.html (accessed April 2016).
78. Yochanan Flusser, "Behold the State where the Socially Vulnerable Suffer," *Haaretz Literary Supplement*, February 28, 2014, p. 4.
79. As per his idiom of bridging Jewish orthodoxy with nineteenth-century European modernity, Hirsch wrote his entire biblical commentary in German, referring to the Hebrew text of the Pentateuch, the Jewish Torah. Given the explicit reference by Justice Arbel and the Israeli Supreme Court to Hirsch's commentary, I have decided to use the same edition referred to by the high court. This is the well-known Hebrew translation by Yitzhaq Breuer of Hirsch's commentary, published in Jerusalem in 1966 and funded by the Memorial Foundation for Jewish Culture in New York, its first publication being facilitated by the then-chairman of the Memorial Fund: of all people, Dr Jacob Robinson! Reprinted with the following reference: Rabbi Samson Raphael Hirsch, *Commentary on The Pentateuch*, new and revised edition (Jerusalem: Yitzhaq Breuer Institute, 2002) {in Hebrew}. This edition also includes, for easy reference, the medieval commentary of Rashi vital for understanding the exact meaning of biblical words which have at times significantly different meanings from modern Hebrew, as well as the late-Antiquity translation into Aramaic by Onkelos (first century AD). All references are made to this edition. English references to the Bible are made, as elsewhere in this book, to the King James Version.
80. Hirsch, *Commentary on The Pentateuch*, Vol. 2 p.רסה {p. 265}
81. Ibid.
82. Shlomo Avineri, "What if Karl Marx had been born under his original family name as 'Karl Halevi': New archive material recently discovered sheds new light on the conversion into Christianity which the Marx family was obliged to undertake – a special report elapsing 130 years since the death of the father of Communism," *Haaretz Literary Supplement*, December 29, 2013.
83. Shlomo Avineri, "What were Karl Marx' Real Thoughts on Jews and Judaism," *Haaretz Literary Supplement*, January 6, 2014.
84. Hirsch, *Commentary on The Pentateuch*, Vol. 2 p. רפ {p. 280}
85. Ilan Lior, "The State to the Supreme Court: We have reached a Settlement with a Country of Secondary Asylum," *Haaretz*, June 2, 2013; Ilan Lior, "Eritreans in Israel: Our Lives will not be Safe in a Third Country," *Haaretz*, June 3, 2013; Ilan Lior, "Testimonies: Migrants Jailed in Israel are Instructed to Prepare for Departure to a Country of Third Asylum," *Haaretz*, June 5, 2013.
86. Barak Ravid, "The Foreign Ministry: We have no Knowledge of any Third Party Agreement for the Transfer of the Eritrean Migrants," *Haaretz*, June 2, 2013.
87. Ilan Lior, "The State Confirms: Negotiations are being Held with an Additional Four Countries Regarding the Deportation of the African Migrants," *Haaretz*, June 9, 2013.

88. See remarks by Advocate Jonathan Bermann at the supreme court hearing on June 9, 2013, quoted by Ilan Lior in ibid.
89. Omry Ephraim, " 'Voluntary Return'? 177 Asylum Seekers left Israel in July," *YNET*, August 6, 2013. See also: Omry Ephraim, "Returning Voluntarily? Dozens of Eritreans have been flown out of Israel," *YNET*, August 6, 2013 (quotation marks in the original). For corroborating reports by another media outlet, see: Ilan Lior, "177 Africans have left Israel in July; a Prisoner at the Saharonim Detention Center: We are being forced to sign," *Haaretz*, August 6, 2013.
90. Ilan Lior, "Reports and Sources in Sudan: The Khartoum Authorities have Interrogated Sudanese Migrants who have Clandestinely Returned from Israel Via Jordan," *Haaretz*, June 13, 2013.
91. "Disgrace and Shame to the Attorney General," *Haaretz*, chief editorial, August 8, 2013. See also the influential column by author Michal Peleg, "The House where Refugee Rights are Trampled Upon," *Haaretz*, August 5, 2013.
92. Ilan Lior, Anshel Pfeffer, and Jonathan Liss, "Permission for Publication Granted: Uganda is the Third Country to which African migrants shall be Deported," *Haaretz*, August 29, 2013.
93. Talila Nesher, "A First Testimony of the Governmental Procedure for 'Voluntary Return': An Eritrean Migrant who Refused to Board a Connecting Flight to Eritrea is Stranded at Cairo Airport," *Haaretz*, March 4, 2013. See also: "The State as a Human–Trafficker," *Haaretz*, chief editorial, February 27, 2013; chief psychiatrist of Physicians for Human Rights, Dr. Ido Luria, "Mental Refugeeness," *Haaretz*, February 26, 2013.
94. Talila Nesher, "Eli Yishai Admits: Over 2000 Sudanese Migrants have 'Left Voluntarily'", *Haaretz*, March 4, 2013. See also: Talila Nesher, "The UN Demands Explanations from Israel over Clandestine Returns of Sudanese back to their Country of Origin," *Haaretz*, February 27, 2013.
95. Talila Nesher, "Following the Publication in *Haaretz:* The Attorney General has ordered a Complete Halt of Migrant Deportations," *Haaretz*, March 5, 2013. See also: Ilan Lior, "Attorney General is Formulating a Procedure which would Enable the Voluntary Return of Migrants Currently Incarcerated," *Haaretz*, May 12, 2013.
96. Anshel Pfeffer, "Uganda Migrants Deal Signed as Military and Business Ties with Israel Balloon: Human Rights Groups Say Migrants from Israel Most Likely Destined for Isolated 'Warehouses for Human Beings' in Uganda," *Haaretz*, August 29, 2013.
97. Lior, Pfeffer, and Liss, "Uganda is the Third Country," p. 2.
98. Ibid., p. 2.
99. Ilan Lior, "Senior Government Officials: The Discussions with Uganda relate to Merely a Few Hundred Migrants: in Direct Contradiction to the Statements Made by Interior Minister Saar," *Haaretz*, September 3, 2013.
100. High Court Ruling 7146/2012, p. 75.

Chapter 8 Incarceration, Forced Resettlement, and the Ensuing Constitutional Crisis

1. For the UNHCR guidelines on durable solutions for refugees, see: www.unhcr.org/pages/49c3646cf8.html (accessed April 2016).
2. See Chapter 7, above.
3. On the border-regime agreements between Italy and Libya, see: Silja Klepp, "Negotiating." For a good discussion of "venue shopping" in general, as well as its specific application to the case of Australia and its agreements with Papua New Guinea, see: Adèle Garnier, "Are states in control of their borders? Testing the venue-shopping approach in the Australian context," Research Academy Leipzig working paper, Series No. 10, University of Leipzig, 2010. On the coinage of the term "venue shopping" and its policy implications, see: Verginie Guiraudon, "European Integration and Migration Policy: Vertical Policy-Making as Venue-Shopping," *Journal of Common Market Studies* 38 (2) (2000), pp. 251–71.
4. On the Italian–Libyan cooperation, see: "Pushed Back Pushed Around," special report from Human Rights Watch, September 21, 2009. Available at: www.hrw.org/sites/default/files/reports/italy0909web_0.pdf (accessed April 2016).
5. Paul Mason, "With EU Funding, Morocco halts Immigration to Europe, and all Means are Justified," *Guardian*, September 8, 2013.
6. "Boat Ride to Detention: Adult and Child Migrants in Malta," Human Rights Watch report, July 18, 2012. Available at: www.hrw.org/report/2012/07/18/boat-ride-detention/adult-and-child-migrants-malta (accessed April 2016).
7. Human Rights Watch, "Pushed Back Pushed Around" p. 11 n. 75.
8. Silja Klepp, *Europa zwischen Grenzkontrolle und Flüchtlingsschutz: Eine Ethnographie der Seegrenze auf dem Mittelmeer* (Frankfurt am Main: Transcript Verlag, 2011): winner of the 2010 Research Academy Leipzig Graduate Prize and the Christiane Rajewsky Prize 2012 for Peace and Conflict Research. See also: Klepp, "Negotiating." Specifically on the Italian case, see: Silja Klepp, *Ankunft und Aufnahme von Flüchtlingen in Italien: Eine ethnographische Reise an die Grenzen Europas* (Munich: Akademiker Verlag, 2012).
9. Klepp, "Negotiating," pp. 5–7.
10. See Chapter 3, above.
11. Paul Adams, "Migrants: What can Europe Achieve?" BBC News report, June 16, 2015. Available at: www.bbc.com/news/world-europe-33103246 (accessed April 2016).
12. "Australia Asylum: Why is it Controversial?" BBC News report, December 5, 2014. Available at: www.bbc.com/news/world-asia-28189608 (accessed April 2016).

13. Lauren Crothers and Ben Doherty, "Australia Signs Controversial Refugee Transfer Deal with Cambodia," *Guardian*, September 26, 2014. Available at: www.theguardian.com/world/2014/sep/26/australia-signs-refugee-deal-cambodia (accessed April 2016).
14. *United States Treaties and Other International Agreements*, Volume 33 (Part 4), Doc. TIAS 10241 pp. 3, 559–66.
15. *Sale* v. *Haitian Centers Council*, 509 US 155 (1993). Available from the Cornell Law School website at: www.law.cornell.edu/supct/html/92-344.ZS.html (accessed April 2016).
16. Kälin Caroni, and Heim, "Article 33, para 1," pp. 1,362–3 n. 247, 248, 249. See also: Ben-Nun, "British–Jewish Roots," p. 101.
17. Tim Butcher, "Sharon Presses for Fence across Sinai," *Daily Telegraph*, December 7, 2005. See also: Shuki Sadeh, "A Fence, but not a Solution."
18. Communiqué of the Israeli Ministry of Foreign Affairs, dated July 1, 2007. See: www.mfa.gov.il/MFA/Government/Communiques/2007/PM+Olmert+holds+discussion+on+infiltrations+into+Israel+via+the+Egyptian+border+1-Jul-2007.htm?DisplayMode=print (accessed April 2016). See also: Human Rights Watch report on the Mubarak–Olmert agreement at the organization's Hebrew website: http://www.hrw.org/he/node/88422/section/6#_ftn73 (accessed April 2016).
19. Maximilian Popp, "Trapped in Apulia: Europe's Deepening Refugee Crisis," *Der Spiegel*, June 21, 2013; see the *Spiegel* English Online edition, available at: www.spiegel.de/international/europe/eu-refugees-the-plight-of-african-migrants-living-in-apulia-italy-a-906950.html (accessed April 2016).
20. The issue of Israeli relations with Africa, and the Israeli view of the continent as "uncivilized" as opposed to Israel's "cultivation" are well researched and lie beyond the scope of this book. See: Eytan Bar-Yosef, *A Villa in the Jungle: Africa in Israeli Culture* (Jerusalem: Van Leer Jerusalem Institute and Hakibbutz Hameuchad Publishers, 2013) [in Hebrew].
21. Olmert's "softness" can be deduced from the State's conciliatory approach when it was caught red-handed as it broke the non-refoulement principle. See: Ruti Sinai, "The State Admits: a Major Failure in the return of 91 Migrants to Egypt," *Haaretz*, September 2, 2008. On Bar-On's naturalization of migrant children, see Chapter 4, above.
22. See: "'Make Their Lives Miserable,' Israel's Coercion of Eritrean and Sudanese Asylum Seekers to Leave Israel," Human Rights Watch report, September 9, 2014. Available at: www.hrw.org/report/2014/09/09/make-their-lives-miserable/israels-coercion-eritrean-and-sudanese-asylum-seekers (accessed April 2016).
23. Talila Nesher, "Eritreans: We are Being Forced to Sign 'Voluntary Repatriation Papers'", *Haaretz*, February 14, 2013.
24. "Voluntary Self-Inflicted Death Sentence," *Haaretz*, editorial, February 15, 2013.
25. Moshe Cohen, "The New Anti Infiltration Act has been approved," *Maariv*, December 9, 2013. Available at: www.maariv.co.il/news/new.aspx?pn6Vq=E&0r9VQ=EIMLM (accessed April 2016) [in Hebrew].

26. High Court Plea 8425/13, tabled on December 15, 2013. Available from the ACRI website at: www.acri.org.il/he/wp-content/uploads/2013/12/hit8425.pdf (accessed April 2016) [in Hebrew].
27. Ibid., p. 41.
28. Oded Shalom, "The Bearers of the Black Flag," *Maariv Weekend Supplement*, January 10, 2014, p. 8.
29. Ilan Lior and Revital Levy-Stein, "Thousands of Migrants Demonstrated on Rabin Square: 1,500 Migrants on Strike in Eilat," *Haaretz*, January 5, 2014.
30. "UN: Israel Breaking Law with Asylum Detentions," South African *Mail & Guardian*, January 10, 2014. See also: the report by UNHCR on its daily news web page, available at: www.unhcr.org/cgi-bin/texis/vtx/refdaily?pass=52fc6fbd5&id=52d38fb45 (accessed April 2016).
31. Ilan Lior, "Record Numbers of Asylum Seekers have Left: 1,705 have Departed from Israel in February," *Haaretz*, February 27, 2014.
32. See the report regarding confrontations between south Tel Aviv inhabitants and the pro-migrant NGO lobby representatives inside the supreme court during its debating session between the pleading attorneys and the State's defense counselors. Omri Ephraim and Ariel Magnazi, "Confrontations during the Court Session regarding the New Anti Infiltration Act," *YNET* News Agency, April 1, 2014.
33. In May 2014, the Israeli State Comptroller published one of the most comprehensive and authoritative reports regarding virtually all the different policy and social aspects concerning the African migrants, including detailed and proof-checked up-to-date statistical data – making this one of the most important factual documents on this matter available for future reference. See: *Israeli State Comptroller Report #ג64: Non Deportable Foreigners in Israel 2014*. Available from the Israeli State Comptroller's website at: www.mevaker.gov.il/he/Reports/Report_248/af07752c-7845-4f1d-ae97-23c45c702624/102-ver-5.pdf?AspxAutoDetectCookieSupport=1 (accessed April 2016) [in Hebrew].
34. Dana Weiler-Polak, "Eritrean Asylum Seekers who had left Israel have been Executed by ISIS," Walla News Agency, April 21, 2015. See also: Ilan Lior, "The Hotline for Migrants and Foreign Workers: Three Eritreans who Left Israel have been executed by ISIS in Libya," *Haaretz*, April 21, 2015.
35. Israeli High Court Ruling 8424/13 – *Eytan Israeli Immigration Policy* v. *The State of Israel Concerning the 4th Amendment to the 1954 Anti Infiltration Act.* (hereinafter: High Court Ruling 8424/13). Available from the *Haaretz* website at: www.haaretz.co.il/st/inter/Hheb/images/mismis.pdf (accessed April 2016) [in Hebrew].
36. See Chapter 4, above.
37. Omri Ephraim, "The Knesset's legal advisor: the new Anti Infiltration law, while more balanced still must undergo changes," *YNET* News Agency, November 26, 2013.
38. Ibid.

39. Revital Choval, "The Debacle of the Women behind the Anti Infiltration Act," *Haaretz*, September 24, 2014.
40. High Court Ruling 8424/13, p. 52 paras 78–9.
41. Ibid., p. 131 para. 3.
42. Choval, "The Debacle."
43. "Israel: High Court Voids Migrant Holding Law. Court Also Limits Detention of New Arrivals," Human Rights Watch communiqué, September 24, 2014. Available at: www.hrw.org/news/2014/09/24/israel-high-court-voids-mi grant-holding-law (accessed April 2016).
44. Jonathan Lis, "Right-wing MKs Promoting Legislation which would Re-enact the Anti Infiltration Act and Allow an Over Ride of the Supreme Court," *Haaretz*, September 23, 2014.
45. Jonathan Lis, "Ministers approve Shaked's Law to Override the Supreme Court," *Haaretz*, October 26, 2014.
46. Oren Yiftachel, *Ethnocracy: Land and Identity Politics in Israel/Palestine* (Philadelphia, PA: University of Pennsylvania Press, 2006). For the contemporary debate at the time, see: Aeyal Gross, "All Signs Point Toward Ethnocracy, Not Democracy, in Israel," *Haaretz*, November 17, 2014.
47. Moran Azoulay and Omri Ephraim, "The New moderated Anti Infiltration law has been approved by the Knesset," *YNET* News Agency, December 9, 2014. For the full text of the law and its official title, which now included mention of the forced expulsion of the migrants under duress, see the official Knesset website: knesset.gov.il/privatelaw/data/19/3/904_3_1.rtf (accessed *April 2016*) [in Hebrew].

Conclusion

1. ISA, Foreign Ministry Files: ISA/RG 130.2.1.1008 Box # 2416/10. Jacob Robinson to Walter Eytan, director general of the Israeli Foreign Ministry, through the division of International Organizations, Ezekiel Gordon, and legal advisor, Shabtai Rosenne – First Report – Ad Hoc Committee on Statelessness and Related Problems, January 23, 1950, p. 2 point 4 a; underlining in the original.
2. Gilad Ben-Nun, "From Ad Hoc to Universal: The International Refugee Regime from Fragmentation to Unity 1922–1954," *Refugee Survey Quarterly* 34 (2) (2015), pp. 23–44.
3. Galia Sabar and Elizabeth Tsurkov, "Israel's Policies toward Asylum-Seekers: 2002–2014," Istituto Affari Internazionali (IAI) Working Paper 20/2015, Rome, May 31, 2015, p. 6. Available at: http://www.iai.it/en/pubblicazioni/is raels-policies-toward-asylum-seekers (accessed April 2016).
4. Ibid., p. 17.
5. Shalailah Medhora, "'Nope, Nope, Nope': Tony Abbott says Australia will take no Rohingya Refugees," *Guardian*, May 21, 2015.

6. Nick Thorpe, "Hungary's Poster War on Immigration," BBC News report, June 14, 2015. Available at: http://www.bbc.com/news/world-europe-33091597; Jean-Philippe Dedieu, "Greece, a Front Line for State-sponsored Racism in Europe," Aljazeera America report, September 29, 2014. Availble at: http://america.aljazeera.com/opinions/2014/9/greece-anti-immigrantsviolenceandracismineurope.html (both accessed April 2016).
7. See UNHCR's communiqué for World Refugee Day, June 20, 2014. Available at: www.unhcr.org/53a155bc6.html (accessed April 2016). See also: Antonio Guterres (United Nations High Commissioner for Refugees), "One Million Syrian Refugees," *New York Times*, March 5, 2013. For the 20,000 deaths estimate, see the quote by Home Affairs Commissioner Cecilia Malmström, available from UNHCR's daily news website at: www.unhcr.org/cgi-bin/texis/vtx/refdaily?pass=52fc6fbd5&id=534e12ac8 (accessed April 2016).
8. See Chapter 6, above.
9. Jonathan Steele, "How Yarmouk Refugee Camp became the Worst Place in Syria," *Guardian*, March 5, 2015.
10. ISA, Ministry of Justice File number 130.4/1- 1829/8: Robinson to Sharett, "Concerning: 'Compensation to the Palestinian refugees out of Palestine'", documental reply to verbal conversation with the minister during his stay in New York, January 9, 1951.
11. C. Goschler, *Wiedergutmachung: Westdeutschland und die Verfolgten des Nationalsozialismus 1945–1954* (Munich: Oldenburg Verlag, 1992), pp. 40–7.
12. ISA, Ministry of Justice File number 130.4/1- 1829/8: Robinson to Sharett, January 9, 1951, point 5.
13. Ibid.: Sharett's reply to Robinson, January 21, 1951.
14. It is noteworthy that Sharett quotes Samuel 2:24, verse 17, although not to the letter. The original verse reads: "and these sheep, what have they done? (ואלה הצאן מה עשו)." Sharett asks, "how have they sinned? (ואלה הצאן במה חטאו)." This change of wording was common within religious Talmudic discourse, and appears from the eighteenth century onwards in Jewish religious literature – most notably, in the writings of Rabbi Meir Simha Hacohen from Dvinsk (nineteenth-century Lithuania) on the Book of Lamentations and those of the late nineteenth-century Rabbi David Zvi Hoffman from Berlin on the Jewish legal principles of laws of torts. With Sharett and Robinson both having enjoyed religious and legal upbringings (Sharett studied law in Istanbul), the subtext of the use of this proverb and the insinuation regarding its Jewish background of legal torts and compensation must have been clear to both men as encoded language for the need to "do the right thing" with the property of Palestinian refugees .
15. Ami Pedahzur, *The Triumph of Israel's Radical Right* (New York: Oxford University Press, 2012).
16. On Yesh Atid (Central Liberals) support for the Anti Infiltration Act *from the opposition benches*see: Ilan Lior, "Even from the Opposition: Yesh Atid will

Support the Anti Infiltration Act in its Current Format," *Haaretz*, December 4, 2014. On Labor's support of the Anti Infiltration Act, see p. 93 n. 312

17. T. Goldstein, "The Building Contractor Association Appeals to the Supreme Court: Block Deportation of 3000 Foreign Workers," *Yediouth Aharonoth*, June 20, 2010. See Also: E. Paz-Frenkel, "A Victory for the Construction Lobby: The Deportation of the Foreign Workers has been Postponed to October by the High Court," *Globes*, July 1, 2010.
18. Y. Yoval Azoulay and Dana Weiler-Polak, "The Netanyahu Administrations are the Record Breakers in Foreign Labor Importation to Israel," *Haaretz*, January 25, 2010.
19. See the article by Advocate Jehoshua Shoffman, former Israeli deputy attorney general, concerning Jewish religious obligations to protect foreign migrants and non-Jewish foreigners at large: Jehoshua Shoffman, "And the Stranger shall dwell amongst you – and yeshall not wrong him," Parashat Kedoshim, reading # 207, Israeli Ministry of Justice 2005 [in Hebrew]. Available at: www.daat.ac.il/mishpat-ivri/skirot/207-2.htm (accessed April 2016). It is noteworthy that the sages of the Talmud in Masechet Baba Meziah pose the question as to why the Torah and the Jewish faith reiterate the commandment to safeguard the migrant stranger–גר–36 times, more than any other repeated legal stipulation in the Torah. Their answer is fascinating in its brevity and meaning. The Talmudic sages answer "because his vulnerability is bad" ("מפני שסורו רע"). As the commentators explain, it is within the nature of society and social interaction to batter the weakest and most vulnerable agent within a given society. It is therefore imperative to provide the most safeguards to he (and, unfortunately, usually also she) who is most vulnerable. See also the wonderful Israeli Labor Court ruling by Justice Eyal Avrahami against the Mordechai Aviv Construction Company, for its harsh and illegal treatment of foreign workers: Israeli Jerusalem Labor Court ruling , 3376 (4)2005 תק-עב 3379–3378 עמ' delivered on December 5, 2005. Available at: index.justice.gov.il/Units/MishpatIvri/Psika/12haiachaslazaravrahami1.doc (accessed April 2016).
20. "The Israeli delegate has been nominated Vice President of the UN General Assembly's Sixth Committee," *Davar*, September 29, 1950. Available at the electronic link to the *Davar* newspaper archive [in Hebrew]: jpress.org.il/Olive/APA/NLI_Heb/SharedView.Article.aspx?parm=o9Sbi1WIsHdoe jWFtHsh3UzLSn4oMbCyYTaFT2WA9U8%2BYJkTkA%2FGFPunNciP YWX3Yw%3D%3D&mode = image&href=DAV%2f1950%2f09%2f29 &page=1&rtl=true (accessed April 2016).
21. See Chapter 1, above.

BIBLIOGRAPHY

Primary Sources (by date order)

Israel State Archives

Israel State Archives (ISA)/Foreign Ministry Files (MFA) RG 93.38/1-31, October 28, 1949 – agreement between the Government of Israel and the International Refugee Organization (IRO) concerning permanent provision for institutional care.

ISA/MFA RG 93.3/1-254, November 9, 1949 – UN Genocide Convention Files, archive address: 02-110-01-03-05, Israeli Foreign Ministry files concerning the UN Genocide Convention – letter from Foreign Ministry legal advisor, Shabtai Rosenne, to Abba Eban, Israel ambassador to the UN.

ISA/MFA RG 93.38/1-31, December 9, 1949 – Memorandum #111, from the Director General, Ministry of Foreign Affairs, to Dr Menachem Kahany, the Israeli delegate to the UN Headquarter offices and ICRC offices1949 – signing of the 4th Geneva Convention for the Protection of Civilians in Times of War.

ISA/RG 130.2.1.1008 Box # 2416/10, January 23 to February 21, 1950 – this filing includes five reports (four in English, one in Hebrew), all from the Ad Hoc Committee deliberations at Lake Success in New York.

ISA/MFA Container 1829/8, September 18, 1950 – Ministry of Foreign Affairs, Legal Advisor – top-secret cable from Shabtai Rosenne, chief legal advisor, to Dr Jacob Robinson in New York.

ISA/MFA Container 2406, October 27 and October 30, 1950 – exchange of letters between Donald Kingsley, director general IRO, to S. Adler-Rudel, representative of the Government of Israel.

ISA/MFA Container 2416, December 13, 1950 – statement by Arthur Lourie, Israeli consul general in New York to the UN General Assembly negotiating committee on contributions to programs of relief and rehabilitation.

ISA/MFA RG, reference: 130.4/1-1829/8, January 9, 1951 – Robinson to Sharett: "Concerning: 'Compensation to the Palestinian refugees out of Palestine'", documental reply to verbal conversation with the minister during his stay in New York.

ISA/MFA Container 2416, doc. 775, July 8, 1951 – Robinson to MFA Director General: "The Convention regarding refugees and stateless people 1st report."

ISA/MFA Container 2416, doc. 782, July 11, 1951 – Robinson to Director General: "The Convention regarding refugees and stateless people 2nd report."

ISA/MFA Container 2416, doc. 788, July 22, 1951 – Robinson to MFA Director General: "The Convention regarding refugees and stateless people 3rd report."

ISA/MFA Container 93.38.1.29 19/8, February 26, 1952 – letter from Dr Paul Weis, chief legal advisor for the UNHCR, to Dr Menachem Kahany, Israeli representative to the UN European office in Geneva, concerning travel documents and the applicability of the law of return revoking the refugee status from Jewish refugees who have obtained citizenship in Israel.

ISA/MFA Container 1976/7, April 1, 1952 – letter from Robinson to Sharett and to Kidron, director of international organizations at the Israeli Foreign Ministry: Letter M/32400, dated March 14, 1952.

ISA/MFA RG93.38/1-31, December 8, 1954 – internal, confidential letter from Kahany to the Director General, confirming Kahany's role as the chair of the UNHCR advisory council on behalf of Israel [Hebrew reference: 2289/ .[יד/מכ].

ISA/MFA Container 1976/7, July 1, 1954 – letter from Robinson to legal advisor Shabtai Rosenne.

ISA/Ministry of Justice Files Container 4524, August 18, 1954 – Jacob Robinson to Israeli Attorney General Chaim Cohn, handwritten doc. 18638: request by Robinson for Israeli ratification of the 1951 Refugee Convention.

Israeli Knesset Documents (Parliamentary Records)

Israeli Anti-Infiltration Act (2008): Proposed legislation by the Israeli Knesset. Available at: www.knesset.gov.il/Laws/Data/BillGoverment/381/381.pdf

Knesset public record of legislative proposals, *Governmental legislation proposal number* 577, dated March 28, 2011 [Hebrew calendar applicable for Knesset records: כ"ב באדר ב' התשע"א in the Hebrew calendar].

Knesset Interior Committee (KIC) Protocol #436, August 10, 2011.

Knesset Interior Committee (KIC) Protocol #448, November 14, 2011.

Knesset Interior Committee (KIC) Protocol #465, December 13, 2011.

Nathan, Dr Gilad, "Aliens in Israel," Special report commissioned by Knesset Member Nitzan Horowitz for the special session of the Knesset Interior Committee concerning alien migrants into Israel, Knesset Research Unit, December 13, 2011.

Knesset Interior Committee (KIC) Protocol #467, December 19, 2011.

Moshe, Neta, "European Union Policy and the Policies of its main Member States, concerning Asylum Seekers: Comparative Perspectives for Israel," Knesset Center for Information, November 21, 2013 [in Hebrew].

United Kingdom National Archives – Kew, Richmond, Surrey

File # BT 271/349 I.O.C. (50) 193: "Steering Committee on International Organizations General Assembly Fifth Session – Draft Brief on Supplementary Agenda Item No. 4," September 25, 1950.

File # BT 271/349 I.O.C. (50) 193 Corr. 1: "Steering Committee on International Organizations General Assembly Fifth Session – Draft Brief on Supplementary Agenda Item No. 4," November 4, 1950.

File # BT 271/349 I.O.C. (51) 68: "Steering Committee on International Organizations, Conference of Plenipotentiaries on the Status of Refugees and Stateless Persons", draft brief for the United Kingdom Representatives: prepared by the Home Office, June 26, 1951.

File # BT 271/349 I.O.C. (51) 125: "Steering Committee on International Organizations, Conference of Plenipotentiaries on the Status of Refugees held at Geneva from 3 to 25 July, 1951," previous reference: I.O.C. (51) 68, and Addendum, August 16, 1951.

File # LCO 2/4317: "Magna Carta for Refugees," UNHCR brochure.

File # HO/274/9: Evans to Hoare, October 16, 1951, following Hoare's request for consultations with Robinson in New York.

United Nations Documents and Records

Ad Hoc Committee on Statelessness and Related Problems, UN doc. E/AC.32/L.25 (1950): "Draft Article on the Prohibition of Refoulement."

ECOSOC Ad Hoc Committee on Statelessness and Related Problems, UN doc. E/1618, E/AC.32/5, February 17, 1950: "Draft Convention Relating to the Status of Refugees and Stateless Persons."

United Nations Archive, New York (UNA), Restricted Document A/AC.41/SR.5 – statement by Arthur Lourie, Israeli consul general in New York, dated December 13, 1950, to the UN General Assembly negotiating committee on contributions to programs of relief and rehabilitation.

UN Conference of Plenipotentiaries on the Status of Refugees and Stateless Persons, *Projet de Convention Relative au Statut des Réfugiés. Suède: Amendement à l'article premier*, July 2, 1951, UN doc. A/CONF.2/9.

UN Conference of Plenipotentiaries on the Status of Refugees and Stateless Persons, *Projet de Convention Relative au Statut des Réfugiés. Belgique: Amendement à l'article 2*, July 2, 1951, UN doc. A/CONF.2/10.

Convention Relating to the Status of Refugees, Conference of Plenipotentiaries: Rules of Procedure for the Conference of Plenipotentiaries, July 2, 1951. Available at: www.unhcr.org/3ae68cd9c.html.

UN Conference of Plenipotentiaries on the Status of Refugees and Stateless Persons, Draft Convention Relating to the Status of Refugees. France: Amendment to Article 2, July 3, 1951, UN doc. A/CONF.2/18.

Convention Relating to the Status of Refugees, Conference of Plenipotentiaries, Draft Convention Relating to the Status of Refugees, report of the committee appointed to study Article 3 (Non-Discrimination) of the Draft Convention. UN doc. A/CONF.2/72, July 11, 1951.

United Nations General Assembly Resolution 3379, adopted November 10, 1975. UN GAOR Res. 3379.

United Nations General Assembly Resolution 46/86, December 16, 1991. UN GAOR Res. 46/86.

UNHCR, The 1951 Convention and Protocol Relating to the Status of Refugees (ed. 2010).

Belgian National Diplomatic Archives – Archives Diplomatiques, Rue des Petits Carmes, Brussels

(All translations from French by the author.)

Les Archives Diplomatiques Royaume de Belgique (ADB), Dossier Numéro PERS: 2159 – Albert Herment (File opened and declassified following the official demand of the author).

ADB/Herment PERS 2159 – letter from Herment to the Secretary General of the Foreign Ministry, December 31, 1939; letter from Herment to Billen, December 13, 1944.

ADB/Herment PERS 2159. The reverse side of the file lists Herment's pension fund remunerations.

ADB/Dossier Numéro 13717 / I: "Apatrides et Definition de Réfugiés."

ADB/ Dossier Numéro 13717 / I: "Apatrides et Definition de Réfugiés," memorandum by Herment: Instructions en vue ECOSOC, Genéve, Juillet–Aôut 1950 (Instructions concerning ECOSOC, Geneva, July–August 1950), dated April 28, 1950.

ADB/Dossier Numéro 13717 / I: "Apatrides et Definition de Réfugiés," memorandum by Herment: Direction de l'Organization Internationale et du Règlement de la Paix, MINUTE – Point 32 Refugiès et Apatrides, October 21, 1950.

Private Archive – Dr Paul Weis, Bodleian Library, Oxford

Biographical note concerning Paul Weis: PW/PR, Intro 1.

Speech by Sir Samuel Hoare in the House of Commons, August 1938. Copy of the speech held in Paul Weis' files: PW/WR/WMSC/2.

Kullmann, Gustav to Martha Biehle, January 17, 1950: PW/PR/IRO-6 doc. 32.

Letter from Doron Kreisel, assistant to the director of the World Jewish Congress Representative Office London to Paul Weis, August 18, 1968, Paul Weis Archive: PW/WR/WMSC/2 doc. 11.

Other Primary Sources

Israeli Jerusalem Labor Court ruling 3379-3378 ' 3376 , עמ (4) עב-תק 2005 by Justice Eyal Avrahami against Mordechai Aviv Construction Company, delivered on December 5, 2005. Available at: www.index.justice.gov.il/Units/MishpatIvri/Psika/12haiachaslazaravrahami1.doc.

Annual report by the Israeli National State Comptroller for 2006, Justice Micha Lindenstraus for the governmental activities and reports of the year 2007 and the fiscal reports for the monetary year 2006. ISSN: 0334-9713, catalogue number: 958/1-2008, published on May 20, 2008. PDF version, pp. 97–120, at p. 98. Available at: www.old.mevaker.gov.il/serve/contentTree.asp?bookid=514&id=190&contentid=9582&parentcid=9581&bctype=1&sw=1366&hw=698.

Association for Civil Rights in Israel (ACRI) and Amnesty International, "The draft Anti Infiltration Act – Lies and reality," position paper published by the Pro-Migrant Coalition, Tel Aviv, 2010. Available for download from the website of the daily newspaper, Maariv, at: www.nrg.co.il/images/news1/report.doc.

Albuquerque, Justice P.P. de, "Concurring Opinion to the Ruling of the European Court of Human Rights," Hirsi Jamaa v. Italy, App. No. 27765/09

(Eur. Ct. H.R. February 23, 2012), 62 – 82, notes 2 – 62. Available at: hudoc.echr.coe.int/sites/eng/pages/search.aspx?i=001-109231.

European Court of Human Rights, Hirsi Jamaa v. Italy, App. No. 27765/09, February 23, 2012. Available at: hudoc.echr.coe.int/sites/eng/pages/search.aspx?i=001-109231#{"itemid":["001-109231"]}.

Israeli Supreme Court Ruling 7146/2012, delivered September 16, 2013, revoking the 2012 Anti-Infiltration Act. Available at: www.elyon2.court.gov.il/files/12/460/071/B24/12071460.B24.htm.

Israeli Supreme Court Ruling 8425/13, delivered September 22, 2014, revoking the 2013 Anti-Infiltration Act. Available from Haaretz website, at: www.haaretz.co.il/st/inter/Hheb/images/mismis.pdf.

Special Israeli State Comptroller Report # 64 ג: "Non Deportable Foreigners in Israel 2014." Available from the Israeli State Comptroller's website: www.mevaker.gov.il/he/Reports/Report_248/af07752c-7845-4f1d-ae97-23c45c702624/102-ver-5.pdf?AspxAutoDetectCookieSupport=1.

Secondary Sources

Adams, P. "Migrants: What can Europe Achieve?" BBC News report, June 16, 2015. Available at: www.bbc.com/news/world-europe-33103246

Alexander, M. *Cities and Labour Responses: Comparing Policy Responses in Amsterdam, Paris, Rome and Tel-Aviv* (Hampshire: Ashgate, 2007).

Amit, H. "Not Faithful: The Knesset is Waging War on the Judicial System and the Justice Minister Remains Silent," *Haaretz*, November 25, 2011.

Amnesty International, Egypt/Sudan: *Refugees and Asylum seekers face Brutal Treatment, Kidnapping for Ransom, and Human Trafficking* (London: 2013).

Amram, A. "Police Suspects Molotov Cocktail – a Vengeance Act against the Rape," Channel 2 News report, April 30, 2012.

——— "Suspected: Rape of an Elderly Woman on her Premises," Israeli Channel 2 News report, December 31, 2013, at 09:02 hours.

Anteby-Yemini, L. "Migrations africaines et nouveaux enjeux de la frontière israélo-égyptienne," *Cultures & Conflits: Frontières et logiques de passage*, 72 (Winter 2008), pp. 77–99.

——— "Les 'réfigiés soudanais' en Israël: discours, representations, mobilizations," *Maghreb-Machrek* 199 (Spring 2009), pp. 71–84.

Arens, M. "African Migrants could Destroy Israel," *Haaretz*, January 14, 2014.

Avineri, S. "What if Karl Marx had been born under his original family name as 'Karl Halevi': New archive material recently discovered sheds new light on the conversion into Christianity which the Marx family was obliged to undertake – a special report elapsing 130 years since the death of the father of Communism," *Haaretz Literary Supplement*, December 29, 2013.

——— "What were Karl Marx's Real Thoughts on Jews and Judaism," *Haaretz Literary Supplement*, January 6, 2014.

Avineri, S., L. Orgad, and A. Rubinstein. *Managing Global Migration: A Strategy for Immigration Policy in Israel* (Jerusalem: Metzilah Center for Jewish Zionist Liberal and Humanist Thought 2009) [in Hebrew].

Azoulay, M. and O. Ephraim. "The New Moderated Anti Infiltration law has been Approved by the Knesset," *YNET News Agency*, December 9, 2014.

Azoulay, Y. and D. Weiler-Polak. "The Netanyahu Administrations are the Record Breakers in Foreign Labor Importation to Israel," *Haaretz*, January 25, 2010.

Barak, A. "The Place of Jewish Law in the Law of State," in H. Cohn and Y. Zamir (eds), *Justice Barak - A Collection of Writings* (Jerusalem: Nevo Publishers, 2000) Vol. 1, pp. 97–105 [in Hebrew].

Bar-Yosef, E. *A Villa in the Jungle: Africa in Israeli Culture* (Jerusalem: Van Leer Jerusalem Institute and Hakibbutz Hameuchad Publishers, 2013) [in Hebrew].

Basok, M. "By Year's End 2012 Israel had 256,000 Foreign Migrants, of whom only 40 Percent were Legal," *Haaretz*, July 30, 2013.

BBC Special Report: "Australia Asylum: Why is it Controversial?" December 5, 2014. Available at: www.bbc.com/news/world-asia-28189608

Beker, Avi. *The United Nations and Israel: From Recognition to Reprehension* (Tel Aviv: Bar Ilan University Press, 1985) [in Hebrew].

Bender, A. "MK Zeev is Inciting and Calling the Murder of Homosexuals," *Maariv* internet portal, "NRG," February 5, 2008.

——— "Knesset Research Unit Report: Over a Quarter of a Million Aliens in Israel," *Maariv*, January 8, 2012.

Bender, A., Yael Friedson, and Yoval Goren. "The Evacuation of the Infiltrators has Begun. Netanyahu: They must either be Locked up or in their Countries," *Maariv*, December 17, 2013.

Bendet, S. "How did the Rape of an Elderly Woman Make Its way into the Electoral Campaign?" Walla News Agency report, December 31, 2012.

Ben-Nun, G. "The Israeli Roots of Article 3 and Article 6 of the 1951 Refugee Convention," *Journal of Refugee Studies* Vol. 27 (1) (2014), pp. 101–25.

——— "The British–Jewish Roots of Non-Refoulement and its True Meaning for the Drafters of the 1951 Refugee Convention," *Journal of Refugee Studies* Vol. 28 (1) (2015), pp. 93–117.

——— "From Ad Hoc to Universal: The International Refugee Regime from Fragmentation to Unity 1922–1954," *Refugee Survey Quarterly* 34 (2) (2015), pp. 23–44.

Bernard, P. "Banlieues: la provocation colonial," *Le Monde*, November 18, 2005.

Bialer, Uri. *Between East and West: Israel's Foreign Policy Orientation 1948–1956* (Cambridge: Cambridge University Press, 1990).

Blatman, D. "If I were an American Jew, I'd Worry about Israel's Racist Cancer," *Haaretz*, March 7, 2014.

Bowen, J. "Israel-Hamas Ceasefire comes into Effect in Gaza," BBC News report, November 21, 2012.

Bulletin of the Association of Jewish Refugees: "Nansen Ring Awarded to Dr Paul Weis," June 1974.

Butcher, T. "Sharon Presses for Fence across Sinai," *Daily Telegraph*, December 7, 2005.

Buzan, B., O. Wæver, and J. de Wilde. *Security: A New Framework for Analysis* (Boulder, CO: Lynne Reinner Publishers, 1998).

Carmi, N. *Immigration and The Law of Return: Immigration Rights and Their Limits* (Tel Aviv: Tel Aviv University Press, 2003) [in Hebrew].

Chetail, V. "Le Principe de Non-Refoulement et le Statut de Réfugié en Droit International," in V. Chetail and J.F. Flauss (eds), *La Convention de Genève du 28 Juillet Relative au Statut des Réfugiés - 50 Ans Après: Bilan et Perspectives* (Brussels: Bruylant, 2001), pp. 3–61.

Chiki-Arad, R. "The Soldiers and the Doctors Looking at Each Other Suspiciously," *Haaretz*, September 7, 2012.

Choval, R. "The Debacle of the Women behind the Anti Infiltration Act," *Haaretz*, September 24, 2014.

Cohen, G. "District Court Authorizes the Deportation of South Sudanese back to their Homeland," *Haaretz*, June 7, 2012.

——— "African Migrants Trapped in the No-Man's Land Zone between Israel and Egypt," *Haaretz*, September 4, 2012.

Cohen, G. and T. Nesher, "A High Court Plea against Defense Minister Barak and Interior Minister Yishai: Explain the Blocking of Entry of the Trapped Migrants at the Border," *Haaretz*, September 5, 2012.

Cohen, M. "The New Anti Infiltration Act has been Approved," *Maariv*, December 9, 2013.

Cohen, T. "Terrorist Organizations are Operating a Money Laundering Scheme using African Migrants," *Haaretz*, July 24, 2012.

Crothers, L. and B. Doherty, "Australia Signs Controversial Refugee Transfer Deal with Cambodia," *Guardian*, September 26, 2014.

Davar newspaper, "The Israeli Delegate has been Nominated as Vice President of the UN General Assembly's Sixth Committee," September 29, 1950 [in Hebrew].

Davy, U. "Article 32 of the 1951 Refugee Convention," in A. Zimmermann, J. Dörschner, and F. Machts, *The 1951 Convention Relating to the Status of Refugees and its 1967 Protocol: A Commentary* (Oxford: Oxford University Press, 2011), pp. 1,277–325.

Dayan, A. *As the Spring Overflows: The Story of SHAS* (Jerusalem: Keter Publishers, 1999) [in Hebrew].

Dedieu, J-P. "Greece, a Front Line for State-Sponsored Racism in Europe," *Aljazeera America* report, September 29, 2014. Available at: www.america.aljazeera.com/opinions/2014/9/greece-anti-immigrantsviolenceandracismineurope.html

Dowty, A. "The Use of Emergency Powers in Israel," *Middle East Review* Vol. 30 (1) (1988), pp. 34–46.

Eckstein, Z. "Report of the Israeli Governmental Inter-Ministerial Committee for the Establishment of Governmental Policy regarding Non-Israeli Workers," published upon the Israeli Government's request by the Israel Democracy Institute – Caesarea Form, June 2010.

Einarsen, T. "The Drafting History of the 1951 Convention and the 1967 Protocol," in Zimmermann, Dörschner, and Machts, *1951 Convention*, pp. 37–74.

Einaudi, J.L. *La Bataille de Paris. 17 octobre 1961* (Paris: Seuil, 1991).

El-Youssef, S. *The Illusion of Return* (London: Halban Publishers, 2008).

Encyclopedia Judaica, "Robinson, Jacob" in Vol. 14, col. 207 (Jerusalem and New York: Macmillan, 1971).

Encyclopedia Judaica, "Robinson, Nehemiah" in, Vol. 14, col. 208.

Ephraim, O. "The Knesset Chief Legal Counsel: The Proposed Anti Infiltration Act is Exceptionally Irregular," *YNET*, December 13, 2011.

——— "'Voluntary Return'? 177 Asylum Seekers left Israel in July," *YNET*, August 6, 2013.

——— "Returning Voluntarily? Dozens of Eritreans have been flown out of Israel," *YNET*, August 6, 2013.

——— "The Knesset's Legal Advisor: The New Anti Infiltration Law, while more Balanced Still must Undergo Changes," *YNET*, November 26, 2013.

Ephraim, O. and A. Magnazi. "Confrontations during the Court Session regarding the new Anti Infiltration Act," *YNET*, April 1, 2014.

Eytan, W. *The First Ten Years: Diplomatic History of Israel* (New York: Weidenfeld & Nicholson, 1958).

Feher, M. "Le Proche-Orient hors les murs. Usage francais du conflit israelo-palestinien," in D. Fassin and E. Fassin (eds), *De la question Sociale a la question Racial* (Paris: La Decouverte, 2009).

Feige, M. *One Space Two Places: Gush Emunim, Peace Now and the Construction of Israeli Space* (Jerusalem: Hebrew University Magnes Press, 2002).

Feldman, A. "My Ideal Supreme Court," *Haaretz*, January 2, 2010.

Finger, S.M. "Beyond the Conflict – the United Nations," in D.S. Wyman and C.H. Rosenzweig (eds), *The World Reacts to the Holocaust* (Baltimore, MD: Johns Hopkins University Press, 1996).

Fisk, R. *Pity the Nation: Lebanon at War* (Oxford: Oxford University Press, 1990).

Flusser, Y. "Behold the State where the Socially Vulnerable Suffer," *Haaretz Literary Supplement*, February 28, 2014.

Friedman, I. *The Question of Palestine 1914–1918* (London: Routledge & Kegan Paul, 1973).

Garnier, A. "Are States in Control of their Borders? Testing the Venue-Shopping Approach in the Australian Context," Research Academy Leipzig, working paper, Series No. 10, University of Leipzig, 2010.

Glickman, A. "Attorney General: South Sudanese can be Deported," *YNET*, May 23, 2012.

Globes Economic News Agency, "Eli Yishai has issued an unprecedented number of working permits for aliens," November 9, 2009.

Glynn, I. "The Genesis and Development of Article 1 of the 1951 Refugee Convention," *Journal of Refugee Studies* 25 (1) (March 2012), pp. 134–48.

Goldstein, T. "The Building Contractor Association Appeal to the High Court of Justice: Block Deportation of 3000 Foreign Workers," *YNET – Yediouth Aharonoth*, June 20, 2010 [in Hebrew].

Goodwin-Gill, G. and J. McAdam. *The Refugee in International Law*, 3rd edition (Oxford: Oxford University Press, 2007).

Goren, Y. "Two Teenagers Murdered in a Youth Event of the Gay and Lesbian Community in Tel Aviv," *Haaretz*, August 2, 2009.

Goschler, C. *Wiedergutmachung: Westdeutschland und die Verfolgten des Nationalsozialismus 1945–1954* (Munich: Oldenburg Verlag, 1992).

Grahl-Madsen, A. *Commentary on the Refugee Convention 1951: Articles 2–11* (Geneva: UNHCR, 1963). Available at: www.unhcr.org/3d4ab5fb9.html

Grimes, W. "Louis Henkin, Leader in Field of Human Rights Law, Dies at 92," *New York Times*, October 16, 2010.

Gross, A. "All Signs Point Toward Ethnocracy, Not Democracy, in Israel," *Haaretz*, November 17, 2014.

Guiraudon, V. "European Integration and Migration Policy: Vertical Policy-Making as Venue-Shopping," *Journal of Common Market Studies* 38 (2) (2000).

Guterres, A. (United Nations High Commissioner for Refugees), "One Million Syrian Refugees," *New York Times*, March 5, 2013.

Guthrie, W.K.C. "The Meno," in *A History of Greek Philosophy*, Vol. 4 (Cambridge: Cambridge University Press, 1975), pp. 236–65.

Haaretz, "Israel's Anti Infiltration Law is a Disgrace," editorial, January 11, 2012.

——— "Mass Jailing," editorial, June 5, 2012.
——— "Let the Refugees in," editorial, September 6, 2012.
——— "Liberalism with Limited Liability – the Removal of Dr Nathan," editorial, January 10, 2013.
——— "Voluntary Self-Inflicted Death Sentence," editorial, February 15, 2013.
——— "The State as a Human–Trafficker," editorial, February 27, 2013.
——— "Disgrace and Shame to the Attorney General," editorial, August 8, 2013.
——— "High Court Exhibits New Commitment to Defending Human Rights," editorial, September 18, 2013.
——— "The High Court has Prevented Shame," editorial, September 18, 2013.
——— "The Minister for Incitement Affairs," editorial, November 20, 2013.
Haaretz Daily News Service, "Eli Yishai: 'We Need to Incarcerate all Migrant Workers and Refugees in Penal Facilities'", May 16, 2012.
——— "Indictment in Court: Beating and Robbing of African Migrants with Clubs," May 31, 2012.
Haberman, C. "Books of the Times: Terrorism Can Be Just Another Point of View," *New York Times*, February 22, 1995.
Hathaway, J. *The Rights of Refugees Under International Law* (Cambridge: Cambridge University Press, 2005).
Hirsch, Rabbi Samson Raphael. *Commentary on The Pentateuch*, new and revised edition (Jerusalem: Yitzhaq Breuer Institute, 2002) [in Hebrew].
Hoare, S. *Nine Troubled Years* (London: Collins, 1954).
Hofnung, M. *Israel - Security Needs vs. The Rule of Law* (Jerusalem: Nevo Publishers, 1991) [in Hebrew].
Human Rights Watch communiqué: "Israel: High Court Voids Migrant Holding Law. Court Also Limits Detention of New Arrivals," September 24, 2014. Available at: www.hrw.org/news/2014/09/24/israel-high-court-voids-migrant-holding-law
Human Rights Watch report: "Pushed back Pushed Around," September 21, 2009. Available at: www.hrw.org/sites/default/files/reports/italy0909web_0.pdf.
——— "Boat Ride to Detention: Adult and Child Migrants in Malta," July 18, 2012. Available at: www.hrw.org/report/2012/07/18/boat-ride-detention/adult-and-child-migrants-malta
——— "I Wanted to Lie Down and Die: Trafficking and Torture of Eritreans in Sudan and Egypt," February 11, 2014. Available at: www.hrw.org/reports/2014/02/11/i-wanted-lie-down-and-die-0
——— "'Make Their Lives Miserable,' Israel's Coercion of Eritrean and Sudanese Asylum Seekers to Leave Israel," September 9, 2014. Available at: www.hrw.org/report/2014/09/09/make-their-lives-miserable/israels-coercion-eritrean-and-sudanese-asylum-seekers
Hundert, G.D. (ed.) *The YIVO Encyclopedia of Jews in Eastern Europe* (New Haven, CT: Yale University Press, 2008).
Ilan, S. "The Naturalization Process has been Concluded," *Haaretz*, June 19, 2007.
——— "First Draft Approved: up to Five Years Incarceration for any Border Trespasser; Seven Years for a Trespasser from Darfur," *Haaretz*, May 20, 2008.
Illouz, E. "Words That Must Never be Uttered," *Haaretz*, June 25, 2012.
International Crisis Group, *Middle East Report No. 25* (Amman/Brussels: International Crisis Group, March 4, 2004). Available at: www.crisisgroup.

org/~/media/Files/Middle%20East%20North%20Africa/Israel%20Palestine/Identity%20Crisis%20Israel%20and%20its%20Arab%20Citizens.ashx

Jabarrin, Y. "A New Politics? Between Conditional Citizenship and Full Equal Citizenship," *Van Leer Institute Bulletin* (1), April 10, 2013 [in Hebrew].

Jehoshua, A.B. "Is there any Practical Meaning to the term Light unto the Nations?" in *Homeland Grasp: Twenty Articles and One Story* (Tel Aviv: Hakibbutz Hameuchad, 2008), pp. 68–73 [in Hebrew].

Kälin, W., M. Caroni, and L. Heim. "Article 33, para 1 (prohibition of Expulsion or Return ('Refoulement')," in Zimmermann, Dörschner, and F. Machts, *1951 Convention*, pp. 1,327–96.

Kaplan-Feuereisen, O. "Im Dienste der jüdischen Nation: Jacob Robinson und das Völkerrecht," *Osteurope* 58th Year/Issue 8–10 (August–October 2008), pp. 279–94.

——— "Robinson, Jacob," in Hundert (ed.), *YIVO Encyclopedia*, pp. 1,567–8.

Kashti, O. "The Campaign to Purge State Bureaucracy of Left-leaning People," *Haaretz*, January 12, 2013.

Kastoryano, R. "Codes of Otherness," *Sociological Review* Vol. 77 (1) (Spring 2010), pp. 79–100.

Kemp, A. and R. Raijman, *Migrants and Workers: The Political Economy of Labor Migrants in Israel* (Jerusalem: Van Leer Institute – Hakibbutz Hameuchad Publishers, 2009) [in Hebrew].

Kershner, I. "Africans Continue to Protest in Israel," *New York Times*, January 6, 2014.

Khadduri, M. "The Alexandretta Dispute," *American Journal of International Law*, Vol. 39 No. 3 (July 1945), pp. 406–25.

Klepp, S. "Negotiating the Principle of Non-Refoulement in the Mediterranean Sea: Mission, Visions, and Policies at the Southern Borders of the European Union," Working Paper Series No. 1 (Leipzig: Global and European Studies Institute – University of Leipzig, 2008).

——— *Europa zwischen Grenzkontrolle und Flüchtlingsschutz: Eine Ethnographie der Seegrenze auf dem Mittelmeer* (Frankfurt am Main: Transcript, 2011).

——— *Ankunft und Aufnahme von Flüchtlingen in Italien: Eine ethnographische Reise an die Grenzen Europas* (Munich: Akademiker Verlag, 2012).

Kobovich, Y. "A Gang of South Tel-Aviv Residents had been Attacking Migrants," *Haaretz*, May 23, 2012.

——— "Aharonovich to Members of the Knesset: Your Words can Incite more Violence Like what we had Yesterday in Jerusalem," *Haaretz*, June 4, 2012.

——— "Yet Another Attack Against Migrants: Fire Bombs Thrown at an Eritrean pub in Tel Aviv," *Haaretz*, June 17, 2012.

——— "Media Ban Lifted: An 83 year old Woman was Raped Near her Apartment in South Tel Aviv," *Haaretz*, December 31, 2012.

Kobovich, Y. and I. Lior. "Molotov Bottles Thrown Last Night at Migrants' Dwellings in south Tel Aviv: A Rise in the Degree of the Onslaught," *Haaretz*, April 27, 2012.

Kobovich, Y. and T. Nesher. "Netanyahu Threatens: We Might Easily Reach 600,000 Foreigners – the PM and the Interior Minister Warn that the Influx of Foreign Migrants Threatens the 'Zionist dream'," *Haaretz*, May 20, 2012.

Koopmans, R. and P. Statham. "Migration and Ethnic Relations as a Field of Political Contention: An Opportunity Structure Approach," in R. Koopmans and P. Statham (eds), *Challenging Immigration and Ethnic Relations Politics* (New York: Oxford University Press, 2000), pp. 13–56.

Lahav, P. "American Influence on Israel's Jurisprudence of Free Speech," *Hastings Constitutional Law Quarterly*, 9 (1981), pp. 21–40.

——— *Judgment in Jerusalem: Chief Justice Simon Agranat and the Zionist Century* (Berkeley, CA: University of California Press, 1991).

Landler, M. "France Declares State of Emergency to Curb Crisis," *New York Times*, November 8, 2005.

Le Monde and Agence France Presse. "En Israël, manifestation monstre de migrants africains clandestins," January 5, 2014.

Lee, V. "What have I Voted?: How do the Members of Parliament Explain their Endorsement for the New Anti Infiltration Act," *Haaretz*, July 30, 2009.

Leibowitch, V. "23 Casualties in a Suicide Bombing in Tel Aviv," *YNET*, January 6, 2003.

Levy, G. "A Larger Danger than the Migrants," *Haaretz*, May 31, 2012.

Lewin, I. *Religious Jewry and the United Nations: Addresses before the United Nations* (New York: Research institute for Post-War Problems of Religious Jewry, 1953).

——— *Ten Years of Hope: Addresses before the United Nations* (New York: Shengold Publishers, 1971).

——— *In Defense of Human Rights* (New York: Research Institute of Religious Jewry, 1992).

Lior, I. "Attorney General is Formulating a Procedure which would Enable the Voluntary Return of Migrants Currently Incarcerated," *Haaretz*, May 12, 2013.

——— "The State to the Supreme Court: We have reached a Settlement with a Country of Secondary Asylum," *Haaretz*, June 2, 2013.

——— "Eritreans in Israel: Our Lives will not be Safe in a Third Country," *Haaretz*, June 3, 2013.

——— "Testimonies: Migrants Jailed in Israel are Instructed to Prepare for Departure to a Country of Third Asylum," *Haaretz*, June 5, 2013.

——— "The State Confirms: Negotiations are being Held with an Additional Four Countries Regarding the Deportation of the African Migrants," *Haaretz*, June 9, 2013.

——— "Reports and Sources in Sudan: The Khartoum Authorities have Interrogated Sudanese Migrants who have Clandestinely Returned from Israel via Jordan," *Haaretz*, June 13, 2013.

——— "177 Africans have left Israel in July; a Prisoner at the Saharonim Detention Center: We are being Forced to Sign," *Haaretz*, August 6, 2013.

——— "Senior Government Officials: The Discussions with Uganda relate to Merely a Few Hundred Migrants: In Direct Contradiction to the Statements made by Interior Minister Sa'ar," *Haaretz*, September 3, 2013.

——— "Israel Examined 250 Asylum Requests out of a Total of 1800: Not one has been Approved," *Haaretz*, January 1, 2014.

——— "Record Numbers of Asylum Seekers have Left: 1705 have Departed from Israel in February," *Haaretz*, February 27, 2014.

——— "The Hotline for Migrants and Foreign Workers: Three Eritreans who Left Israel have been Executed by ISIS in Libya," *Haaretz*, April 21, 2015.

——— "Even from the Opposition: Yesh Atid will Support the Anti Infiltration Act in its Current Format," *Haaretz*, December 4, 2014.

Lior, I. and R. Levy-Stein. "Tens of Thousands of African Migrants Protest in Central Tel Aviv," *Haaretz*, January 5, 2014.

Lior, I. and R. Levy-Stein. "Thousands of Migrants Demonstrated on Rabin Square: 1,500 Migrants on Strike in Eilat," *Haaretz*, January 5, 2014.

Lior, I., A. Pfeffer, and J. Lis. "Permission for Publication Granted: Uganda is the Third Country to which African Migrants shall be Deported," *Haaretz*, August 29, 2013.

Lis, J. "A Stormy Knesset Debate – Police Representative at the Knesset Confirms: A Rise in Migrant Crime Rates – the State must allow them Employment," *Haaretz*, May 21, 2012.

——— "Right-Wing MKs Promoting Legislation which would Re-enact the Anti Infiltration Act and allow an Over Ride of the Supreme Court," *Haaretz*, September 23, 2014.

——— "Ministers approve Shaked's Law to Override the Supreme Court," *Haaretz*, October 26, 2014.

Lis J. and Talila Nesher, "After a Negative Right-Wing Campaign: A Researcher in the Knesset's Research Authority has been Removed from Office Due to his Left-Leaning Opinions," *Haaretz*, January 6, 2013.

Luria, I. "Mental Refugeeness," *Haaretz*, February 26, 2013.

Maariv – NRG News Agency. "Following the Rape of an Elderly Woman: SHAS Launches an Anti-Migrant Campaign," December 31, 2012.

Marciano, I. "MK Zeev against the 'Disgusting Homosexual'," *YNET*, July 23, 2003.

Margalit, D. *Awakening* (Tel Aviv: Kineret – Zmora Bitan Publishers, 2009) [in Hebrew].

Marrus, M. *The Unwanted: European Refugees from the First World War Through the Cold War* (Philadelphia: Temple University Press, 2002).

——— "A Jewish Lobby at Nuremberg: Jacob Robinson and the Institute of Jewish Affairs 1945–1946," paper prepared for The Cardozo Law Review Conference: "The Nuremberg Trials: A Reappraisal and Their Legacy," Benjamin N. Cardozo School of Law, New York, March 27–29, 2011.

Marton, K. *A Death in Jerusalem* (New York: Pantheon Books, 1994).

Marx, R. and F. Machts, "Article 6 of the 1951 Refugee Convention," in A. Zimmermann, J. Dörschner & F. Machts, *The 1951 Convention Relating to the Status of Refugees and its 1967 Protocol: A Commentary* (Oxford: Oxford University Press, 2011), pp. 707–14.

Marx, R. & W. Staff. "Article 3 of the 1951 Refugee Convention," in Zimmermann, Dörschner, and Machts, *1951 Convention*, pp. 643–56.

Mason, P. "With EU Funding, Morocco halts Immigration to Europe, and all Means are Justified," *Guardian*, September 8, 2013.

Mazower, M. *No Enchanted Palace: The End of Empire and the Ideological Origins of the United Nations* (Princeton, NJ: Princeton University Press, 2009).

Mbembe, A. "The Republic and its Beast," in C. Tshimanga, C.D. Godola, and P.J. Bloom (eds), *Frenchness and the African Diaspora: Identity and Uprising in Contemporary France* (Bloomington, IN: Indiana University Press, 2009).

McAdam, J. "The Interpretation of the 1951 Convention," in Zimmermann, Dörschner, and Machts, *1951 Convention*, pp. 75–116.

Médecins Sans Frontières, "Violence, Vulnerability and Migration: Trapped at the Gates of Europe, A report on the situation of sub-Saharan migrants in an irregular situation in Morocco," March 2013. Available at: http://www.msf.org.uk/sites/uk/files/Migration_Morocco_2013_201303132441.pdf

Medhora, S. "'Nope, Nope, Nope': Tony Abbott says Australia will take no Rohingya Refugees," *Guardian*, May 21, 2015.
Melamed, A. "The African Migrants have not Infiltrated Anybody's Political Campaign," *YNET*, December 20, 2012.
——— "My Home and SHAS Racism," *YNET* News Agency, January 16, 2013.
Meranda, A. "SHAS Condemns Attack on Gay Center," *YNET*, August 2, 2009.
Misgav, U. "I am pacifist," *Haaretz*, May 21, 2012.
Mizrachi, S. "MK Zeev: 'One should Treat Homosexuals Like Bird Flu'," *Maariv* internet portal, "NRG," January 29, 2008.
Morris, B. *Israel's Border Wars 1949–1956* (Oxford: Oxford University Press, 1997).
Morsink, J. "The Dawn of Human Rights: the Universal Declaration and the Conscience of Humanity," in R. Huhle (ed.), *Human Rights and History: A challenge for Education* (Berlin: EVZ Stiftung, 2010), pp. 25–56.
Mosse, George L. *Nationalism and Sexuality: Middle-Class Morality and Sexual Norms in Modern Europe* (Madison, WI: Wisconsin University Press, 1988).
Nakrumah, G. "Here Today Gone Tomorrow: Why are Increasing Numbers of Sudanese refugees fleeing Egypt for Israel," *Al Ahram Weekly*, issue No. 856, August 2–8, 2007.
Nathanson, R. and L. Achdut (eds). *The New Workers: Wage Earners from Foreign Countries in Israel* (Tel Aviv: Friedrich Ebert Stiftung – Hakibbutz Hameuchad, 1999) [in Hebrew].
Nesher, T. "First Testimony by the African Female Migrants Stranded at the Border: the Army Refouled and Actively Pushed the Male Migrants Back into Egyptian territory," *Haaretz*, September 11, 2012.
——— "'State Attorney: Yishai's Declarations Concerning the Mass Incarceration of the Sudanese Migrants, were Misguide," *Haaretz*, October 25, 2012.
——— "Amid Drop in Entry of African Migrants: 80,000 Working Permits for Aliens were Issued this year by the Interior Ministry," *Haaretz*, December 31, 2012.
——— "Eritreans: We are Being Forced to Sign 'Voluntary Repatriation Papers'," *Haaretz*, February 14, 2013.
——— "The UN Demands Explanations from Israel over Clandestine Returns of Sudanese Back to their Country of Origin," *Haaretz*, February 27, 2013.
——— "A First Testimony of the Governmental Procedure for 'Voluntary Return': an Eritrean Migrant who Refused to Board a Connecting Flight to Eritrea is Stranded at Cairo Airport," *Haaretz*, March 4, 2013.
——— "Eli Yishai Admits: Over 2000 Sudanese Migrants have 'Left Voluntarily'," *Haaretz*, March 4, 2013.
——— "Following the Publication in Haaretz: The Attorney General has Ordered a Complete Halt of Migrant Deportations," *Haaretz*, March 5, 2013.
——— "The High Court Suspends the Application of the Anti Infiltration Act," *Haaretz*, March 12, 2013.
Nesher, T. and G. Cohen. "UNHCR: Israel must Grant Immediate Entry to the Stranded Migrants on the Border Fence," *Haaretz*, September 6, 2012.
Nettleship, R.L. *The Theory of Education in Plato's Republic* (Oxford: Oxford University Press, 1935).
Neumann, K. *Refuge Australia: Australia's Humanitarian Record* (Sydney: University of New South Wales Press, 2004).
New York Times, Obituary: Rabbi Dr Isaac Lewin, August 25, 1995.

Nir, Y. *Arye Deri: The Rise, The Crisis and the Pain* (Tel Aviv: Yediot Aharonot, 1999) [in Hebrew].
Niv, S. "Objection in the Knesset Rising Towards Endorsement of the 'Infiltration Law'," *Globes*, February 3, 2010.
Novik, A. "Yishai's 'Doomsday Electoral Weapon': Watch SHAS' Secret Campaign Pitch," *YNET* News Agency, December 31, 2012.
Obert, M. and Moises Saman, "Im Reich des Todes," *Suddeutsche Zeitung*, March 29, 2013.
Ortar, I. *Uprooting, Refugeeism and Immigration* (Herzliya Museum of Contemporary Art, Herzliya: Hakibbutz Hameuchad, 2005) [in English/French/Hebrew].
Ozanne, Juian. "Unflinching Supporter of Greater Israel," *Financial Times*, June 30, 2012.
Paz-Frenkel, E. "A Victory for the Construction Lobby: The Deportation of the Foreign Workers has been Postponed to October by the High Court," *Globes*, July 1, 2010 [in Hebrew].
Pedahzur, A. *The Triumph of Israel's Radical Right* (New York: Oxford University Press, 2012).
Peleg, M. "The House where Refugee Rights are Trampled Upon," *Haaretz*, August 5, 2013.
Perry, A. "Solving Israel's African Refugee Crisis," *Virginia Journal of International Law*, Vol. 51 (1), pp. 157–84.
Pfeffer, A. "Uganda Migrants Deal Signed as Military and Business Ties with Israel Balloon: Human Rights Groups Say Migrants from Israel most Likely Destined for isolated 'Warehouses for Human Beings' in Uganda," *Haaretz*, August 29, 2013.
——— "Reserve Soldiers Actively Opposed the Forceful Refoulement of Infiltrators to Egypt – and the Order has been Suspended," *Haaretz*, April 22, 2011.
Pico Della Mirandola. *Oration on the Dignity of Man*, paras 1–7. Available at: www.fordham.edu/halsall/med/oration.asp
Popp, M. "Trapped in Apulia: Europe's Deepening Refugee Crisis," *Der Spiegel*, June 21, 2013. *Spiegel* English Online edition available at: www.spiegel.de/international/europe/eu-refugees-the-plight-of-african-migrants-living-in-apulia-italy-a-906950.html
Power, S. *A Problem from Hell: America and the Age of Genocide* (New York: Harper Perennial, 2002).
Pundik, H. *Die Flucht der dänischen Juden 1943 nach Schweden* (Husum: Husum Verlag, 1995).
Rabinovich, I. *The Road Not Taken: Early Arab-Israeli Negotiations 1949–1952* (Jerusalem: Maxwell-Macmillan-Keter, 1991), p. 27 [in Hebrew].
——— *Waging Peace: Israel and the Arabs 1948–2003* (Princeton, NJ: Princeton University Press, 2004).
——— *The Lingering Conflict: Israel, The Arabs, and the Middle East 1948–2012* (Washington, DC: Brookings Institute Press, 2012).
Rahat, M. *SHAS the Spirit and the Power* (Tel Aviv: Alfa Communications Publications, 1998) [in Hebrew].
Rahav-Meir, S. "After the Jewish Festivals: Tens of Thousands of Migrant Trespassers will be Jailed," *Channel 2 News* report, August 29, 2012.
Ravid, B. "Israel's Pillar of Defense achieved its Goals," *Haaretz*, November 22, 2012.
——— "The Foreign Ministry: We have no Knowledge of any Third Party Agreement for the Transfer of the Eritrean Migrants," *Haaretz*, June 2, 2013.

Rice, C. *No Higher Honor: A Memoir of My Years in Washington* (New York: Random House, 2011).

Robinson, J. *Das Minoritäten-Problem und seine Literatur; kritische Einführung in die Quellen und die Literatur der europäischen Nationalitätenfrage der Nachkriegszeit, unter besonderer Berücksichtigung des Völkerrechtlichen Minderheitenschutzes* (Berlin and Leipzig: Institut für ausländisches öffentliches Recht und Völkerrecht in Berlin, Walter de Gruyter & Co., 1928).

——— *Kommentar der Konvention über das Memelgebiet* (Kaunas: Verlag Spaudos Fondas, 1934).

——— *Minorities and the League of Nations* (Washington, DC: American Council on Public Affairs, 1941).

——— "Book Review – Knud Larsen 'Nationality Laws'," *American Journal of International Law* Vol. 45 (July 1951), pp. 617–18.

——— *The Metamorphosis of the United Nations: Extract of the Recueil des Cours* (Leiden: The Hague Academy of International Law A.W. Sijthoff, 1958).

——— *The Holocaust and After: Sources and Literature in English*, (Jerusalem Yad Vashem Memorial Authority and YIVO Institute for Jewish Research: Israel University Press 1973).

Robinson, J. and Y. Bauer. *Guide to Unpublished Materials of the Holocaust Period* (Jerusalem: Hebrew University Press, 1970).

Robinson, J., O. Karbach, M. M. Laserson, N. Robinson, and M. Vichniak, *Were the Minorities Treaties a Failure?* (New York: Institute of Jewish Affairs, 1943).

Robinson, N. *The Convention Relating to the Status of Refugees. Its History, Contents and Interpretation: A Commentary* (New York: Institute for Jewish affairs and World Jewish Congress, 1953).

Rosenhek, Z. "Challenging Exclusionary Migration Regimes," in S. Willen (ed.), *Transnational Migration to Israel in a Global Comparative Context* (Lanham, MD: Lexington Books, 2007), pp. 217–32.

Ross, D. "Stop Giving Palestinians a Pass," *New York Times*, January 4, 2015.

Rotem, T. "Lessons in Incitement: Migrant Children Speak of their Life in Fear," *Haaretz*, June 3, 2012.

Rubenstein, E. *Judges of the Land* (Tel Aviv: Schoken, 1980) [in Hebrew].

Sabar, G. "The Rise and Fall of African Migrant Churches: Transformations in African Religious Discourse and Practice in Tel Aviv," in Willen (ed.), *Transnational Migration*, pp. 185–202.

——— "*'We're not Here to Stay': African Migrant Workers in Israel and Back in Africa* (Tel Aviv: Tel Aviv University Press, 2008) [in Hebrew].

Sabar, G. and E. Tsurkov, "Israel's Policies toward Asylum-Seekers: 2002–2014," Istituto Affari Internazionali (IAI) Working Paper 20/2015, presented Rome, May 31, 2015. Available at: www.iai.it/en/pubblicazioni/israels-policies-toward-asylum-seekers

Sadeh, S. "A Fence, but not a Solution on the Israel-Egypt Border," *Haaretz*, November 25, 2011.

Salzberger, F.O. and E. Salzberger, "The Secret German Roots of the Israeli Supreme Court," *Israel Studies* Vol. 3, No. 2 (Fall 1998), pp. 159–92.

Sarid, Y. "Nice to Meet You, Israel the Deporter," *Haaretz*, June 12, 2012.

——— "Open them a Gate while Locking Gates," *Haaretz*, September 6, 2012.

Sartre, J.-P. *Existentialism & Humanism*, translated by Philip Mairet (London: Methuen Press, 2007).

Schechter, A. *Rothschild Boulevard: The Anatomy of Protest* (Tel Aviv: Hakibbutz Hameuchad Publishing House, 2012) [in Hebrew].

Schlezinger, L. "The UN: 90 percent of Asylum Seekers in Israel are Considered Under Refugee Status," *Maariv*, February 2, 2010.

Senior, E. and G. Morag, "A Ninth Suspect Apprehended Regarding the Attack on Migrants in Tel Aviv," *YNET*, May 25, 2012.

Shalev, A. and M. Shimoni, "Molotov Cocktails Thrown at Migrant Dwellings and an African Kindergarten in South Tel Aviv," *Walla News Agency* report, April 27, 2012.

Shalom, O. "The Bearers of the Black Flag," *Yediot Aharonot Weekend Supplement*, January 10, 2014 [in Hebrew].

Sheffer, G. *Moshe Sharett: Biography of a Political Moderate* (Oxford: Oxford University Press, 1996).

Shoffman, J. "And the Stranger shall dwell amongst you – and ye shall not wrong him," Parashat Kedoshim, reading #207, Israeli Ministry of Justice, 2005 [in Hebrew]. Available at: www.daat.ac.il/mishpat-ivri/skirot/207-2.htm

Shumfalvi, A. "Eli Yishai: Homosexuals and Lesbians are People with an Illness," *YNET*, February 22, 2006.

Shumfalvi, A. and G. Morag. "A Counter Demonstration in Jerusalem following Yesterday's Anti-Migrant Riots: Racism in the Knesset and the Country is Collapsing," *YNET News Service* report, May 24, 2012.

Shuval, J. and E. Leshem (eds). *Immigration to Israel: Sociological Perspectives* (New Brunswick, NJ: Transaction Publishers, 1998).

Sinai, R. "The High Court of Justice Forbids Keeping the Sudanese Refugees in Administrative Detention without Recourse to Judicial Due Process," *Haaretz*, May 9, 2006.

——— "The State Admits: A Major Failure in the return of 91 Migrants to Egypt," *Haaretz*, September 2, 2008.

Smith, D. "Uganda Proposes Ban on Miniskirts in move against Women's Rights," *Guardian*, April 5, 2013.

Smith, S. "A day between Locals and Foreigners at the Helm of the Conflict in the Shapira Neighborhood," *Haaretz*, May 18, 2012.

Sofer, A. (ed.) *Refugees or Migrant Workers from African States?* (Tel Aviv: Research Center of the Academy for National Security, 2009) [in Hebrew].

Steele, J. "How Yarmouk Refugee Camp became the Worst Place in Syria," *Guardian*, March 5, 2015.

Sussman, G. "The Challenge to the Two-State Solution," *Middle East Report* (34) (2004). Available at: www.merip.org/mer/mer231/challenge-two-state-solution

Takkenberg, A. and C.C. Tahbaz. *The Collected Travaux Pre?paratoires of the 1951 Geneva Convention Relating to the Status of Refugees*, Vols I–III (Amsterdam: Dutch Refugee Council/European Legal Network on Asylum, 1990).

Thorpe, N. "Hungary's Poster War on Immigration," BBC News report, June 14, 2015. Available at: www.bbc.com/news/world-europe-33091597

Trägårdh, L. and M.D. Carpini. "The Juridification of Politics in the United States and Europe: Historical Roots, Contemporary Debates and Future Prospects," in L. Trägårdh (ed.), *After National Democracy: Rights, Law and Power in America and the New Europe* (Oxford: Oñati International Institute for the Sociology of Law and Oxford University Press, 2004), Ch. 3 pp. 41–78.

Troebst, S. "Speichermedium der Konflikterinnerung zur Ost (Mittel) Europäischen Prägung des Modernen Völkerrechts," in M. Keilbach (ed.), *IPP Colloquium Papers Winter 2012* (Graduate Institute for Global and European Studies, University of Leipzig, 2012).

Troebst, S. "Lemkin and Lauterpacht in Lemberg and Later: Pre- and Post-Holocaust Careers of Two East European International Lawyers," paper given at the Annual Conference of the Imre Kertész Kolleg at Friedrich Schiller University, Jena on "Catastrophe and Utopia: Central and Eastern European Intellectual Horizons 1933 to 1958," Budapest, June 13–15, 2013. Available at: www.iwm.at/read-listen-watch/transit-online/lemkin-and-lauterpacht-in-lemberg-and-later-pre-and-post-holocaust-careers-of-two-east-european-international-lawyers

Tshimanga, C., C.D. Godola, and P.J. Bloom (eds). *Frenchness and the African Diaspora: Identity and Uprising in Contemporary France* (Bloomington, IN: Indiana University Press, 2009).

UNHCR, *Guidelines on the Applicable Criteria and Standards relating to the Detention of Asylum-Seekers and Alternatives to Detention* (Geneva: UNHCR, 2012). Available at: www.refworld.org/docid/503489533b8.html

Van Reisen, M., M. Estefanos, and C. Rijken. *The Human Trafficking Cycle: Sinai and Beyond* (Oisterwijk: Wolf Legal Publishers, 2013).

Vilnai, O. and G. Meroz. *Suddenly a People Arises* (Tel Aviv: Modan Publishers, 2011) [in Hebrew].

Von Thadden, Elisabeth. "Am Seelenmarkt: Was macht die moderne Ökonomie mit unseren Gefühlen?" *Die Zeit*, April 16, 2009.

Walla News Agency, "MK Zeev: 'Homosexuals are sick people who have a serious defect'," March 19, 2001.

——— "Rape of an Elderly Women Concludes an Excessively Violent Year in South Tel Aviv," 31 December 2012.

Weiler-Polak, D. "Knesset Member Katz Deliberately Withheld a Report Contradicting Prime Minister Netanyahu's Claims for a Refugee Tidal Wave," *Haaretz*, February 19, 2010.

——— "The Government has Decided to Withdraw the Anti Infiltration Act," *Haaretz*, July 29, 2010.

——— "Interior Minister Eli Yishai has Issued a Record Number of Working Permits for aliens this year," *Haaretz*, November 9, 2011.

——— "Yishai: Many Women who have been Raped by Migrants are Afraid to Come Forward and Report their Abuse for Fear of Being Tagged as AIDS Carriers," *Haaretz*, May 31, 2012.

——— "From Today: New African Migrants shall be Immediately Incarcerated for up to 3 years," *Haaretz*, June 3, 2012.

——— "Growing Concern in the Migrant Community: We're Afraid to Exit Leave our Homes," *Haaretz*, June 11, 2012.

——— "Eritrean Asylum Seekers who had Left Israel have been Executed by ISIS," *Walla News Agency* Report, April 21, 2015.

Weiler-Pollack, D. and I. Lior. "Tension in the South Tel Aviv Neighborhoods: After the Molotov Cocktails Thrown at Migrant Dwellings – Threats to Humanitarian Aid Workers," *Haaretz*, May 7, 2012.

Weis, P. *Nationality and Statelessness in International Law* (London: Stevenson and Sons, 1956).

——— *The Refugee Convention, 1951: The Travaux Pre?paratoires Analyzed, with a Commentary* (Cambridge: Cambridge University Press, 1995).

Wieseltier, L. "Fevers," *New Republic*, January 25, 2012.

Willen, S. "Introduction," in Willen (ed.), *Transnational Migration*, pp. 1–27.

——— "Flesh of our Flesh," in Willen (ed.), *Transnational Migration*, pp. 159–84.

——— "L'hyperpolitique du 'Plus jamais ça!': demandeurs d'asile soudanais, turbulence gouvernementale et politiques de contrôle des réfugiés en Israël," *Cultures & Conflits* No. 71 (Fall 2008), pp. 93–112.

——— "Blood rhetoric and Danger: Labor migrants, Suicide Bombings and the Politics of Visibility in the Realm of Mourning," in E. Lomsky-Feder and T. Rapoport (eds), *Visibility in Migration: Body, Gaze, Representation* (Jerusalem: Van Leer Institute and Hakibbutz Hameuchad, 2010), pp. 329–53 [in Hebrew].

——— "Darfur through the Shoa Lens: Sudanese Asylum Seekers, Unruly Biopolitical Dramas, and the Politics of Humanitarian Compassion in Israel," in B.J. Good, M.M.J. Fischer, S.S. Willen, and M.-J. DelVecchio Good (eds), *A Reader in Medical Anthropology: Theoretical Trajectories – Emergent Realities* (New York: Wiley – Blackwell, 2010), pp. 505–18.

Willen S. (ed.) *Transnational Migration to Israel in a Global Comparative Context* (Lanham, MD: Lexington Books, 2007), pp. 1–27.

Wyman, D.S. and C.H. Rosenzweig (eds). *The World Reacts to the Holocaust* (Baltimore, MD: Johns Hopkins University Press, 1996).

Ya'ari E. and Z. Schiff. *Israel's Lebanon War* (New York: Touchstone Books, 1985).

Yacobi, H. "From Non-Policy to Politics of Fear," in H. Yacobi, *African Refugee's Influx in Israel from a Socio-Political Perspective* (Florence: European University Institute, Robert Schuman Center for Advanced Studies, 2009).

——— "Let Me Go to the City: African Asylum Seekers and the Politics of Space in Israel," *Journal of Refugee Studies* Vol. 24 (1) (2011), pp. 48–68.

Yagne, Y. "Yishai: A State which does not Want Infiltrators shall not allow them Employment," *Haaretz*, May 22, 2013.

Yalon, Y. "Betar Shall Remain Clean of Arabs," *Israel Today*, February 1, 2013.

Yerasimos, S. "Le sandjak d'Alexandrette: formation et integration d'un territoire," *Revue de l'Occident musulman et de la Mèditerranée* No. 48–49 (1988), pp. 198–212.

Yerushalmi, S. "Eli Yishai in a special Interview: its either us or them," *Maariv*, June 1, 2012.

Yiftachel, O. *Ethnocracy: Land and Identity Politics in Israel/Palestine* (Philadelphia, PA: University of Pennsylvania Press, 2006).

Die Zeit, "Tausende Flüchtlinge demonstrieren gegen israelische Lagerhaft," January 6, 2014.

Zimmermann, A., J. Dörschner, and F. Machts. *The 1951 Convention Relating to the Status of Refugees and its 1967 Protocol: A Commentary* (Oxford: Oxford University Press, 2011).

Zimmermann, A. and P. Wennholz, "Article 33, para 2 (prohibition of Expulsion or Return ('Refoulement'))," in Zimmermann, Dörschner, and Machts, *1951 Convention*, pp. 1397–423.

Zimmermann, M. "Between the Fences 1938, 2012," *Haaretz*, September 9, 2012.

INDEX